WHAT CONSTITUTES THE
PATIENT IN PSYCHOTHERAPY

Also by Richard D. Chessick, M.D., Ph.D.

Agonie: Diary of a Twentieth Century Man (1976)

Intensive Psychotherapy of the Borderline Patient (1977)

Freud Teaches Psychotherapy (1980)

How Psychotherapy Heals (1969, 1983)

Why Psychotherapists Fail (1971, 1983)

A Brief Introduction to the Genius of Nietzsche (1983)

Psychology of the Self and the Treatment of Narcissism (1985)

Great Ideas in Psychotherapy (1977, 1987)

The Technique and Practice of Listening in Intensive Psychotherapy (1989)

The Technique and Practice of Intensive Psychotherapy (1974, 1983, 1991)

WHAT CONSTITUTES THE PATIENT IN PSYCHOTHERAPY: ALTERNATIVE APPROACHES TO UNDERSTANDING HUMANS

RICHARD D. CHESSICK, M.D., Ph.D.

JASON ARONSON INC.
Northvale, New Jersey
London

The author gratefully acknowledges permission to reprint the following:

"The Unfortunate Case of Dr. Z: How to Succeed in Medical Practice in 1984," by J. Bernum. Copyright © 1984 by *The New England Journal of Medicine*, volume 310, pp. 729–730. Reprinted by permission of *The New England Journal of Medicine*.

Ezra Pound: *Personae*. Copyright © 1926 by Ezra Pound. Reprinted by permission of New Directions Publishing Corporation.

Production Editor: Judith D. Cohen

This book was set in 10/12 Goudy by Lind Graphics of Upper Saddle River, New Jersey, and printed and bound by Haddon Craftsmen of Scranton, Pennsylvania.

Library of Congress Cataloging-in-Publication Data

Chessick, Richard D., 1931–
    What constitutes the patient in psychotherapy : alternative
approaches to understanding humans / by Richard D. Chessick.
      p. cm.
    Includes bibliographical references and index.
    ISBN 0-87668-549-1
    1. Psychotherapy—Philosophy. 2. Psychology and philosophy—
History—20th century. 3. Philosophical anthropology—
History—20th century. 4. Phenomenological psychology.
5. Therapist and patient. I. Title.
    [DNLM: 1. Psychoanalytic Theory. 2. Psychotherapy—methods. WM
460 C524w]
    RC437.5.C48 1992
    616.89′ 14′ 01—dc20
    DNLM/DLC
    for Library of Congress   91-41341

Manufactured in the United States of America. Jason Aronson Inc. offers books and cassettes. For information and catalog write to Jason Aronson Inc., 230 Livingston Street, Northvale, New Jersey 07647.

This book is dedicated to the memory of
the late Dr. Franz Alexander and
the late Dr. Karl Menninger
who volunteered their friendship and support
at times when I needed them most

CONTENTS

PREFACE AND
ACKNOWLEDGMENTS

T HIS BOOK IS THE RESULT OF many years and long evenings of intensive study, inspired by the exciting new work that has appeared over the past half century in a number of disciplines, all seeming to converge on a new or "postmodern" view of the human. This "human" is of course the subject and object of our investigations in all the so-called human sciences. This "human" is the patient in the psychotherapy process and also is the psychotherapist or psychoanalyst. In classical science the investigator or therapist was conceived of as a neutral, objective recipient of sense data, who then verified hypotheses or came up with interpretations that arose strictly from a value-free inspection of the data. Freud (1912) began the slide away from this view in psychotherapy when, in his famous telephone receiver analogy, he spoke of the doctor's unconscious reconstructing of the patient's unconscious. The emerging popularity of his predecessor Nietzsche precipitated a reinvestigation of the classical or "Cartesian" dichotomy between subject and object, or therapist and patient.

As I immersed myself more and more in the thought of the authors covered in this book, I began to question my presuppositions in my clinical work and found myself listening to patients in new ways. I began to question the very function of psychiatry and psychotherapy in our society and found the experience important and humbling, for many of the received "truths" about humans turned out to be far less self-evident than Descartes believed and that a whole

xi

tradition that followed him took for granted. I began sharing these views with colleagues, and, because most of them were from the United States, I found they had little background in continental thought; then the idea of introducing them to it emerged. So I presented the views of these authors for several years in all-day courses at the annual meetings of the American Psychiatric Association.

I was surprised at how well received these courses were, considering the naive pronouncements often found in the "official" psychiatric literature that want to view psychiatry as proudly marching back to the nineteenth century. I realize that my audience was self-selected and not representative, but it gave me the hope that future psychiatrists and psychotherapists, students now in training, and practicing psychiatrists and psychotherapists might still be open to the new and unfamiliar ideas emerging from the thought of the distinguished authors reviewed here. This led me to attempt the present book, believing that a combination of these new ideas with clinical experience might be the best way to appeal to psychotherapists and psychiatrists who suspect that something has been left out in the approach to humans touted by the insurance companies and the drug corporations.

What has been left out turns out to be revolutionary, and requires an openness on the part of the reader to new ideas and unfamiliar ways of looking at the world and at humans. At the basis of it all is the Hegelian concept that we are defined by the "Other," by a dark edge or by background practices that we can never get clear about; so, for example, as madness is defined by sanity, sanity is defined by madness. In this postmodern view, to contrast it with the classical scientific view, every science is intertwined with an ideology under all conditions, and both the science and the ideology arise from the same presubjective source, the background practices that constitute the culture into which we are born. It is the interaction between our desires and these background practices that forms the human. This interaction is always at work, both in the continual constituting of the human subject or patient and in the therapist–patient interaction, generating the very "data" or experience upon which our clinical work is based. It is more than just an intersubjective field, for both the therapist and patient are themselves formed and continuing to be formed by the cultural background practices, whether these are characterized as the "name-of-the-father," "narcissistic woundings," "biopower," "epistemes," "politics of experience," or whatever.

This opens up an entire new area of investigation of the psychotherapy situation, one not amenable to study by classical or natural sciences methodology, and so raises the issue of what else there is to the human besides a biological organism and how to explore this "what else." This is where phenomenology and hermeneutics have been most successfully employed, although the combination of jargon, obscure writing, and difficulty of the subject has led most United

States clinicians not to be bothered with the publications on the subject. I have attempted to clarify some of the concepts and give applications of these methods here. No teacher, investigator, therapist, or psychiatrist who deals with the human sciences will ever be the same after grasping some of these concepts, and we all know how all of us attempt to avoid change, since it forces the ego to make new compromise formations and lose the gain we received from the old compromises; the price of undoing these compromises is what Kierkegaard called the "dizziness of freedom," or anxiety.

This work could not have been accomplished without the interaction and contributions of my American colleagues during the course presentations, and I wish to express my appreciation for their interest and generosity. I wish to express my thanks and gratitude to the many scholars and colleagues who were so kind and helpful in discussing my recent presentations of some of this material in Germany and Czechoslovakia, as well as serving as gracious hosts: Professor Doctors Alfred Kraus, Christoph Mundt, and Walter Bräutigam at the University of Heidelberg; Professor Doctor Hermann Lang and Doctors Hermann Faller and Aaron Mishara at the University of Würzburg; Professor Hans-Georg Gadamer, Emeritus Professor at the University of Heidelberg (now living near Würzburg); Doctor Daniel Devreese of Belgium; Professor Doctors Wolfgang Blankenburg and Wolfram Schüffel at the University of Marburg; Professor Doctor Hana Junova of the Psychologic Department at Charles University in Prague; and Doctor Vaclav Zeman of Prague. The enormous task of assembling books and references fell on the capable shoulders of my administrative assistant, Ms. Elizabeth Grudzien, and I want to thank her very much for her devoted hard work and help. My thanks also to Ms. Wanda Sauerman, who conscientiously transcribed, typed, and retyped the manuscript. Above all I wish to express my love and gratitude to my wife Marcia, without whose patience, tolerance, support, and love this work would not have been possible.

INTRODUCTION

O VER THE PAST CENTURY SOME psychoanalysts and a number of continental philosophers, among them Husserl, Heidegger, Foucault, Ricoeur, Lacan, Sartre, Merleau-Ponty, Federn, Lukács, Patočka, Gadamer, Laing, and Kohut, have rethought what it is to be human. The purpose of this book is to stimulate the reader to think about what their controversial ideas, which fall more or less out of the mainstream of psychoanalytic thinking, imply for the mental health professions and the practice of psychotherapy.

I have concentrated on presenting the views of these important thinkers rather than arguing for or against them. I have been selective in two ways. First, I have focused only on what in their work I believe to be of interest or pertinent to mental health professionals and the practice of psychotherapy. Second, I have chosen those thinkers who directly influenced me in my clinical practice or indirectly affected my conceptions of what constitutes the human, the person who is either the psychotherapist or the patient. Some readers will miss their favorites here, such as Binswanger, Boss, Buber, or Jaspers, but, much as I admire them as thinkers and human beings, I found their "existential" work to be too vague and general for my taste as far as day-to-day clinical work is concerned. This is of course a matter of preference, and, like all one's choices, is determined by one's intrapsychic dynamics. I have also not referred at length to a number of important contemporary thinkers such as Spence or Schafer, again as a matter of preference, although their ideas certainly are related to these topics.

All the authors I discuss have some affinity to phenomenology and differ from the traditional psychoanalytic view of the patient. It is interesting to note that Freud's *Interpretation of Dreams* and Husserl's *Logical Investigations* appeared at the same time. Freud seemed unfamiliar with phenomenology, but the term does appear twice in his (1940) last work. Jaspers (1972), in his monumental work of 1923, gets the credit for introducing it into the field of psychiatry, although he minimized the work of Husserl and used the term in his own idiosyncratic fashion, which was really that of a descriptive psychology. Federn, as we shall see in Chapter 8, was one of the first psychoanalytic pioneers to study the ego by a "precise and minute description of inner experience, rather than theoretical hypotheses" (Alexander and Selesnick 1966, p. 302).

There will be an explanation of technical terms used by these thinkers, and inevitably some oversimplification. I have tried to strike a balance between ensuring accessibility on the one hand, and capturing the complexity and depth of their ideas on the other. References are included for those who wish to study these matters further. The text begins with abstract material and generally moves increasingly to the clinical area of psychotherapy and psychoanalysis, and this is the reason for the sequence in which the authors are discussed. I will indicate how one thinker may have influenced another, but the order of presentation is not meant to imply the occurrence of a natural or logical progression from the thought of one author to that of the one in the next chapter.

BRIEF OVERVIEW

Reacting to the horror of World War I and the subsequent breakdown of nineteenth century culture, Heidegger profoundly influenced continental psychiatrists and philosophers after him, producing a reorientation comparable to that of Freud's work in the fields of psychiatry and psychology.

The line of thought that Heidegger originated was reworked in his own way by Sartre, and came to clinical fruition through the writings of R. D. Laing. The self in their view is taken to be a conscious or preconscious choosing agent. In their explanations of psychopathology these thinkers were the first to explicitly emphasize the self; in psychoanalysis Winnicott mentioned it repeatedly *en passant*, and Fairbairn's "ego" is perhaps the same thing. Freud used "self" and "ego" interchangeably.

Gadamer, Ricoeur, and Kohut all moved toward a new theory of knowledge for psychiatric investigation, away from one that strove to emulate the nineteenth-century natural sciences. More radically, Foucault and Lacan, again under the influence of Heidegger, decentered the subject of psychiatric investigation entirely. In a project that began with Feuerbach, Marx, and Nietzsche, a key principle was that the subject *human* is constructed by the culture. That is to say, there exists no *essence* to humans, no universal fixed human nature as a starting point.

All of these authors also force a new focus on both the method and the role of psychiatry in a culture. This is not to deny the importance of *DSM-III-R* and biology, but to insist there is something more to psychiatry and psychotherapy than can be encompassed by straightforward empirical science. The investigation of this "something more," which constitutes the human subject, forms the topic of this book.

Vico (1668–1744) was one of the first thinkers to realize that science must investigate its own origins, and that because we are participants and authors of our own and others' experinces, there is a sense in which we can know more about these than we can ever know about non-human nature, which we can only observe from the outside. Whitehead (1861–1947) said, "When you understand all about the sun and all about the atmosphere and all about the rotation of the earth, you may still miss the radiance of the sunset." (1967, p. 199).

Before reviewing the arguments of various authors and the clinical implications of their positions, I will briefly define some terms used in this book. These are nontechnical working definitions, sufficient for our purposes.

Metaphysics asks:

1. Is there a structure or order to the universe as a whole, beyond or behind the immediate and locally observable entities of our everyday experience?
2. What are the things that are? The search for answers to this question is ontology (coming from the Greek word ὤν [ōn] a participle of the verb "to be"). Ontology is referred to as the study of Being, a term used to indicate the ground or originating principles or sources of all our experience. By way of contrast, "ontic" knowledge refers to ordinary scientific knowledge, which is always grounded on an overt or covert ontology.
3. How are the things that must exist interrelated? The mind–body problem and the problem of free will are well-known instances of this type of question, which has been debated for centuries.

Ideally, metaphysical statements are supported not by dogma and revelation but by sound proofs. This standard of rigor leads quickly to the question of what is proof, an aspect of philosophy known as epistemology.

Epistemology comes from the Greek word ἐπιστήμη *(epistēmē)*, meaning absolute or "scientific" knowledge, and is compared in ancient Greek philosophy to δόξα *(doxa)*, approximation or right opinion. The physician-philosopher John Locke defined epistemology in 1690 as a study of the extent, powers, and limitations of human understanding. Psychology asks why people hold certain beliefs and how they come to hold them; so, for example, a cruel father may lead a person to a revolutionary hatred of authority. Epistemology, however, is not concerned with the etiology of particular beliefs, but questions the grounds for various classes of beliefs, what constitutes "proof."

Some examples of epistemological positions from classical eighteenth century philosophy are rationalism and empiricism. *Rationalism* was an approach founded by Descartes and carried on by Leibniz and Spinoza. It regards the truth as coming from what is clear and distinct to a rational mind: intuition of first principles, and deductions from them.

Empiricists, on the other hand, viewed the truth as obtainable only from empirical data. Locke (1690) wrote, "There is nothing in the mind that is not first in the senses" (p. 91). The philosophy of Hume carried this position to an extreme and ended in skepticism. Kant tried to bring these two approaches together and establish that all knowledge is to some extent a function of our mental processes, so that unlimited absolute knowledge through either empiricism or pure reason is impossible. Hence his claim that his purpose was to make room for faith.

Piaget (1970), in the approach he called genetic epistemology, demonstrated that what we consider self-evident truth changes with the development of our thought processes as we mature. Thus every theory, every scientific discipline, carries with it an implicit metaphysics and epistemology. No truth is ever context-free or value-free.

SCIENCE AND THE MODERN WORLD

Even now the basic situation is not so different from the one confronted by Kant in 1781 when he wrote the *Critique of Pure Reason*. We are still faced with two conflicting world models or views. The first model states that our scientific conception of the world, including humans as physical-chemical machines subject to mechanical causality, is sufficient to explain everything. For example, Freud's "metapsychology" was an attempt to describe mental functioning according to orderly scientific laws, a hydrodynamic model using forces, energies, and quantities. He saw himself as a natural scientist in that tradition, and that is how modern United States psychiatry increasingly sees itself.

In the second world view, the human is conceived of as free-willed and creative, unfolding a basic preconscious or unconscious project of his or her nuclear self (as Kohut would put it) or a prereflective self (as Sartre would say), with the capacity for wondering, enjoying beauty, and experiencing a sense of the joy of being alive. This model emphasizes the human as having a solid sense of self with—as one of my patients metaphorized—"an iron rod of being" that withstands the vicissitudes of mental conflicts and compromise formations and still preserves a feeling of being joyously alive and even a part of something greater than oneself. Freud himself oscillated between these models, and mysteriously once commented to Binswanger, "Spirit is everything" (Spiegelberg 1972, p. 199).

Since the central curative aspect of psychotherapy rests on our ability to understand the patient and communicate this understanding back to him or her, then if these thinkers are correct we must not ignore the second model with its focus on a nonmechanistic mode of being human. Although many mental health professionals give lip service to this, the exigencies of a busy practice lead one to tend to disregard this model. As one young psychiatrist recently told me, "I might as well put a Prozac dispenser outside my door."

The crucial problem is how to approach these nonmechanical or "spiritual" aspects of humans, and it poses a central issue in all the human sciences, including psychology, economics, politics, sociology, anthropology, and philosophy. Certainly it is a crucial issue for the practice of intensive psychotherapy.

How does human being differ from all other being? Or, as Heidegger asks (here using the term *Dasein* loosely as human being), "What are the constitutive properties of *Dasein?*" The answer to this question remains unresolved. Leakey and Lewin (1978), for instance, argue that the constitutive properties of *Dasein* are as follows: (1) an awareness of the passage of time; (2) spoken language and our use of it to question our place in nature, or, as Heidegger put it, "to ask the Being question of Schelling, 'Why is there something rather than nothing at all' "; and (3) conscious awareness of the world around us and of ourselves. Some argue that the latter seems to be an evolutionary matter of degree. (For example, chimpanzees can recognize themselves in a mirror, whereas other primates cannot.) If this is true, conscious awareness may not be a constitutive property of *Dasein*.

Here also is where Freud the neurologist failed. His neurone system, elaborated in *Project for a Scientific Psychology* (1895), could not account for consciousness, so he gave it up and turned to psychoanalysis without reference to the neurological substrate at all. Freud's turn formed the starting point of psychiatry and psychology as a nonmedical, nonnaturalistic science, one that also developed in the works of Heidegger, Foucault, Ricoeur, Lacan, Sartre, Laing, and Kohut, among others, in a variety of ways not envisioned by Freud, who insisted repeatedly that psychoanalysis was a "natural science."

All of this emphasis on self and consciousness originated with Hegel's masterpiece, *Phenomenology of Spirit* (1807). It was taken up by the "left" Hegelians, among them Feuerbach and Marx (Conway 1987). Feuerbach stated that "species consciousness" is the crucial difference between humans and animals, and that the more human you are the more other-regarding you are. Marx (1844) pointed out that humans have no essence, only potentials (for autonomy, species consciousness, aesthetic appreciation, and philosophy).

Brentano (1838–1917) was a philosopher–psychologist who gave a series of courses that Freud eagerly attended for a couple of years when he was an 18-year-old medical student (Jones 1953). Brentano began his views with a study of Aquinas's famous statement, "Mental phenomena all include an intentionality," that is to say, a direction upon an object, in three ways:

1. *Ideas*: One may think of A, that is, present A to one's consciousness.
2. *Judgments*: One may take an intellectual stance to A, for example, accept it or reject it as a proposition.
3. *Emotions*: One may take an emotional stance with respect to A, for example, to love it, to hate it, and so on.

What is crucial here is that no mental phenomena are passively experienced – all are directed upon something, they always posit a representation of something or somebody "out there."

These ideas eventually led to *phenomenology*, which was first developed by Husserl in 1900. The term itself has been used differently by Heidegger, Sartre, Jaspers, and many others since that time. I will discuss it in detail in Chapter 10. In brief, Husserl's conceptions are as follows: A phenomenon is whatever appears to us immediately in experience. No "reduction" is permitted, no selecting out of experience is allowed. Such items as things, sensations, feelings, entities, and so forth, are not selected out of the flow of phenomena or stream of consciousness, since this already assumes certain classification principles about the world. Thus no *DSM-II or DSM-III* is to be allowed in the back of the therapist's mind. Husserl believed he found a new epistemological method, for these phenomenological statements could not be called empirical in that empiricism already assumes "things" or "entities" out there, as, for example, when we speak of a "case" of depression or schizophrenia.

Husserl argued that there is such a thing as presuppositionless inquiry, and it occurs in his phenomenology. That is to say, there are no theories, and one just describes the phenomena as they present themselves to an unprejudiced view. The technique of doing this employed the phenomenological stance – just register and react to what is simply there in immediate experience. One does not disconnect, isolate, interpret, or classify any aspects of the experience.

Epochē, a Greek word meaning suspension, is taken from stoic philosophy, and is called by Husserl phenomenological reduction or bracketing of being. With this technique one refrains from judgment about diagnosis, morals, values, cause, background, and subject. The patient is not seen as separate and different from the objective observer or therapist. Instead there exists an "intersubjective field" in which, for example, the therapist pays special attention to his or her own state of consciousness in the presence of the patient. This was applied in clinical psychiatry at Chestnut Lodge by Pao (1978) when he wrote about "the feel of a schizophrenic," the special intersubjective atmosphere created by a schizophrenic patient.

Husserl (1913) used this technique in an obsessive attempt to gain absolute knowledge. As such it fell into philosophical disrepute, but this new method became the principal alternative in one form or another to the empirical study of humans as objects of natural science. The empirical study of humans in practice often ignores the vivid immediacy of the lived world of the person in its effort to abstract out mechanical, scientific laws, reducing that person to a thing to be studied, dissected, manipulated, or liquidated – with all that implies for the history of the twentieth century and for the course now taken by United States psychiatry. I will illustrate this by turning first to Heidegger and then to Foucault to show how different their approach to humans is from that of the natural sciences. My argument is not directed against the natural-sciences approach but is intended to establish that this can never be a totally sufficient approach to humans for mental health professionals who practice psychiatry and psychotherapy. Heidegger and Foucault claim further that the current immersion of the world in science carries dangerous consequences for human relationships in general, for the very future of our species, and even for the planet on which we dwell.

The world is darkening. The essential episodes of this darkening are: the flights of the gods, the destruction of the earth, the standardization of man, the preeminence of the mediocre . . . (and) the misinterpretation of the spirit.

—Martin Heidegger (1961, p. 37)

By introducing such themes as Being, *Dasein*, world, time, and death, Heidegger placed man and his psyche before a vast cosmic background that psychology had never before considered in this manner. What now emerged was that a real understanding of man, normal or abnormal, was possible only by seeing him in relation to this most comprehensive setting. . . . Heidegger's phenomenological hermeneutics provides the horizon against which man's psyche stands out in depth. . . . It is thus Heidegger's new ontology which has ultimately revolutionized psychology and psychiatry.

—Herbert Spiegelberg (1972, p. 21)

Our world has been transformed by the material, spiritual, and intellectual impact of science and science-based technologies. Its reaction to the transformation (and a strange reaction it is!) is that we are stuck in a scientific environment. . . . My point is that these consequences are not grounded in an "objective" nature, but come from a complicated interplay between an unknown and relatively pliable material and researchers who affect and are affected and changed by the material which, after all, is the material from which they have been shaped. . . . The "subjective" side of knowledge, being inextricably intertwined with its material manifestations, cannot be just blown away . . . a look at history shows that this world is not a static world populated by thinking (and publishing) ants who, crawling all over its crevices, gradually discover its features without affecting them in any way. . . . It was once full of gods; it then became a drab material world; and it can be changed again, if its inhabitants have the determination, the intelligence, and the heart to take necessary steps.

—Paul Feyerabend (1989, p. 406)

1

HEIDEGGER

MARTIN HEIDEGGER (1889–1976), who died at the age of 86, was the most difficult and controversial of all the thinkers discussed in this book. There exists total disagreement about him; some call him a charlatan, whereas others claim his philosophy has the stature of Plato's and Aristotle's thought. Born near Freiburg, he spent his life in southwest Germany and remained a nasty and narrow provincial man to the end of his life. His father was Catholic and he had one younger brother. He was married (although an unfaithful husband) and had two sons, born between 1917 and 1919.

In November, 1918, Germany lost World War I. In that year Spengler's (1962) enormously influential *Decline of the West* appeared, explaining this decline (rather inconsistently and near the end of the work) as due to the rise of science and the technological society that resulted from it. In 1927 Heidegger published *Being and Time* (1962a) and became instantly famous. From 1933 to 1934 he was the Rector of the University of Freiburg and a member of the Nazi party. He resigned from the rectorship after nine months. After World War II he was not reinstated because of his Nazi affiliation (see Farias 1989) and he lived in a lonely cottage in isolation. In all the years he lived after World War II he never uttered a word about being a Nazi, he never said anything significant about the Holocaust, and he even refused to answer questions about the Holocaust and what it meant for philosophy and human beings. A generous explanation of this would be that he considered these questions to be "ontic," as we shall see, and he was interested in the ontological instead.

His basic preoccupation was with the ontological question of Being. How does Being manifest itself through both animate and inanimate beings? He replaced God with Being in writing that was dogmatic, authoritative, and sometimes plainly dishonest. He assumed without any argument that this question of Being is meaningful and in this sense, as Waterhouse (1981) called it, he introduced "a second religiousness," although some commentators (Llewelyn 1985) warn that his work is not simply a secularized theology.

HEIDEGGER'S METHOD

The unique approach of Heidegger, who was a great and inspiring teacher but morally a small person and thus a very odd combination, was that philosophy must arise out of and return to lived experience. That is what gives it value and ensures its truth. For Heidegger the method of phenomenology was to let that which shows itself directly appear without prejudices; in this he borrowed from his teacher, Husserl, but he used this method for quite a different purpose. Whereas Husserl (see Chapter 10) attempted to found philosophy as an exact science, Heidegger used phenomenology to explore the human condition, as we shall see. When one exercises that sort of phenomenology, it reveals, claims Heidegger, that human lived experience is temporal and depends for meaning on memory and anticipation. Therefore it contains a unity of understanding that is *prior* to any natural scientific knowledge of any person.

The human lived world and language are a system shared with others and are historical, which implies they are born of a long tradition whose meaning we can only discuss from the inside, since we are always a part of it. We are thrown into this system at birth, says Heidegger.

By way of illustration, he explains that each and every truly great philosophical, literary, or psychological text such as the complete *Standard Edition* of Freud's collected works, or the complete works of Plato, or the novels of Dostoevsky, expresses an insight or vision into the way things are. To read such texts we must grasp the intuition of our lived world that the author expresses in his or her historical moment. By approaching texts in this way, as a teacher Heidegger also brought into contemporary importance ancient and medieval works that the modern age had obscured or lost. Every great system of thought, explains Heidegger, contains, either expressed or unexpressed, an implicit driving idea, a star on which that philosopher is fixed at the time.

At first he collaborated with his teacher, the Jewish philosopher Husserl

(1859–1938) who was 30 years older, but although both claimed to use the "phenomenological" method, as mentioned, they are entirely different in their conception of it and how to apply it. This led initially to confusion and then a break-up of their friendship.

Another important friend, Karl Jaspers (1883–1969), was a psychiatrist and philosopher. Heidegger and Jaspers were friends until 1933. Jaspers had a Jewish wife and consequently lost all his academic positions because he would not divorce her as the Nazis demanded. Heidegger became a Nazi and never helped Jaspers. From Jaspers (1932a, 1932b, 1932c) he took the idea that truth begins in certain fundamental experiences in the lived world, so-called boundary or limit situations, such as death, anguish, guilt, and suffering.

HUMAN BEING AND THE WORLD

Among the critically important points that Heidegger makes are, first, the static entities that are related by the laws of science, such as diagnoses, research objects, and so forth, are actually *abstractions* from two crucial "horizons" that form a background out of which all natural science emerges. These horizons are (1) the temporal, the awareness of time that always accompanies conscious awareness, and (2) the lived world of human everyday background practices of every culture.

Heidegger describes the *mitwelt*, our with-world, or "being-with-others" as it can be for each of us, in two ways. It can be inauthentic, that is to say, represented by a concern for people as things or objects. (The word "concern" [*Sorge, Besorgen*][1] here means interestedness, a term he borrowed without attribution from Kierkegaard. It has no moral connotation and implies simply involvement or curiosity.) Or one's being-with-others can be authentic, a binding with people by devotion to common causes that Heidegger labels solicitude (*Fürsorge*). It is this solicitude that has been lost in our modern age, he says, and in place of it, inauthentically, we have our "relationships" with people that are based on, as Heidegger (1962a) writes, (1) *competitiveness*, which sets us apart from each other; (2) *publicness*, which suppresses the exceptional and implies an obsession with being a well-rounded personality, with what one "ought" to do to fit in, to adapt, to achieve an *averageness*; all of which results in (3) *fallenness (Verfallenheit)* into the "they" (*das Man*), or the public world, as

---

[1]Heidegger used German words in his special way. I have included some of his terms in parentheses for accuracy and have chosen translations from the references cited.

Heidegger puts it, which relieves one of personal responsibility because "every-body does it" or "I was just following orders." Heidegger's notion of fallenness was taken, again without attribution, from the work of Kierkegaard; a number of Heidegger's ideas are borrowed from Kierkegaard and reshaped.

Heidegger introduces the special term *Dasein*, or human being. He wants to avoid the preconception of an essential "human" by using this term, which means literally "to be there in the world." *Dasein* is always immersed in the world, grounded in it. The mode of being of *Dasein*, or human being, is to raise the question of Being; but *Dasein* is always influenced by the social world and *Dasein*, Heidegger says, is always in a mood, a state of mind. What is meant here by a state of mind is "where you are at" affect-wise at a given time.

The term *facticity* is used to denote the way *Dasein* experiences the facts which are true of it. For example, consider one's self-image, which is determined by one's place in history, in the family, and in the culture, since *Dasein* is always from birth already in the world. This is Heidegger's concept that he calls "throwness" (*Geworfenheit*). We are inescapably cast into the world; the stories of Franz Kafka give marvelous illustrations of "throwness." So the human is an event or happening caught up in the flow of a shared historical project.

It follows that there is no separately independent ego. The human is always interrelated with the world of things and other persons. Thus the human is an activity or a process, never a subject or an essence, claims Heidegger, never an "object" that can be studied under a microscope without losing its very human being.

A mood can only be replaced, he says, by another mood, not by cognitive insights, and in this, as we shall see, there is a similarity to the value systems of Kohut and Foucault in their deconstruction of the central role of reason and insight, which prevailed since the enlightenment. Our perception of the world varies from mood to mood. A mood for Heidegger is a style of activity, for example, approaching everything in a fearful, cringing way or a paranoid way, and so forth. This has been suggested in psychiatry by Shapiro (1965) in his book *Neurotic Styles*, but Shapiro concentrates more on cognitive styles than on affect. Heidegger concludes that we must face and overcome moods and become master of our moods, but he never explains how to do this.

In discussing "understanding," Heidegger claims that one's chosen capac-ities are displayed in one's activities. Understanding, then, for Heidegger, is not cognitive. We are not rational animals. This is very similar to Kohut's (1977) notion of action thought, in which intrapsychic change during psychoanalysis is displayed in the case he presents of Mr. M., whose efforts to find a bridge between the poles of his bipolar self are described; these efforts or manifest activities shift as he goes through phases of analysis. Action thought is also demonstrated in Kohut's (1984) claim that the proof of the transformation of narcissism and successful treatment is not in the gaining of cognitive insights but occurs when one has actively built an empathic matrix.

For Heidegger "understanding" develops through interpretation of the world and expresses itself through discourse or the choice of being silent, but it always contains prescientific presuppositions. So there exist no neutral facts in the sciences of man. "Truths" or "facts" are always determined by background cultural practices, which provide the basic unarticulated background of meaning in that culture. That is to say, the practices of each culture carry an implicit interpretation of what it is to be a person, object, or society. The belief systems each person has are embodied in these practices, which carry a pre-theoretical understanding.

Heidegger continues by claiming that genuine discourse for most people is replaced by idle chatter of the public world or by the media, which Heidegger labels "a repetitious prattling on," or by superficial activity, such as what one "must" do and see according to convention, like collecting dolls or watching sports. This is the being of everyday *Dasein* which Heidegger labels fallenness: self-distraction, frantic meaningless activities, or, as one of my patients put it, "My life consists of lunching and shopping on the North Shore," activity which has a self-generating, accelerating quality that Heidegger calls turbulence *(Wirbel)*, a whirlpool effect.

In his idiosyncratic use of the term "anxiety," again borrowed from Kierkegaard, Heidegger labels anxiety as desirable and as occurring primarily about fallenness. It has the tendency to pull the person back from absorption in the public world. For example, being-towards-death as it is described in Tolstoy's great story, *The Death of Iván Ilých*, raises anxiety and stirs what Heidegger calls conscience to get us to face, in a manner he calls "resolutely," death, nothingness at the heart of one's being—all is vanity, and one can never reach one's own potential fully because one dies first.

Heidegger concludes that one must be resolute, although he does not say how. It is a dangerous concept because it contains a hint of the blond goose-stepping Nazi superman, which some authors (Waterhouse 1981, Farias 1989) argue is just what he had in mind at the time, pointing to his application of it in his (1985b) infamous speech, "Self-assertion of the German University," in 1933.

BEING AND TIME

Being and Time, published in 1927, is an unfinished obscure masterpiece that made Heidegger quickly famous. It appealed to philosophers, theologians, psychiatrists, and psychologists, profoundly influencing all of these on the European continent. Only now is it gaining influence in England and the United States (Chessick 1986). In this work Heidegger reopens the question of Being, which was last formulated implicitly but wrongly (he says) in Aristotle, and lost since then because the West has gone off in a technological direction. For Heidegger, Being is the transcendent unity of all things. It is self-evident and one cannot encapsulate it in any definition. For the early pre-Socratic Greeks, he says, it was an object of wonder and awe, and indeed there exists a sense of awe in Heidegger regarding Being through all of his work (for the best overview of his thought, see Richardson 1974).

Because the Being-question implies a questioner, this investigation, says Heidegger, is only open to humans. He hoped by a study of the manifest phenomena of human being, *Dasein*, to demonstrate that time is the horizon for any study of Being and to get some idea of Being as it shows itself through a phenomenological study of human being (Heidegger 1982).

Heidegger (Heidegger 1968a, Kocklemans 1984) gave up this approach midway, however, because his very conclusions indicate that Being can only appear when we retire from active investigation and achieve a state of *Gelassenheit* ("releasement"; see Heidegger 1969, p. 54n) — serenity, composure, release, a state of relaxation, a disposition that lets be, rather reminiscent of Bion's (1963, 1967) exhortation to approach each therapy session without memory, desire, or understanding. Yet there is active investigation in *Being and Time*. Heidegger's "existential analytic" is an analysis of how we live our lives, and this rather than the investigation of Being is what made the book famous, much to Heidegger's anger and constant disclaimers that he was not an existentialist.

Heidegger (1975a) goes back to the early Greeks. The trouble began with Plato, who interprets Being as Idea, a word that comes from the Greek word *eidō* (εἰδω), meaning to see, implying a separation of the subject who sees from an object of study or knowledge. Heidegger says Aristotle was wrong also, replacing Being with a static "substance" or *ousia* (οὐσία), another Greek term, the participle of the Greek verb "to be" (εἶναι). But the crucial point is in Heidegger's reading of the history of philosophy as having taken with Plato a wrong turn that requires rethinking. Rorty (1979) has also discussed this topic and yet he (Murray 1978) also agrees with Heidegger that "to cease thinking about what Plato and Kant were thinking about is to be diminished, to lose hold of what is most important, to sink into darkness" (p. 257).

In Heidegger's method of "existential analytic" in *Being and Time*, which is really a study by Heidegger of himself (a method similar to that of Freud and Kierkegaard), he uses what he calls phenomenology, for Heidegger a description of the actual lives of human beings, especially his own. He borrows the philosopher Windelband's (1848–1915) epistemological distinction, which is based on the fact that any real object such as the human can be viewed either *nomothetically*, that is, falling under general laws, the descriptions of empirical natural science which constitute the biology of humans; or *ideographically*. In stressing specific and unique individuality we are viewing humans ideographically, and Heidegger would ask from this viewpoint, "What is specific and unique about the being of man *(Dasein)?*"

A similar distinction is used by Meissner (1971), who describes Freud's psychoanalysis as a scientific hybrid resting on and trying to combine two poles: (1) nomothetic–using rules, laws, mathematical physics, and energy, and (2) ideographic–representing ideas by symbols that are unique, individual, characteristically human, and have subjective meaning.

The point being made by all these thinkers is that every human science–economics, social science, psychology, psychiatry, history, political science, and so forth–by its very nature must be such a hybrid. The contemporary psychiatrist cannot ever be, by virtue of his or her subject matter, the human mind, only a medical specialist. If he or she tries to be, the very subject of the study, the human being, will disappear and the psychiatrist end up studying a thing, a machine, an apparatus, a central nervous system. So we have a quasi-science attempting to gain respectability in our culture. Thus the term crypto-biologist, as Sulloway (1979) calls Freud, a secret biologist, rests on a slight misunderstanding of Freud and the data of psychiatry. The phrase "quasi- or imitative biologist" would be better. As Kohut (1984) says, "Scientific objectivity in the sciences of man must always include the objective assessment of the observer–the influence of the observed on the observer and, especially, the influence of the observer on the field that he observes" (p. 40).

If we agree that the human sciences have to be more than natural sciences, the obvious question would be, What other approaches and methods must we also use? Heidegger's "existential analytic" was an early, admittedly nonscientific, attempt to do this. It did not use laboratory or instrumental observation and experiment. It was not nomothetic. Its method was phenomenology, borrowed from Husserl (1913), and used ingeniously for a different purpose.

For Heidegger phenomenology is a method giving access to the being of entities, to an understanding of Being. Phenomenology first concerns itself with matters of concrete existence that Heidegger labels the ontic dimension. This yields "existentiells." From such phenomenological descriptions, by "hermeneutic analysis" he proceeds to uncover what he calls basic structures or "existentials" of Being. So for Heidegger, phenomenology moves from ontic inquiry to ontological inquiry, and this is the key method of his early philosophy. For Heidegger phenomenology does not, as in Husserl, lead to any transcendental subject or ego, a fundamental difference between them.

"EXISTENTIAL ANALYTIC"

Let us take a closer look at Heidegger's "existential analytic." Here are some of his conclusions, simply announced by him on the basis of his phenomenological study. All other entities besides *Dasein* have essential properties. That is to say, they have *presence-at-hand (Verhandenheit)*. *Dasein* does not; it only has "characteristics," possible ways to be. *Dasein* can choose to appropriate its being and be authentic; otherwise an inauthentic way of being becomes pervasive.

The concept of "everydayness" for Heidegger means *Dasein's* way of being, when it is actively living in a developed culture. This already carries certain basic inarticulated structures and influences how the human understands himself or herself to be. In order to understand the human you must understand these existentials, as Heidegger calls them, for any given culture. The existentials are:

1. *Being-in:* The human is absorbed in the world as a dwelling place. He or she cannot avoid an encounter with the world. Objects can, for they can exist in space inertly alongside each other. Thus, as for Lacan (see Chapter 5), cultural practices for Heidegger determine meanings and values and represent a background that we are born into and that entirely shapes our thought and beliefs. These can never be fully articulated, since they even underlie our use of language.
2. *At-homeness:* This is implied in our always dwelling somewhere in the world specifically, and not somewhere else.
3. *Concern:* A human is always absorbed in something that matters to him or her.
4. *Worldhood:* This is implied, since to all of us a world around us appears always—the *Umwelt*, things encountered in our practical activities. Heidegger's (1962a) term for these things encountered in everyday practical activity is *Zeug*, gear or equipment, which is ready-to-hand and is used for our purposes. This is not value free, because equipment is used for the goals of practical activity and is prescientifically understood. When, however, gear is damaged, missing, or does not work right—or, in Heidegger's terms, it becomes "obstinate" (*Aufässigkeit*, obstinacy)—our purposeful activity is interrupted. Then we stand back and study, and from this, science and the objects of science arise and technological language and communication develop.

THE FUNDAMENTAL ERROR

Dasein mistakenly understands itself as objectlike, by false analogy from studying other entities (*Zeug*) in the above situation. *Dasein* mistakenly conceives of its relationship to objects as knowing or scientific study. But knowing or science only arises *secondarily* when the human pulls back from concernful involvement and practical activity and just looks or studies. This produces a false dichotomy between the human observer and "objects" of study in the world, and makes possible the human as an "object" of such study. It loses sight of the crucial background practices that determine the human in each culture, which can only be grasped from the inside by empathy, as Kohut would say, or hermeneutics, as Heidegger would say, not through scientific detachment. Heidegger argues that the human is not, as Descartes claimed, primarily a subject, a scientific knower disengaged from the world.

The same mistaken attitude held by Descartes has inevitably, from the time of Plato, led to the age of technology, according to Heidegger (1954); Russia and the United States are in a "technological frenzy" (Heidegger 1961), which leads to an increased unrestricted organization of the average man into "stock" for use (perhaps currently we might de-emphasize Russia and add Japan and Germany, which is *not* what Heidegger hoped for from Germany). Heidegger's (1954) term for this process is *Ge-stell*, or enframing. Technology entrenches itself everywhere, leaves man out, runs away with man (Mitcham 1985). This leads to a darkening of our world (Heidegger 1961) and produces the modern world picture, as Heidegger (1954) calls it in his essay, "The Age of the World Picture." He points out how the scholar is replaced by the "researcher" with his or her academic power struggles, meetings, publications, and grants, and how the human becomes conceptualized at that point as only another object for study and manipulation. Thus technology makes humans into "raw material." It destroys the spiritual part of humans and leads to nihilism, as Nietzsche pointed out so dramatically. This "darkening of the world" (Heidegger 1961) is similar to Arendt's (his student) concern with the banality of evil or Marcuse's (1964) "one dimensional man," and similar to Spengler's (1962) thought.

As a concrete example, consider the Being of a tree. For the Greeks, says Heidegger, it was the power to emerge from non-presence, grow, and maintain its presence in the face of a possible lapse into non-presence. For the medievals, it fills a fixed place in a divinely created hierarchy. For modern man, beginning with Descartes, it is classified by botany and viewed as a useful physico-chemical product, transformable into a commodity. The task of humans today, maintains Heidegger, is to prepare ourselves for a new disclosure of the presence of things. This is a radical utopian vision arising from his revulsion at the present situation. But it is quite passive, for Heidegger concludes in his later thought that there is nothing for us to do but wait and hope for the grace of a better dawn (lighting of Being) since the light has gone out in the West.

Heidegger insists that humans must recover authentic engagement or attunement, which is not far from Kohut's (1978) call for our empathy with each other and with the world. But for Heidegger (1985a) empathy is a "pseudo-problem" (p. 243). We need not feel ourselves into another subject. We understand him or her because the world in which he or she is in is also in us. Technology, however, cuts us off from our roots and our culture. Ours is a society of the spectacle, and we are incapable of authentic dwelling, in which space is an ancient landscape providing a context for everyday life, and time is a historical realm for deeds and events (Zimmerman 1990). Heidegger in his later writings (1968a, 1975b) argues that great art, especially poetry, rather than empathy, recovers our authentic attunement with the world, for poetic expression both presents things and reveals their relationship to humans and how humans experience them. Indeed, poetic vision becomes central to the revelation of meaning in the later work of Heidegger (Kockelmans 1985), and is the main antidote to technological frenzy. For him poetry can lead to the illumination of Being, and it has what he calls a healing function among the arts. This is discussed at length in his (contained in 1975b) essay *The Origin of the Work of Art*, based on courses originally presented in 1935 and 1936. In the introduction, the translator tells us how the basic creative function "obtains its creativeness from its willingness to stop, listen, hear, remember, and respond to the call that comes from Being" (p. xvi). Heidegger's notion of thinking hopes for a complete opening of the human spirit, in contrast to the "calculative thinking" of science (Halliburton 1981). This essay and *Being and Time* constitute Heidegger's most extraordinary and original publications. The student should be warned not to read this essay in *Basic Writings* (Heidegger 1977a) where it is badly abridged, but in *Poetry, Language, Thought* (Heidegger 1975b).

OBJECTIONS TO HEIDEGGER'S THEORIES

A number of powerful objections have been raised to Heidegger's theories. How does one validate his claims, which after all just describe his existence and experience? He idealizes primitive peasant work as primary and in some way, like poetry, close to Being—a simplistic notion which has an appeal to mindless fundamentalists. This romanticism over the *"volk,"* or the primeval world of ancient Germans, is a common tendency in German writers, for example, Spengler (1962). He presents mystic visions of Being that seem impossible to validate but have great appeal to some religious Catholics, and he (in Sheehan 1981) concludes, "Only a god can save us" (p. 45), presenting perhaps a kind of secularized theology, and implying the advocacy of passivity in the face of human problems (Chessick 1989b) or leading to nihilism (Bernstein 1988b).

Unconvincingly, he (1954) blames corruption by the ideology of science for the inauthentic shift from the craftsman at work to the detached scientist or technician making missiles. He seems unaware that Marx wrote extensively about this shift, and it has since become the subject of many conflicting sociological treatises.

It is not true that everybody relates as inauthentically as Heidegger did. Not all professors cheat on their wives and have sexual affairs with their students as he did (Young-Bruehl 1982). People do love their children, families, and friends, and do show solicitude for the human community, and do try to improve the world—at least to some degree some people do. There is a kind of schizoid ingredient in Heidegger's thought, suggesting social withdrawal, mystical visions, and waiting for a god. At the same time his ideas are so cleverly formulated that, once studied, they have a way of adhering and reorienting one's interests and interpretations, even in clinical work!

A certain vacuity pervades Heidegger's concepts, as in his important notion of authenticity. Heidegger was morally a very small man, and he proved that thinking on Being does not make a person ethical. He himself was not authentic in any sense of the term. His Greek etymologies and his readings of the great poet Hölderlin are unacceptable to scholars and are generally indefensible. Caputo (1988) points out there is no evidence for Heidegger's claim that the Greeks had a moment of illumination and that our era is a dead end. He argues that no epoch is privileged.

To all of this Heidegger, who admired "Hitler's wonderful hands," answered that one star had caught his eye as the light went out in the West, the question of Being. One could argue, however, that it is in the apocalypse at Auschwitz that the essence of the West is revealed—and it was the uniquely evil thought guiding this event that Heidegger entirely failed to recognize. Reading Heidegger leaves the best minds, such as Steiner (1979), troubled and unsure whether he simply plays on words or has uncovered something of fundamental importance. The profound influence he has exercised on those who followed him in many fields, including psychology and psychiatry, indicates that he has indeed touched on a universal theme.

HEIDEGGER'S LATER THOUGHT

Hölderlin (1770–1843), who greatly influenced Heidegger, pointed out that art can be a source of truth, and that through the power of poetry and song humans draw goals and meanings from nature and primitive chaos. Nietzsche (1844–1900) invented a literary-philosophical language to illustrate that all "knowledge" is a creative perspective. Heidegger concluded that art could be a counterforce to technology and insisted that poetry is the highest manifestation of art. It sensitizes us to the world and it sets up a possible world as "truths becoming." Language gives the world to us (Bruns 1989). It is not simply a tool, but actually generates a template through which we come to understand ourselves and the world, a concept taken up by Lacan.

Thus science leaves something out. The entities that scientists encounter are shaped by their projections. Scientists must not forget their pervasive constituting role in the creation of the "entities" that they study. Even *Being and Time*, Heidegger says, got caught up in what he (1969) calls "calculative thinking" in a search for total clarity. But truth is always accompanied by hiddenness; in Heidegger's mysterious terms, Being conceals while it reveals.

Being, for Heidegger in his later writing (1958, 1977b), is a lighting process by which beings are illuminated as beings. It is a power. *Dasein* is endowed with the unique prerogative of ecstatic openness to this lighting process. *Dasein* or there-being is where it takes place, in a clearing, a breach in the darkness which itself changes in each cultural era and is completed through language. There is a mutual presence of *Dasein* and Being; there is no subject–object dichotomy. Heidegger's later method requires a docility to Being found only, he says, in poets and true thinkers who engage in a "talking-listening." For Heidegger (1977a) language is the house of Being—that is, the space where Being is able to appear.

This is not the humanism that sees man as a separate subject and a rational animal, or as a Cartesian starting point and a creator of values. It is not at all the view of Sartre (see Chapter 6), and Heidegger, as he repeatedly insisted, is not an "existentialist." The human for Heidegger (1977a) is only the "shepherd of being." This philosophy is not a "metaphysics" which from the time of Plato, says Heidegger, was grounded in the subject–object polarity. It is not philosophical anthropology, which places the human at the center and affirms his or her fundamental individuality and sociability, as in the theories of Kierkegaard, Marx, and Nietzsche, although even Nietzsche wanted revalued values (Chessick 1983a).

Rilke (1875–1926), according to Heidegger (1975b), was the first poet attempting to evade technicity, a technicity that treats humans as raw material. (Historians of literature would certainly disagree.) Rilke looks for the realm of the heart, in an imitation of Pascal, which locks him unfortunately even deeper into subjectivism because his source is the heart of the subject. At any rate, Heidegger calls him a poet "on the way for a troubled time" (see Richardson 1974, Part 3, Section A, Ch. 8 and Section B, Ch. 11).

Heidegger's (see Kockelmans 1984, p. 71) obscure notion of "mittence" *(Geschick)* (Richardson 1974, pp. 20–21, 435) is defined as an event *(Ereignis)* in which Being is disclosed on the initiative of Being (Llewelyn 1985). "Mittence" is a neologism used by Richardson (1974, p. 435) to refer to Heidegger's concept of coming-to-pass or self-emitting (p. 20), an event by which Being sends itself to man. As Heidegger (Richardson 1974, p. xxii) remarks, it is ambiguous and must be. The mystery of Being is its self-concealing revelation. This leads to what Heidegger calls poetizing: In a mittence the Holy (Being) addresses the poet, and he or she responds by forming this address into words (White 1978). The same is true for what Heidegger calls "foundational thinkers" in philosophy. We are each free to respond to the hail of Being, and authenticity in Heidegger's (1968a) later version indicates an individual's docile consent to facilitate and consent to the appeal of Being, an acquiescent response to this hail of Being. Each person, however, must experience this for him- or herself, and it is always tentative and requires "ever-renewed watchfulness" (Heidegger 1977a). Heidegger's (1958) writing on the Being-question becomes increasingly mystical, in the direction of Meister Eckhart (1260–1328).[2]

Being presents itself in the fourfold (earth, sky, gods, and mortals) which mutually mirror each other (Heidegger 1975b, Zimmerman 1981) to produce the richness of Being. The human subject is decentered as Being-towards-death, on the way to not-being. Authenticity is to heed this, and to realize that *Dasein* dwells in nearness to things. It tends Being in beings. *Augenblick,* or a moment of vision, is the time when an individual is chosen to receive a new manifestation of Being. For example, when we let a work of art be what it is, we allow ourselves to be transported by what flows from the work itself, deemphasizing the artist. Then for us in each art work the truth leaps forth in an original leap, says Heidegger, and he claimed that art ended with Wagner, who expressed frenzied feelings in art, not truth. For Heidegger art is over, but his position on this is ambiguous (Kockelmans 1985).

Heidegger's later notion of the self moves farther and farther away from any ontic notion such as that of Kohut. It begins in the "Letter on Humanism" (Heidegger 1977a), although it is already implicit in some of his essays after *Being and Time.* To understand it, some recapitulation and preliminary explanations are in order.

The "clearing" *(Lichtung)* is defined as a place where a releasing, a setting free of entities happens so they may come to light, a free space. But for this to occur, man must ek-sist, open himself to entities as they appear in the clearing. *Dasein* (being there) must stand in the open and "endure" (Biemel 1976) the clearing that comes to pass.

The clearing itself changes, for in each era beings have made their appearance in different ways. Man has no control over this; all we can do is

---

[2]See, for example, Heidegger's essay "The Pathway" (in Sheehan 1981), or "Conversation on a Country Path About Thinking" (Heidegger 1969).

think about it, which, says Heidegger, makes the history of metaphysics our history. We ask, what is the nature of the particular clearing that has occurred at any given time? In which clearing does a given philosopher stand (although each philosopher thinks not of clearings but of entities, without realizing that he is in a clearing)?

So the human cannot be thought of with respect to his or her character—behaving and doing—or with respect to social behavior and political action. For Heidegger, the nature of man can only be defined with respect to the clearing. As *Dasein*, man is the being to whom it is given to stand outside of himself in the clearing, his ek-sistence. This is a change from his earlier definition of *Dasein*, employing a different terminology, hopefully more free of metaphysical concepts. Also, Heidegger claims that man is used by the clearing as its trustee or guard. This active function of *Dasein* authenticates the human character; he performs it by way of thinking and by the production of art, especially poetry. He experiences the clearing and articulates it in language.

Being, clearing, truth of Being, and ἀλήθεια are the same (in Heidegger). Standing in the clearing is the ek-sistence of man, and man's efforts concerning his selfhood, the projecting of himself on his possibilities, to use Heidegger's language, are no longer of central importance. It is a mistake for a person to consider himself or herself as an independent subject, or "ego," or center of initiative, a theme of Heidegger's developed later by Lacan.

But the later Heidegger invests man with a dignity far surpassing any humanism, stressing his "nearness" to Being. Man is no longer conceived as a subject or a self. In contrast, metaphysics is a technique of explanation dealing with beings but not the truth of Being itself. A clearing is conceived as changing due to a "destiny" (*Geschick*), or a mittence, which man must endure. In the age of technicity, man never encounters his true self or nature, which, as defined above, stems from his relationship to the unconcealed. In his last work, Heidegger writes Being crossed out to emphasize the inextricable relationship between Being and *Dasein*.

The supremacy of *Ge-stell* (enframing) in the age of technology poses a threat that man cannot enter the primordial mode of disclosing because this mode produces nothing, and man in *Ge-stell* is sucked up in a frenzy of disposing, the placing of stock for material use and production. This mode of disposing, says Heidegger, was preceded by an epoch in which entities became objects, with man as a subject. Knowledge supposedly obtained by the subject about objects now becomes replaced by mastery—the power of having something at one's disposal, and so objects or things become viewed as stock for this purpose. This is not to be interpreted as a total condemnation of the age of technicity, for Heidegger sees even this as a manner in which Being chooses to show itself in our era. Reflecting on this, he believes, offers the chance of liberation of man, so for Heidegger in some of his essays, it seems that the human is not a slave of destiny or the mittence of Being.

This reveals an ambiguity in Heidegger's later conception of man, since on the one hand he is used by unconcealedness but on the other hand he contributes the activities of thinking and art. Is man delivered up to his destiny or does he determine it? Heidegger would answer that the question is wrong because it assumes the opposition of the active and the passive and traditional metaphysical conceptual dichotomies such as subject and object. Both must be true, but if man is simply used there is no hope to escape the age of technicity.

The later Heidegger moves into a resigned mood and the realm of poetry and "releasment" (Gelassenheit). He concludes with the all-moving, all-generating Being or fourfold, which in their interplay constitute the world: earth, sky, gods, mortals. This is held together by language, the "primordial gathering," which should not be understood in the language of metaphysics as a sort of transcendental force but rather as contained within the fourfold. It is a form of soundless speech, which Dasein in the clearing gathers and articulates in poetry. Ereignis (event) is the primal source of poetry; it is the mode of disclosure in which appropriation in the clearing occurs when Being "gives." This "giving" also should not be thought of as a cause or effect or force, but built into the very essence of Being itself.

These concepts are extremely difficult for us and appear to be mystical and meaningless because we are steeped in the assumptions that constitute the metaphysical stance of the Western world. Heidegger has attempted to think his way out of that stance by returning to its alleged origins in the presocratic Greek thinkers, and for him these concepts emerged out of a lifetime of what he would call genuine or foundational thinking (as contrasted to the calculative thinking and logic that constitute Western scientific thought). To the end of his life he regarded himself as "on the way" but with an unfinished task always before him.

CLINICAL ASPECTS

Heidegger never considers the problem of the unconscious. He would probably repudiate the question because it is ontic – about persons, not about Being. One could say as does Richardson (1965) that the unconscious is the ontological-existential dimension of the onto-conscious self, but this is stretching Heidegger's meanings. Freud, on the other hand, was utterly oblivious to what

Heidegger would call the being-dimension of humans, and worked only with the ontic aspects of humans, considering himself a natural scientist (Chessick 1980).

Why is the ultimate meaning of *Dasein* for Heidegger temporal? First, there is *Dasein's* future, which is always coming back to Being through beings. Then there is *Dasein's* past which already has been, its throwness. Finally, there is *Dasein's* present, in which Being renders beings manifest. The unity of *Dasein's* future, past, and present is the unity of time and it is what gives unity and meaning to *Dasein.*

According to Heidegger, there are three aspects of being-in-the-world. First, *Befindlichkeit,* or the discovering of one's self as already in the world, the recognition of one's facticity. It constitutes a state of mind so as to be affected by what happens in the world. Next, *Verstehen* (understanding), the realization of one's *Existenz* or ontological possibilities. This concept is again quite different from Sartre, who sees each human as freely constituting himself or herself ontically in the world. So Heidegger's ontology and investigation of Being is for him the central issue and is to be conceived of as quite different from Sartre's ontic existential preoccupation, with each person making one's self as a project in the world that one lives in (Fell 1979). The final aspect of being-in-the-world for Heidegger is discourse, or *Rede,* the capacity to articulate our being tuned-in to the world and what understanding discloses to us. But psychotherapists should note that *Rede* for Heidegger includes speaking out, hearing and listening, heeding, and being silent and attentive.

In *Basic Problems of Phenomenology,* lectures given just after the publication of *Being and Time,* Heidegger (1982) points out that *Dasein* is transcendent because by being-in-the-world it is out beyond itself. It has an "ek-static" structure, standing outside of itself and toward Being. The self cannot be separated from being-in-the-world and includes a precognitional intimacy with others. Therefore the ego-self is not primary. *Dasein* is not a "thing." Studies of people in the human sciences are ontic and reveal only "existentiells." They miss the transcendental aspects of *Dasein.* Pursuing this line of thought, Heidegger labels as the "ontological difference" the fact that beings are not the same as Being. *Dasein* is characterized by transcendence, finitude (being thrown into the world and dependent on others), and temporality (a person lives on a time scale and dies). So for Heidegger *Dasein,* or the self, is a process, a goal-directed activity.

This has extremely important implications for our clinical work, as it emphasizes the human interaction, intersubjectivity, and precognitional intimacy and avoids the nineteenth century notion of the detached scientist-doctor "objectively" studying the object-patient. It sets the stage for all the other approaches outlined in this book (for a detailed comparison of the notion of the "self" in Heidegger and Kohut, see Chessick 1988a). Heidegger's goal is "re-trieve" or what he later calls "dialogue" ("talking-listening"), one of the principal modes of foundational (as opposed to calculative) thought: a wringing of the un-said from the said.

Every clinician who takes the time and trouble to study Heidegger's work, with the aid of such commentaries as Richardson (1974), Kockelmans (1984, 1985), Kaelin (1988), Pöggeler (1987), and Mehta (1971, 1976), will find his or her fundamental conception of what constitutes the patient in psychotherapy profoundly altered, just as happened to those famous pioneers in psychotherapy, Binswanger and Boss (see for example Binswanger's case of Ellen West in May 1958 and discussed in Binswanger 1963, Boss 1963, 1979, Chessick 1989a), as well as to the thinkers discussed in this book and many, many others. This brief chapter does not do justice to the depth and originality of Heidegger's thought. He is one of those seminal thinkers with contemporary significance, like Nietzsche, Marx, and Freud, who demands a lifetime of study and restudy. At each point in one's life that one returns to such thinkers, one is stimulated by different aspects of their vision and again forced to rethink one's own preconceptions, practices, and values.

2

FOUCAULT

MICHEL FOUCAULT WAS A homosexual who died of AIDS at the age of 57. His father was a physician. He was born in France, spent his childhood under the Nazi occupation, and began his career as a psychologist, working with state hospital psychiatrists. Eventually he became a prestigious professor of philosophy specializing in the history of thought. Foucault called the entire history of psychiatry into question and studied the rise of the human sciences. A unique, original thinker, he defies classification and is elusive and exasperating, like Nietzsche, of whom he is the greatest modern disciple. In later years he did much work on behalf of prisoners and penal reform and to help dissidents and deviants. Eribon (1991) nicely reviews his controversial career.

Foucault employed a terrible literary style, working always across the disciplinary boundaries of the human sciences: psychiatry, psychology, linguistics, education, economics, social science, penology, administration, philosophy, and politics. He concluded that power and knowledge determine each other and resonate to produce these "disciplines." He employed two methods in his investigations, so there is an "earlier" and a "later" Foucault, and he was developing a third method, which was unfinished when he died prematurely.

Foucault, especially in his earlier writing, used many Marxist-sounding terms such as class, political economy, capital, labor, and struggle, but he was not a committed Marxist. He was a communist for two years after World War II and then withdrew from the party. By Foucault's own philosophy Marx belongs to the nineteenth century "episteme," as we shall see. For those with an interest in the philosophy of science, the best review of the background and development of Foucault's earlier thought is by Gutting (1989). He also offers a balanced criticism of Foucault's views on the concept of madness and correctly warns us not to misconstrue his writing as a denial of the legitimate progress being made in scientific psychology and psychiatry, both in neurobiology and psychoanalysis. He wants to call into question how these disciplines characterize themselves, and what constitutes the patient, the subject of their investigations.

GENERAL APPROACH

Using his initial method Foucault began as a structuralist, publishing his first important critical book, *Madness and Civilization* (1973a) in 1961. This approach peaked in his books, *The Order of Things* (1973b) in 1966 and *The Archaeology of Knowledge* (1972) in 1969. The 1968 Paris student riots and the subsequent rise of various poststructuralism approaches in Paris had a great influence on Foucault, and no books by him appeared for 6 years. All these poststructural approaches decenter the subject and represent movements that arose after 1968, when the student revolt in France failed. His contemporaries, Derrida, who is the most nihilistic of all, and Lacan, who was in many ways an extraordinary Parisian "happening," especially influenced Foucault. Poststructuralist authors share the definition that a human action is not an expression of intentions of a person but a strategy determined by social forces utilizing human desire. There is no abstract "structure" in a human and there exists no such thing as an apolitical person. There is no essence and no fixed human nature.

His second method appeared in his famous 1970 essay, "Discourse on Language" (in Foucault 1972; see also discussion in Foucault 1980a) and was brought to its fullest applications in *Discipline and Punish* (1979) first published in 1975 and volume 1 of *The History of Sexuality* (1980b) published first in 1976. These works focus on power as immanent in knowledge and discourse, power coming not from above but from below. Thus discourses or the human sciences arise out of endless power struggles, and Foucault (1979) writes that "carceral practices" give birth to the sciences of man.

Foucault, rather weakly and vaguely, opposes to power (1) "bodies and pleasures," in which he exhorts us to deplore conformism, oppression, and racism, and promotes individuality, attributing a positive role to psychoanalysis and psychiatry in this struggle; (2) "laughter," which he takes from Nietzsche, a concept similar to Kohut's (1978) hope for the transformation of narcissism; (3)

"praxis"—the history of events with their ruptures and reversals do produce, at times, "regimes of truth," so that political action to support these is needed; and (4) "philosophy," which keeps watch over power, explains how it works, and finds ways to thwart it.

In his first method, which he labels *archaeology*, Foucault tries for each culture and over the historical past to the present to study the serious documents of the so-called experts, for example, psychiatrists, in the human sciences. He calls these discursive practices or serious speech acts, and he studies them without regard to their truth. He does this in order to ferret out hidden "epistemes" or paradigms of the culture. This method eventually proved inadequate because it leaves out the influence of society on the epistemes, ignores social concerns except for certain rhetorical claims by Foucault, and gives no explanation of why epistemes change.

In his second method, which he took from Nietzsche and labeled *genealogy*, Foucault (1971) asks: How are these discourses used? What role do they play in the governing systems of a given society? In his view the power practices of the culture produce the discourses or human sciences and determine the epistemes that govern their nature. More technically, as Foucault puts it, they determine the conditions of the possibility of knowledge for that culture.

FINDINGS FROM ARCHAEOLOGY

Foucault's early work, culminating in *The Order of Things*, which some authors (Gutting 1989) including myself consider to be Foucault's masterpiece, is close to structuralism and, as stated, uses the method of *archaeology* to unearth epistemes. The result is summarized in Table 2-1, which I hope will help orient the reader to the various movements, historical events, and authors mentioned in this book.

These epistemes, or codes of knowledge, undergo unexplained epistemological shifts that occur rather suddenly. They represent the world view for each age, and are rather arbitrarily outlined by Foucault (1973b). He takes examples from psychiatry in *Madness and Civilization* (1973a), but in later writing (1973b, 1975) he applies the epistemes to all the human sciences.

The first episteme, from the sixteenth century, is that of the Renaissance. Resemblance is the crucial criterion. In the Renaissance, madness was separated from the Middle Ages' belief that divine truth was contained in it. Madness was made human and so, for example, the wise fool, a person who is wise and mad but human, appears in the plays of Shakespeare. There is a search in this

Table 2-1. Historical Table

	Early 19th Century	Later 19th Century	20th Century	Mid 20th Century	Late 20th Century	21st Century
World History:	French Revolution (1789) Napoléon Mozart Beethoven	Wagner	W.W. I Europe in crisis Spengler	W.W. II 1968 Paris riots Cold war	Collapse of Soviet Union	
Philosophy:	Kant (1724–1804) Hegel Goethe Kierkegaard	Marx Nietzsche	Husserl Heidegger Jaspers Phenomenology	Sartre Structuralism Foucault Hermeneutics Gadamer	Failure of European Marxism and existentialism. Poststructuralism Derrida Ricoeur	
Psychiatry:	German romantic idealism → Organic psychiatry and medicine. Separation of syphilitic paresis from other psychoses.	→ Scientific positivism and optimism Freud	Rise of psychoanalysis	Ego psychology in U.S.A. R. D. Laing in England	Kohut in U.S.A. Rise of psychopharmacology in U.S. and England Lacan and psychoanalysis in France	
Episteme: (Foucault)	"Classic" age ends "Modern" Age →	→ Rise of the "medical personage"	"Modern" Contemporary age—"find reason in unreason" "Human sciences" predominant—the "expert"	"The Future" "Mad artists" (Kafka, Kleist, etc.) as heralds of the future.		"Future" age—decentering or erasure of man as a subject

episteme for superficial similarities and resemblances and an ordering of things in this fashion.

The period in Paris from 1656 when the poor and the sick and the mad were put in a catch-all Hôpital-Général to that of the French Revolution in 1789, covering roughly the latter seventeenth and all of the eighteenth century, constitutes the episteme of the Classic Age, according to Foucault. In this episteme madness or "delirious discourse" was set off against "reason" in which the rational man speaks. Language now becomes critical. The insane were confined as bestial along with deviants and criminals. They were social lepers, outside the work ethic. The episteme of the Classic Age is based on tables, contiguities, identity and difference, and relationships as ordering principles in a world created by God. Man's role here is only to clarify; there is no creating subject needed, since God did this already.

The Modern Age, spanning the nineteenth century, begins, according to Foucault, with Kant. In this era occurs the emergence of man at the center; focus on the finitude of human life and human knowledge appears. Pinel and Tuke emerge in the history of psychiatry, illustrious pioneers who indicate that the mad are sick. Foucault calls this *medicalization*, in which the mad are accepted as a faulty part of humanity and placed in hospitals or special asylums—hence "the birth of the asylum." The inevitable consequence of this is the rise of "the medical personage" and the discovery of the mind, which, according to Foucault, came out of the need of industrial society to impose "norms" for effective workers. Foucault labels this *homocentrism*. The episteme of the Modern Age is the search for analogies and successions—cause and effect—experiments, and the general stance of gazing at or dissecting. Here originates "the birth of the medical clinic" (Foucault 1975), and the same approach prevails in the field of other human sciences, such as economics, characterized by the work of Ricardo and Marx.

Freud forms the bridge from the Modern Age to the Modern Contemporary Age. In the twentieth century, or the Modern Contemporary Age, as Foucault calls it, Freud retains the medical authority but now stresses the similarity between the sane and the insane, placing the neurotics in between. The episteme of the twentieth century or the Modern Contemporary Age is to find the reason in the unreason, to search from the surfaces to the depth through a dialogue with unreason.

Foucault labels the period from 1950 "The Future." He regards this as unpredictable and heralded by the mad artists of the last 150 years. This is similar to Kohut's (1978) description of Kafka's stories and the role of modern art. For Foucault, modern art heralds the final disappearance of "man" as a "subject" of study (not as a species), as a fixed essence, as the object that constitutes the world of objects, and the fragmentation of our entire culture. As in the work of Heidegger, who greatly influenced Foucault (Dreyfus and Rabinow 1983), a very important role is given to our poets and artists. Foucault concludes from artistic fragmentation in our century that "man" will be either decentered or "erased, like a face drawn in sand at the edge of the sea" (1973b, p. 387), a quite pessimistic view. In his very last work (1985, 1986), some commentators (Bernauer and Rasmussen 1990) claim to detect a more hopeful note that humans may reconstitute themselves.

FIRST CONCLUSIONS

Foucault's early conclusions are based on his discovery that a series of discontinuous unexplained shifts in epistemes takes place. The history of madness rests on these epistemes and becomes the history of how each culture defines itself. This is taken from Hegel (1807), who states that we are defined by the Other. Thus for Foucault, in a direct head-on collision with modern psychiatric thinking, there is no objective definition of madness possible, since the judgment of madness is always a matter of judgment between an "expert" and a subject. This view has led to severe criticism of Foucault by establishment psychiatrists, and a tendency to disregard his important insights.

Foucault insists that all human sciences fail as pure natural sciences because of the three doubles in the aspect of humans. This is explained in *The Order of Things* (1973b), in the section known (Dreyfus and Rabinow 1983) as Foucault's "analytic of finitude." The first of these three doubles is the "transcendental/empirical." The human is seen as a set of "facts" to be studied, but he or she also forms the transcendental condition of knowledge for any culture at the time of the study. Thus, if we reduce the human to the empirical, we cannot become clear about how to obtain knowledge. For example, the question, Where do assumptions about the validity of empirical study come from? cannot be answered by empirical study.

The second double Foucault labels the "cogito/unthought." Although the human has a potential for lucid thought, the human is always surrounded by unfathomable limits that he or she can never be clear about. Foucault writes that the human wanders in distress; there is no complete knowledge and no final truths and the human is dominated by conditions of his or her life history and language.

The final double is the "retreat/return of origin." The human is a product of history whose beginning he or she can never reach. Yet the human is the source of that very history. We have here an essential mystery, says Foucault, because the beginning keeps receding as we study it. Therefore, he argues, in the human sciences there are many competing pseudoparadigms that arise, and they never agree. This is different from the natural sciences and Kuhn's (1962) account of their paradigms, and presents an insoluble validation problem.

Foucault states his basic question: "By what modes in our culture are human beings made into subjects?" He gives a threefold answer to this question. The first mode, making humans into subjects in our culture, he calls "dividing practices," the use of categorizing, distributing, and manipulating, as the result of which a person is given a social and personal identity by being divided from others. Examples of such categories are the poor, the sick, the mad, the yuppies, the gays, and so on. The second mode is "scientific classification." The human sciences, taking humans as subjects or the body as an object, go on to try to understand ourselves "scientifically" and produce results such as *DSM-III-R*. Finally there is the mode of "subjectification," in which a human turns himself or herself into a subject with the help of "experts" and so-called statistical norms, in order to give meaning to his or her life. Here a person actively gives him- or herself a self, attempting to become an acceptable average subject, not so different from Heidegger's concept of inauthentic averageness, discussed in the previous chapter.

WHAT IS "MEANING" IN THE HUMAN SCIENCES?

Certain crucial definitions are necessary if one is to understand Foucault. In *The Order of Things* (1973b) he defines what he calls "anthropological sleep." The human is seen as a controlling center and creates an illusion of pure truth, which dulls the mind to the disruptive effects of power and death on human life. Foucault hopes to wake us from this anthropological sleep. For Foucault the science of anthropology is an ideology that privileges the human as the center and source of philosophy and human sciences. More generally, all sciences are accompanied by an ideology intertwined within them.

The word "disciplines" is a deliberately chosen double-meaning term employed by Foucault. The "scientific disciplines" of the human sciences discipline human power for economic needs of the industrial society. Behind "man" as a subject of study in human sciences are tactics to control persons so as to produce a disciplined population of workers.

Foucault's concept of "transgression" is based on the fact that there is no such thing as pure knowledge. Knowledge for Foucault is always suffused with power and history. Knowledge is gained only by criticism of knowledge. Thinking, even by definition, is a continual transgression of established norms of truth. Furthermore, since these norms are socially constructed and maintained, thinking is a political act, always challenging the established and the accepted. For this reason Nietzsche thought of himself as "dynamite" (Chessick 1983a). Foucault (1980a) proclaims,

> Each society has its regime of truth, its "general politics" of truth; that is, the types of discourse which it accepts and makes function as true; the mechanisms, and instances which enable one to distinguish true and false statements, the means by which each is sanctioned; the techniques and procedures accorded value in the acquisition of truth; the status of those who are charged with saying what counts as true. [p. 131]

It is appropriate at this point to pose a critical question for all mental health professionals. How does "meaning" given to human thought and behavior arise and how do we study it? Here are five views from continental philosophy:

In Husserl's (1913) phenomenology the transcendental ego gives meaning, and for Husserl man is a "meaning-giving transcendental subject." From Heidegger on all the philosophers attack this conception, and even Husserl, in my opinion, was never completely satisfied with it, revising it many times.

A second view is that of structuralism, in which objective laws are seen to govern human activity, laws that are hidden by the false notion of a subject giving meaning. Structuralists claim there exist hidden built-in universal structures in the very nervous system of the human being that determine everything else.

A third view, from hermeneutics, agrees that there is such a thing as meaning but claims that it is preserved in man's social practices and texts and must be ferreted out; there is no Husserlian transcendental subject. So, for example, Ricoeur (1970) writes that psychoanalysis is interpretation from beginning to end (to be discussed in the next two chapters).

A fourth view is known as existential phenomenology and also represents a countermovement to Husserl's view given above. For example, Merleau-Ponty (discussed in Chapter 10) claims that the lived body, not the transcendental ego, organizes and allows meaning to our experience; his is an unfinished and ambiguous theory but in some ways is surprisingly close to modern infant research. The work of Heidegger also belongs here. Human subjects are formed by historical cultural background practices in which they develop. These practices contain a primordial meaning, a way of understanding and coping with the world around us, and are prescientific.

The final view is that of the later Foucault, in a way similar to that of the late writing of Heidegger. The obsession with meaning and knowledge in human sciences, says Foucault, is an expression of "bio-technico-power." This complex term is defined as an increased ordering in the guise of improving the welfare of people. It is for Foucault a strategy with nobody directing it and all of us are increasingly enmeshed in it; the only end of it is the increase of power and order itself. This concept is similar to Heidegger's (1954) notion of today's runaway technology. Foucault argues that the examination of the treatment of the body by human sciences demonstrates this viewpoint, and he convincingly urges us to study the modern hospital or the prison. Only a personal sojourn in each of these institutions can demonstrate just how cogent Foucault's descriptions are. As one who trained in a large hospital and later spent two years as a physician and psychiatrist in a federal prison, I can attest to the validity of Foucault's claims.

FINDINGS FROM GENEALOGY

This brings us directly to the later Foucault, using *genealogy* as his method. Now he inverts the priority of theory (epistemes) and practice. Biopower or social practices become the ground of human science theories and produce humans in a given culture. Foucault calls this a microphysics of power. It follows that *the investigator is always involved in and produced by the social practices that he or she studies.* The genealogist, such as Foucault, concentrates on the relation of power, knowledge, and treatment of the body in any given society, in order to show the lowest undirected motives as the ground for the human sciences including philosophy—which, now exposed, becomes all over, a discipline of the study of essences that has come to an end, since there are no essences.

This is a view that began with Nietzsche's postulate of the will to power in individuals as behind all our "disciplines," but it moves on to a meaningless operation of bio-power with no goal except *more,** an extreme nihilism. Foucault writes about micromechanisms of power operating through techniques of normalization and control. As Foucault reads Nietzsche, "History is the story of petty malice, of violently imposed interpretations, of vicious intentions, of high-sounding stories masking the lowest of motives" (Dreyfus and Rabinow 1983, p. 108).

Foucault gives us detailed and gory examples of all this in his book, *Discipline and Punish* (1979). A docile and mute body is needed for industrial

---

*Movie buffs will no doubt remember *Key Largo*, in which Edward G. Robinson, playing the gangster, is asked what he wants, what are his goals. The answer: "more." Apparently, even charity organization executives are vulnerable.

growth of power. Thus, especially in the nineteenth century, prisons shift torture and punishment to treatment, a discipline of the body. This requires penology and social studies and factory surveillance technology. So Foucault explains that strategies, technologies and programs must arise and provide knowledge for this purpose of disciplining the body. The psychiatrist is brought in to determine responsibility and to decide on the treatment. Furthermore, since crime is a sickness, we now must examine and police everybody under the excuse of "protecting" the public good. This, Foucault points out, leads to meticulous rituals of power and to the rise of the bureaucrat and the administrator. Thus power and knowledge are one mutually generative process.

Another major example of this is presented in his book, *The History of Sexuality* (1980b), vol. 1. Here he claims that sex began as a "family matter," not a "drive," but due to the need for organization and control of the population for war, labor, and so forth, became the subject of statistics and administrative control in the eighteenth century. In the nineteenth century it becomes "the individual sex instinct," regarded as an object of medical study. Thus the "sex instinct" notion is not biological but a historical construct out of the needs of bio-power.

A new host of human sciences arises for this purpose of incitement to sexual discourse in the nineteenth century. These are (1) the "hysterization" of the female body—the female body is sexualized, considered saturated with sex, and mysterious, and must be explored and dissected; (2) the "pedigogization" of children's sex—"experts" (remember this is the nineteenth century) fight masturbation with the aid of medical science warnings and impressive documents, which Foucault quotes at length; (3) "socialization" of procreation—the theory of eugenics, the worry over hereditary degeneracy, and the biological theory of mental illness arise at this point. Only psychoanalysis resisted this, which is a plus for psychoanalysis, says Foucault.

Finally occurs the rise of the sexual sciences, which Foucault calls a pseudobiology or a psychiatrization of perverse pleasures. This in the nineteenth century consisted of a detached pejorative naming and classifying and a chronicling and regulation of individual sex life, leading to today's worry over what is normal and what is not normal, the precise timing of mutual simultaneous orgasms, and so on. It results ultimately in the Western human as a confessing animal. Foucault is suspicious of the motives of the confessor and the analyst, who represent the "centralization of power." The rise of the specialist in interpretation of confessions is also the result of the need for an "expert" to hear the confessions, one who has a specialized knowledge of *DSM-III-R* (the psychiatrist), or the psychoanalyst, who bases his or her work on the assumption that desire is the final deep truth in humans. So Foucault in this is against both Freud and Lacan because he claims that their concept of desire as the final deep truth of humans is also a knowledge/power historical construct, not a biological or essential quality of humans.

SUMMARY

For Foucault the crucial question of philosophy is the question of what we ourselves are. Since we have only cultural practices that made us what we are, contemporary philosophy, he says, must be political, historical, and interpretive. He concludes that human sciences are always to some extent pseudosciences because, while claiming to be advancing under legitimate banners of science, they have remained intimately involved with the micropractices of power. They use what he calls the "repressive hypothesis," the view that truth is intrinsically opposed to power, and can play a liberating role. An example of the repressive hypothesis is found in Freud's claim that knowledge will cure, a cognitive ideal of the nineteenth century, or in Habermas's (1971) philosophy of self-reflection.

For Foucault the human sciences are always unstable, derived, epistemologically complex, precarious, and full of disagreement. This is due to the double nature of man. Human sciences are dubious and can never be "normal" like natural sciences. There will never be agreement on a paradigm (Kuhn 1962) in the human sciences, as there is in the natural sciences. He says that the psychiatrist as "embodied investigator," as well as the objects he or she studies, have *both* been produced by bio-power of their culture, its manipulations and interactions. Background power practices produce the investigator, with his or her values and interests, who studies the human. Therefore, "knowledge" in the human sciences depends on discursive practices or epistemes or on nondiscursive practices or bio-power in any given culture at the time: no context-free, value-free, "objective" human science like the natural sciences is possible. In fact, to try as Max Weber did to make background practices the object of social sciences is circular, since the knower is produced by the very practices he attempts to analyze. In the natural sciences, the background practices that make science possible can be more or less ignored. But the human sciences must take account of the human activities that make possible their own disciplines. If an unchallenged "normal" human science develops, it only means that an "orthodoxy" has been temporarily established (see Dreyfus and Rabinow 1983, pp. 162–167).

OBJECTIONS

Certain objections to Foucault are obvious. Foucault does not account for the cumulative progressive knowledge in the sciences and technology as compared to philosophy and the arts, or for shifts in epistemes. Furthermore, what is "power"? How can this be kept from being used as just another metaphysical principle or essence? How does one resist power? And why do we have a natural need to resist it? This is not explained by Foucault's theory.

Foucault is vague, nihilistic, pessimistic about runaway technology and the future, and he represents an extreme view. All people, he contends, are shaped by bio-power and all human disciplines are seen as emerging in the service of bio-power. He ignores the empirical and experience value of the human sciences as a constructive force even to combat power. Finally, a philosopher would point out that Foucault's work suffers from the Nietzsche paradox. If there is no such thing as truth, then how can Foucault's study claim to be true? On what grounds would Foucault's methods and conclusions be justified?

Foucault's archaeology ends in the perspectivism and relativism of all truth. His genealogy offers no antidotes or cures for the biopower problem. In this sense both of his methods have been called unserious or irresponsible. He leaves out all in human history that might have been animated by civic humanism, rationalism, or enlightened thought.

CONCLUSIONS

From a study of these authors my conclusion is that the history of human sciences, for example, psychiatry, viewed according to all basic psychiatric models, leads to an unveiling of the nonconscious as constitutive both of humans generally and of the human scientist who investigates the human. Revealed as built in to us is a danger of the use of human sciences in the service of micropower practices, normalization, and oppression by the investigator so constituted in that service. *We must always be alert to this danger.*

Certain models can be used as basic examples of these human science approaches. The *biological* model sees the human as an organic "thing" and groups as "bodies," as in the studies of sociobiology and ethology. An *economic* model views the human as an expression of class and other economic conflicts, as in the work of Marx and Lukács. The *philological* model utilizes hermeneutics and began with Freud in psychiatry. Here hidden meanings are discovered by interpretation, and we seek to explore the history of desire. The *linguistic* model claims that there exist hidden universal structures in humans and their signifying systems, such as language, myths, and so forth. Semiotics is the study of these systems.

There are *hybrid system* models, such as that of the mature work of Freud, which combines natural-science biological notions of the "mental apparatus" with the hermeneutic approach, or that of Kohut, which combines data from empathy in which the self is seen as a supraordinate configuration, with postulated developmental forces such as the *Zeigarnik* effect (see Chessick 1985). The *political* model of R. D. Laing considers diagnosis a repressive political act, and it unfortunately pervaded Soviet psychiatry at the time of this writing, although the Soviet psychiatric system is rapidly disintegrating.

Foucault offers two models. The method of *archaeology* reveals that hidden epistemes determine what we call knowledge. The method of *genealogy* reveals that hidden micropower practices determine and produce "knowledge." Finally, in a line of thought developing from Nietzsche through Derrida there arises an utter nihilism, in which an inherent paradox in all systems is revealed by deconstruction of their texts. Thus Derrida writes that history is already over.

The psychiatrist or the mental health professional can never be only another medical specialist. If one understands the history of psychiatry, one must be aware of all these other models and of the dangers involved in thinking that one possesses the "scientific truth" about any person. The danger in assuming that the psychiatrist or mental health professional possesses the truth is that instead of fighting "normalization," oppression, racism, and so on, by active engagement, laughter, pleasure, freedom, and transformations of narcissism, the psychiatrist or mental health professional becomes an instrument of biotechnical power and participates in the erasure of humans, along with the insurance companies, drug companies, and certain politicians. This is illustrated in the following case reported by Bernum (1984) in the prestigious *New England Journal of Medicine*:

The Unfortunate Case of Dr. Z:
How to Succeed in Medical Practice in 1984

The following address was given by Merin Gip, the Regional Inspector Commissioner of the Bureau of Health Care Delivery, at the 1984 inaugural meeting of the Coalition of Health-Care providers and Consumers.

As a Regional Inspector Commissioner of the Bureau of Health-Care Delivery, I wish to give an account of the unfortunate case of Dr. Z. This material is drawn from the hearing in which he was stripped of his hospital privileges and placed on probationary office practice because of failure to adjust to the new medicine. The hearing was occasioned by conjoined charges brought by the National Board of Hospital Administrators and ourselves, the state.

Amici curiae included the U.S. Advertising Council and Statistical Analysands, Inc.

Dr. Z's rebellious obstinacy first came to our attention in the early 1970s. His dossier was soon swollen with complaints from many quarters—from our PSRO-PRO secretarial corps and data coordinators to high officials in the business and management of the medical industry. From the very outset, he failed to submit diagnoses that matched the computer disease and procedure codes. What was more, he refused to accept the guiding principles of the new medicine: that the encounter with the patient—the illness episode—is accurately and completely defined by a disease diagnosis (along with its accompanying tests and procedures), and that for every such disease there is a corresponding technological treatment.

Dr. Z insisted that patients came to see him for many reasons other than the presence of a specific disease. According to him, some wanted to establish themselves with a physician, so that if they were to become ill, they would have someone to call on who was familiar with them and their medical history. Others came for a medical evaluation, as a wise health practice or as a practical necessity, before embarking on a new business venture. Dr. Z believed that many patients came because of fear: if a good friend had just been found to have inoperable cancer, they might wish to know whether they had the same illness or whether their chest pain was due to heart disease. Many others came for genetic counseling, for advice on precautions to take when traveling abroad, for help in trying to decide whether to have surgery or take a new drug for gallstones, or for one of the many other reasons that people seek expert knowledge from professionals. Finally, according to Dr. Z, a visit whose purpose was disguised by an account of physical symptoms may simply have been made for the purpose of talking about the patient's troubles.

Moreover, Dr. Z claimed that when a disease *was* present, it was often just one of many diseases, each varying in severity from patient to patient, and usually inextricably mixed with emotional distress and adjustment difficulties—all components of the illness. Dr. Z claimed that illness is therefore unique and difficult to define by disease codes. Two similar patients may have identical grades of emphysema as described by pulmonary-function tests, but one may work without complaints and the other may apply for early retirement benefits; thus, the patients' feelings, their reactions to their disease, count.

Dr. Z's heretical views and his failure to code properly struck at the very heart of the new medicine: the data-collecting computer network. I need hardly remind you that in addition to using disease codes to pay for services and define treatment, we profile all physicians by these code numbers and corresponding costs per case. As a statistician, I can assure that this gives us a complete picture of every physician's professional life and value to the health-delivery system. There is little that happens in American medicine that is not known to us. Therefore, Dr. Z was quickly singled out as a dyscodic outlier and heterogenicist. He was exposed as the shameless statistical deviate that he is.

With PSRO-PRO and then DRGs, Dr. Z's alienation from the new medicine worsened. Patients go to hospitals for acute illnesses, and naming their disease tells us all we need to know about the patients and their treatment. Dr. Z always seemed to be bogged down in the *process* of health-care delivery — in taking care of the patient, as he puts it — instead of stressing outcome. When asked by the review clerk for a patient's diagnosis and treatment plan, Dr. Z was known to reply that he was thinking, that he was trying to figure out what was wrong with the patient, and that this would involve studying and choosing the most appropriate tests to reach a diagnosis. He would then spend more time reading about the best treatment of the disorder, which in some cases might be nothing — that is, no technologic intervention. How can our peer-review data collectors deal with this kind of talk?

On another occasion Dr. Z said that explanation was the treatment. A patient with vertigo, who had been rushed to the hospital on several occasions thinking that he was dying, was told of the painful but harmless nature of the attacks and that he required no subsequent hospital care. Dr. Z asserted that, in addition to providing scientific expertise, physicians should express concern about their patients, gain their confidence and cooperation, and give them — and their families — peace of mind.

My answer to Dr. Z, of course, is that we have no code or audit criteria for explanation and reassurance or for what he calls "personal care." Our audit criteria were configured by experts and have

been declared accurate and complete. Dr. Z's lame defense has been
to say that the patient is not a disease and that the care of the patient
is what counts. Tell that to a computer!

Despite mandatory attendance at indoctrination sessions, Dr.
Z seemed incapable of understanding and participating in the new
mission of hospitals—thus, his loss of hospital privileges. He was
never able to think of medicine as an industry and view a hospital as
a business. He was rude to the hospital's vice-president for marketing
and opposed the plans to operate a health spa, give free cardiovas-
cular stress tests to executives, and sell aloe tonic in the hospital gift
shop, as well as all the other numerous publicity and selling strategies proposed by the marketing department. He could not see that
hospitals have to be consumer-oriented, that they must sell what the
consumer wants, nor would he support the hospital's policy, determined by strict cost accounting, of providing services to the public
that are profitable and eliminating those that are not. His opposition
to dropping the teaching program was particularly offensive.

Dr. Z is wrong. Hospitals are businesses, and the success of a
doctor depends on the success of the hospital. Professional qualifications are not enough. The bottom line is whether the doctor can
contribute to the hospital's overall marketing plan. Promotions and
staff privileges will depend on whether doctors are winners or losers
for the hospital. Low-paying-DRG profilers must go. The practice of
medicine must change. There must be greater emphasis on hospital
productivity and efficiency. Cost accounting must be part of physicians' grand rounds.

In today's world doctors and hospitals cannot succeed without
computers. We must think in terms of DRG trees, outliers, hard-
ware, and software; indeed, we must learn to think like computers.
We can no longer look at patients as persons, but must view them as
output or input, or as products. We must learn to manage product
lines, to get into the habit of defining our output by product. Heart
failure and shock, DRG 127, are now products.

We have made Dr. Z a test case in behavior modification and
rehabilitation. He first felt the impact of monetary disincentives
when he lost his hospital privileges. After thinking-adjustment
sessions, he was given training in computer coding, advertising,
market analysis, and selling strategies. At first I was optimistic about

his progress, but I am told that he recently turned down our suggestion that he retain a publicity agent for his practice. When requested to be a preferred provider, he pulled out the old saw that physicians should be preferred for no reason other than their professional qualifications and abilities and that he did not like to be called a health-care provider in the first place. He has failed to understand the necessity of shifting the emphasis in medicine from personal services to a return on capital. He clings to the archaic belief that medicine is an ethical rather than a commercial enterprise. Our proposed time frame for developing his new mind set is short. If he cannot adapt to the new medicine, that is too bad; there are plenty coming along who will.

The test of the moral worth of a society is the way in which it treats the poor and the sick and the mad. Foucault says that the history of madness or of the poor or of deviants for a given culture is the means by which a culture defines itself. Dreyfus and Rabinow (1983) present the best overview of Foucault's work; less technical reviews with more emphasis on his sociological contributions abound. Among these I recommend Smart (1985) and Sheridan (1980) as good starting points. The "sampler" edited by Rabinow (1984) offers an overview of Foucault's ideas in his own words.

FOUCAULT'S THIRD METHOD

All of the authors reviewed in this book tried to explore the unrepresentable or nondiscursive sources of experience, which arise in a fashion that cannot easily be represented in language. For Marx this was known as the anti-bourgeois. For Heidegger focus on it constitutes the post-Cartesian era of philosophy. Nietzsche referred to it as the Dionysian, and Freud's theory would label it as from the preoedipal period of life. Foucault approached this exploration using three different methods.

Volumes 2 and 3 of *The History of Sexuality*, published eight years after volume 1, and volume 4, which came just before Foucault's death in 1984, present his third and unfinished method (see Foucault 1985, 1986). During a period of eight years he studied ancient Greek, Roman, and Christian texts and devised this method, which examines the self-constitution of the subject. He became interested now in the forms, the modulation, and the recasting of the relation to the self by which an individual constitutes and recognizes himself or herself as a subject from the Greek to the Victorian age. This third method seeks to trace the historical continuity and modifications of the "problematizations" through which the human being offers itself to be thought of as a subject, and the values and practices on the basis of which these problematizations are formed.

To recapitulate, the method of *archaeology* examines the forms of discourse themselves. The method of *genealogy* examines the formation of these forms out of practices and modifications of these practices from below, via an invisible hand of biotechnical power. The third method or "problematization" or "ethics" studies, for example, the problematization of madness and illness, which arises from social and medical practices and defines the normal. Or it studies the problematization of life, language, and labor, which arises in discursive practices that conform to epistemes, and the rules for the care of the self and sexual behavior that arise from the given episteme of the culture. The problematization of crime and criminal behavior arises from punitive practices conforming to the disciplinary model of the particular culture. The problematizations of the sex act and pleasure arise through the practices of the self based on an aesthetics of existence, that is to say, a style that is fashioned out of the use of pleasure that differs with values in various historical eras.

Volumes 2 through 4 of *The History of Sexuality* do not deal with the power aspects of knowledge and are more of an old-fashioned academic discourse based on selected classical texts. In volume 2 he claims there were the same prohibitions on sexual behavior in the fourth century B.C. as in the writing of the church fathers. But the Greeks used these prohibitions for aesthetic purposes as the personal choice of an elite, and made no attempt to normalize the population. In volume 3 he studies how it was believed the self should be constituted in Greco-Roman times. Here also, ascetic themes develop before Christianity, but again in Greco-Roman times it is a matter of choice and no attempt is made to normalize the population. Foucault says the goal of ethical life for the Greeks was a beautiful life. Techniques were developed to accomplish this by operating on "ethical substance," which he defines for the Greeks as acts, pleasure, and desire.

Scholars attacked Foucault's secondhand familiarity with this immense topic. For example, he neglected the plays of Aristophanes and the Greek vase paintings and certain other texts of the Greeks and Romans. His supporters retort that he did grasp the main trends, and that is sufficient.

Foucault's tragic and premature death unfortunately cut short his development of these new and fertile ideas, which, like his other contributions, force us to rethink our most fundamental premises of discourse and practice in the human sciences. Foucault distinguishes among three kinds of intellectuals. The "universal intellectual" speaks for the conscience of the collectivity. Sartre was the last of these, says Foucault. The "specific intellectual," a type that emerged since the Second World War, is an "expert" in a specific field. Foucault says the first of these was Oppenheimer. A third rare type is "the social thinker" such as Marx and Freud. These, Foucault (1984) says, are "founders of discursivity" (p. 114) and work only in the human sciences. One returns repeatedly to their texts even if the texts contain errors, and each reexamination of these texts modifies their field. These authors have "established an endless possibility of discourse" (p. 114), and I believe Foucault deserves to be considered a member of this third rare group of intellectuals.

3

HERMENEUTICS

WHAT IS "HERMENEUTICS"?

Hermeneutics is usually defined as the art and science of interpretation. It emerged in the seventeenth century as a discipline devoted to establishing the correct interpretation of biblical scripture with the aim of uncovering and reconstructing the message from God that biblical scripture supposedly contains. The term hermeneutics is often traced to Hermes, the messenger of the Greek gods—and also the god of cheats, thieves, and gamblers—but the actual etymology of the word is disputed, since there exists the important Greek verb ἑρμηνεύω and its derivatives, which refer directly to the explication of meaning and to interpretation. So probably all these descend from a common earlier root word. By the end of the eighteenth century, hermeneutics began to be expanded to apply to literary texts and historical periods and, as is well known, it was Dilthey (1831–1911) who brought hermeneutics into the service of understanding human motivations and behavior, and attempted to introduce it as an alternative "method" from that of the natural sciences.

Dilthey, who based his views on those of Vico, is sometimes called the father of modern hermeneutics. Vico was an unappreciated seventeenth century Italian genius who introduced the concepts of "inner" and "outer" knowledge.

Following his ideas, Dilthey (1978) distinguished the natural sciences, the rigorous empirical sciences that observed the human *qua* natural object (as, for example, in behavioristic psychology) from *Geisteswissenschaften* or the human sciences. The method used by *Geisteswissenschaften* is different and left somewhat vague by Dilthey, who labeled it as empathy or *Verstehen*. One must remember that Dilthey's manuscripts were in fragments, but his main point was that there exist two "standpoints" of experience, two ways of experiencing the world: (1) standing back separately and observing a world conceived as composed of natural objects, and (2) living in the world—we cannot ever live and interact with people and things without adopting a stance towards them, an inextricable involvement.

To these there correspond two ways of being aware of experience, which Dilthey called (1) *Erklären*, knowledge of the laws of the causal order of natural phenomena, rigorous scientific knowledge, and (2) *Verstehen*, knowledge of the inner mental life of humans, a function of our "world-view," or system of value-laden and meaningful existence, and a consequence of our being-in-the-world.

Dilthey tried to establish *Verstehen* as a method by using the so-called hermeneutical circle: beginning with a preliminary notion of the whole, one then moves to an ever more probing analysis and synthesis of the parts, which in turn leads to an evolving, ever-changing concept of the whole. This affords an increasingly internalized and thought-through understanding of the whole. *Verstehen* for Dilthey requires *Nacherleben*, an empathic reliving.

From the time of Dilthey we have realized more fully that meaning and understanding are subject to time and change, and that we always survey the past from within our own horizon, which is always shifting. This has become a central tenet of the hermeneutic approach, namely, that meanings change and that the historical and cultural past is inextricably tied to the present orientation of the interpreter. Therefore the interpreter brings to the data a complete set of preconceptions or, as Gadamer (1982) calls them, "prejudices," which form a sort of foreknowledge and serve as a matrix or prism through which the data are organized and interpreted.

Meichenbaum (1988) tells us,

> In the same way that a biblical or literary scholar attempts to understand a particular passage by referring to the corpus of the work, the student of human behavior must refer to the historical and cultural context that is constantly changing. The same ostensible behavior may have quite different meanings, and there is a need to assess and determine these meanings if we are to understand the nature of human behavior. [p. 117]

Thus emphasis from the hermeneutic approach continually reminds us that the "prejudice" or horizon of the investigator or interpreter contributes fundamentally to the nature of the interpretation and the meaning that he or she assigns to the data.

From these basic principles a vast literature has developed, as well as a substantial amount of argument and disagreement. There are three general modern uses of the term "hermeneutics," as explained by Messer and colleagues (1988). One of these uses, from Vico and Dilthey, emphasizes hermeneutics as a methodological alternative to the natural sciences, an art or science of interpretation especially suitable to the domain of the human sciences. Unlike those human science approaches that attempt to emulate that of the natural sciences, "methodological hermeneutics" does not strive for "objective facts" but emphasizes meanings as developed by investigators whose activities are rooted in a given socio-historical setting. The consequence of this approach is to emphasize the inseparability of fact and value, detail and context, and observation and theory: "Methodological hermeneutics utilizes qualitative description, analogical understanding, and narrative modes of exposition. It deemphasizes quantification and controlled experimentation, and does not seek a neutral objective vocabulary with which to characterize social phenomena" (p. xiv).

Another use of the term, from Heidegger, is labeled "ontological hermeneutics" and concerns itself with the very basis of human existence. This aspect of Heidegger's work has been developed by Gadamer and rests on the premise that our fundamental mode of being in the world is that of understanding and interpreting; there is no knowledge free of presuppositions. Thus human knowing or understanding, which is definitive of our species, always is interpretive and always takes place within an at best dimly perceived horizon. This horizon consists, depending on which author one reads, of bodily activities, symbol systems, cultural practices and institutions, or "superstructure" and "base." The consequence of ontological hermeneutics is to call into question the standard Cartesian world view separating a knowing subject from an object of study, a view that carries with it the implication that it is possible to have a neutral subject recording in an unprejudiced fashion observed objective "facts." This view is of course the fundamental epistemological tenet of nineteenth century natural science.

A third usage, that of "critical hermeneutics," has a more political and moral aim in that it attempts to reveal the ideological underpinnings of the culture, the intellectual practices, the social institutions, and the prevalent economic system of exchange itself, with the goal of fostering consciousness of these underpinnings, and hence will lead to a hoped-for emancipation from arbitrary forms of political domination and cultural pressures. The assumption behind critical hermeneutics is also that made by Breuer and Freud (1893–1895) in *Studies On Hysteria*—knowledge of one's self will allow the ego to make realistic choices and, in the case of the psychoneuroses, permit freedom from bondage to unconscious childhood conflicts. Habermas (1971) applied this tenet of Freud to a philosophy of self-reflection, in the hope that a useful critical theory and practice could be developed in order to free human beings from blindly following the social institutions into which they are thrown by the accident of birth.

The hope is that hermeneutics can function as a corrective to what Heidegger (1954) has called the age of technicity and the modern proclivity to view the natural sciences as models for all forms of inquiry. In some ways it represents a revolt against this technicity: against quantification, objectivism, ahistoricism, and technology, which Heidegger (1961) has told us led to the "darkening of the world" in our time. To put it another way, Gadamer (1991) pointed out that to have a method is already to have an interpretation. Hermeneutics forces psychological investigators to confront their false sense of objectivity and epistemological privilege.

Thus methodological hermeneutics attempts to reform, broaden, and humanize the social sciences; ontological hermeneutics, employing phenomenological methods, seeks truths that are foundational for all inquiry including science; and critical hermeneutics attempts in particular to reveal sources of domination and coercion by exposing and criticizing the ideological underpinnings of all social practices, including political and scientific activity.

THE DEVELOPMENT OF MODERN HERMENEUTICS

The origin of modern hermeneutics is frequently attributed to Hegel's (1807) youthful, ingenious, philosophical vision expressed in his *Phenomenology of Spirit*, in which a conceptual prototype is presented that was later adopted and developed in various ways by Heidegger, Gadamer, and Habermas. Hegel recognized that any critique of knowledge itself presupposes knowledge, and therefore any epistemology that seeks to identify some ultimate foundation for knowledge must be grievously flawed. This is aimed primarily at the epistemology of empiricism, in which perception is viewed as a passive registration of atomic "facts" that are allegedly gathered objectively by a neutral observer. Heidegger and Gadamer point out that no ultimate ground of knowledge outside of history and culture is possible, and they challenge the predominant correspondence theory of truth, a theory that identifies truth as a matching between a physical state of affairs on the one hand and a mental representation or verbal description produced by the investigator on the other. I think it is fair

to say that the entire dialectical approach of Hegel, putting aside his precon-
ceived wish to demonstrate the unfolding of an Absolute Spirit, is a demonstra-
tion of how *any* method contains within it presuppositions about truth and
falsity, and about how these are determined, that cannot be established by the
method itself and that represent "prejudices" of the investigator.

Authors rarely cite a much earlier source of this discovery. Francis Bacon
(1620) is usually cited as first delineating the principles of the inductive method
in the natural sciences, principles that are of course more often honored in the
breach than the observance, but are even today given lip service by naive
investigators. His concept of "idols," however, is rarely brought to the attention
of modern medical students and residents. He distinguished "idols of the tribe,"
which represent unreasonable expectations in human observers, such as ex-
pecting that every effect must have an identifiable single natural cause; "idols of
the cave," which represent cultural prejudices such as chauvinism, feminism,
racism, and so on and vastly distort the interpretation of data; "idols of the
marketplace," which point to our immersion in language and the impossibility of
getting away from current linguistic practices in trying to describe meanings and
interpretations; "idols of the theater," in which appeal is made to established
authority, such as systems of philosophy that have become famous because they
are "classical"; and, finally, "idols of the schools," in which appeal is made to
authoritative rules rather than reason and judgment.

Hermeneutics as a methodology begins with the work of Friedrich
Schleiermacher (1768–1834), who proposed that a literary text could not be
understood unless one understood the sociocultural context in which the work
was created and whatever factors in addition gave rise to and made meaningful
the author's productions. It was also Schleiermacher who first described the
"hermeneutic circle": since understanding always involves reference to that
which is already known, the understanding must operate in a circular, dialectical fashion. A fact never stands on its own, independent from its context or
interpreter, but is always partially constituted by them, since it can be evaluated
only in relation to a larger theory or argument of which it is a part. Therefore we
go back and forth between the part and the whole as we attempt to understand
the given "facts."

From this, Dilthey, as explained above, attempted to develop a method of
understanding in human sciences that involved a kind of empathic reliving of
the culture or historical epoch that produced whatever was being studied. To
put it another way, according to Dilthey a radically different method from that
utilized in the natural sciences was required, one based on an empathic
identification with the subject under study rather than on an attempt to remain
separate and "objective" as one might watch an insect under the microscope.
Although his theories have been criticized from many directions, they still

present in outline a debate between whether the psychological study of humans should be carried on in a natural sciences fashion or through the method of hermeneutics and empathy. Authors disagree, some stressing one pole and some the other, and some trying to make the methods complementary and therefore synergistic—which is very difficult to do because their premises contain a basic epistemological opposition (Chessick 1980b).

Hans-Georg Gadamer is the foremost expositor of hermeneutics living today. Gadamer's primary interest, in contrast to that of Dilthey, is not the reformation of scientific understanding but rather an elucidation and extension of the hermeneutic aspects of Heidegger's philosophy, especially Heidegger's notion of preunderstanding, which is a central concept of Heidegger's work. Gadamer's quest is to make explicit as much as possible the preunderstanding that guides science at any time. In order to understand Gadamer, certain concepts originating with the genius of Heidegger must first be reviewed (for details see Chapter 1).

In the famous section of *Being and Time* (1962a) entitled "Existential Analytic," the thesis is advanced that all scientific activity arises in a context of preunderstanding that derives from practical dealings in the lived world of various activities. Practical dealings and activities are achieved in a taken-for-granted cultural and historical background consisting of practices, habits, and skills, which is not spelled out explicitly and comprehensively but really constitutes the fundamental mode of human existence. Thus not detached knowing but practical engagement and activity mark the fundamental mode of human existence, in contrast to the Cartesian "I think, therefore I am."

A misunderstanding of this, according to Heidegger, has led to erroneous philosophical assumptions from the time of Plato and a dead end in western metaphysics, as well as to the development of the age of technicity. Objects of equipment, such as a hammer, are termed "ready-to-hand" by Heidegger. A hammer becomes a hammer when it is imbued with human purpose and meaning, not as a copy of some Platonic Form or because of some essence "in itself." This mode of existence is contrasted with another form that Heidegger calls "present-at-hand," which corresponds to the isolated perceptual object studied by a detached uninvolved observer. This kind of detachment only takes place when there is some sort of failure, or as Heidegger puts it, "obstinacy" of a tool during an activity, which forces us to stand back and study it in a detached fashion in order to repair or replace it. It is not, however, a fundamental mode of human activity.

According to Heidegger, therefore, human being always involves a context or cultural totality within which experience occurs that is labeled by him alternatively "ground," "horizon," or "clearing." This "horizon" is the essential concept of modern hermeneutics because it undercuts the Cartesian opposition of subject and object and is the very condition or possibility of anything at all appearing or being known. According to Heidegger, the horizon involves the customs, institutions, and language of a given culture, not the idiosyncratic perspectives of isolated individuals.

HANS-GEORG GADAMER

Hans-Georg Gadamer was born in 1900 and presently teaches at the University of Heidelberg. He separated out Heidegger's hermeneutics from his phenomenology, in contrast to Heidegger, for whom these are essentially the same. He attempted to move entirely away from a natural sciences approach to understanding humans by the use of hermeneutic theory, that is to say, from an approach assuming a subject without preconceptions studying a text—for example, the "objective" psychoanalytic authority studying a patient's dream—to an approach realizing that "understanding" arises out of our preconceptions, our position in historical tradition. Thus to understand the patient's narrative and associations we must merge or fuse our horizons with the patient and his society, which always give a new meaning each time there is an encounter between a patient and a doctor, a reader and a text, or an historian with historical "facts."

These communal horizons channel and constitute individual human experience. It follows, as Gadamer explains, that our self-knowledge is not freely chosen but actually deeply imbedded in culture, history, and our bodily being, aspects that are so pervasive as to be nearly invisible. Gadamer (1982) writes, "History does not belong to us, but we belong to it. Long before we understand ourselves through the process of self-examination, we understand ourselves in a self-evident way in the family, society and state in which we live. . . . The self-awareness of the individual is only a flickering in the closed circuits of historical life" (p. 245).

In *Truth and Method* (1991), his major work, he points out how there is a dialectic or mutual influence between the subject of interpretation and the interpreter, in which, as the horizons of each coparticipate, meaning is generated in that particular dyadic pair at that particular time and place. What is known is always known by a knower situated within history and society, and therefore interpretation is always conditioned and influenced by the tradition and the horizon of understanding within which one operates. Gadamer proclaims that one should not attempt to overcome the "prejudices" that constitute our socio-historical vantage point, because no technique and method can ever secure absolute objectivity in interpretation.

The crucial concept of "prejudices" *(Vorurteile)* or "prejudgments" is discussed in *Truth and Method* (1982) on pages 238–253. These are inherited from
tradition, constitute what we now "see," and have an anticipatory aspect. They
are forestructures with which we approach any new data. "Even a scientific
approach to an object places it within a certain context and takes a certain
attitude towards it" (p. 77), explains Warnke (1987). The meaning of an object is
co-determined by one's own circumstances and expectations. "Knowledge" is
based on tradition, "facts" are based on context, and all "subjects" are situated in
history and are finite.

In a later section Gadamer adds that the reader of a text is always a part of
the meaning of the text, and the same is true in the social and other human
sciences (p. 322). A critical "openness" (p. 324) is needed, and there is a
"conversation" (p. 341) as the key model of hermeneutic studies. Language is at
the center and a communion must occur, which changes both participants.
Gadamer writes, "To reach an understanding with one's partner in a dialogue is
not merely a matter of total self-expression and the successful assertion of one's
point of view, but a transformation into a communion, in which we do not
remain what we were" (p. 341). We test and risk our prejudices by dialogical
encounter.

Gadamer's use of the word "prejudices" here I think is unfortunate because
this term has a pejorative connotation, at least in English. What he really means
is the socio-historical vantage point that we are all born into when we acquire
language, as Lacan has so cogently described it, our own particular tradition and
history, which are indispensable to all understanding. But since our socio-
historical vantage point constantly changes, there is no such thing as final
knowledge or absolute truth; this is Gadamer's argument. Understanding is
essentially historical, for that which is to be understood has a history and the
interpreter is also situated within history, within a tradition (Roqué 1988). He
believes there are legitimate prejudices based on tradition, and these prejudices
constitute the historical reality of the individual.

Gadamer outlines what he calls "the prejudice against prejudice." For
Gadamer this refers to the scientific conviction that truth demands the bringing
forward and removal of all assumptions so that absolute objectivity toward the
facts may be obtained. It was one of Heidegger's most important contentions
that because we are always immersed in a horizon of understanding any such
attempt would be impossible. If the hermeneutic circle is the critical way in
which human meaning, interpretation, and knowledge arises, then of course
"prejudice" or "foreknowledge" is always present and always must be present and
required to provide devices to organize and orient the perception and collection
of data. To have a method is already to have an interpretation. Even in the

collection of so-called "raw data" there are an inherent interpretation, meaning, and human values. We belong to history.

For Gadamer in *Truth and Method* (1991), science is perceived as "method," whereas hermeneutics is dialectical and rests on uninterrupted listening. He hopes to take up the task left by Leibniz and Hegel, to supplement science through the study of the hermeneutics in human sciences. This is based on a dissatisfaction with modern "methodology" in the natural sciences. Because all understanding contains prejudices or prejudgments, the scientific method does not guarantee truth. Especially in the human sciences, the knower's own being is involved. "Method" does not lead to certain truth; according to Gadamer, even questioning and hermeneutic research lead only to a kind of truth. Thus he disagrees with Dilthey, who tried to find a method in the human sciences. This approach employed by Gadamer leaves us in an unsatisfactory position because it does not really help to explain how truth emerges in a given historical situation. There is a certain self-contradiction in Gadamer's work: How does one know when the truth has been found and what to do when one has found it? There is a threat of relativism lurking in the hermeneutic circle.

Hermeneutics as applied to a text, says Gadamer, implies that the meaning of the text is never exhausted by the intentions of the author. As it passes from one culture or historical context to another, new meanings are culled from it not anticipated by the author or its contemporary audience. Thus instability is a part of the character of the work itself and all the interpretation of a work or a text is a dialogue between the past and the present.

An important aspect of the hermeneutic stance is to allow, by proper listening (Chessick 1989a), the text or narrative to speak to us. What we hear depends on the kind of questions we ask from our vantage point in history. It also depends on our ability to reconstruct the problems that the text or patient narrative is attempting to communicate and to answer. The present is only understandable through the past, with which it has a living continuity. The event of understanding comes when our horizon of historical meanings and assumptions fuses with the horizon within which the text or narrative is placed. At such a moment we enter into an alien world, but at the same time we gather into our own realm, reaching a more complete understanding of ourselves. This assumes that history is a continuity and that what holds us apart in understanding others and texts from the past is ideology, in which there is a failure of communication between the cultures, or the conflict between the powerful ideology of one individual or culture versus the powerful ideology of another.

Gadamer, in *Reason in the Age of Science* (1984), points out that the task of philosophy is to join together science and "man's knowledge of himself" as it streams towards us out of the great historical tradition, to achieve a new

self-understanding of humanity. This is especially needed owing to the condition that we live in today of an ever-increasing self-estrangement. This alienation is due not only to capitalism, as Marx would have it, but also to our
ever-growing worldwide dependency on technological civilization, as Heidegger
pointed out. Gadamer argues that we must demythologize science, which
controls what is proper to it but cannot know the person whom it serves. He
argues that only self-knowledge can save our freedom, not only from rulers but
from domination by and dependence on everything we think we control. Thus
Gadamer changes our understanding through the use of hermeneutic theory,
from visualizing a subject without preconceptions studying a text, to realizing
that all understanding arises out of our preconceptions, our position in a
historical tradition.

The prejudices of an individual are the historical reality of his being, and
the issue of how to distinguish legitimate and illegitimate prejudices is obviously
crucial. The great value of the study of the "classical" texts is that they stimulate
us to become conscious of our current prejudices. In *Why Psychotherapists Fail*
(1983b), I discussed in detail the importance of such study specifically for
psychotherapists, and suggested a model curriculum to introduce the student
mental health professional to hermeneutic inquiry in addition to scientific
inquiry.

Gadamer (1982) defines "horizons" (pp. 269-270) as the limits to our
vantage point, the limits of our empathy. For the ideas of another person to
become intelligible we must discover the standpoint and horizon of that person.
Furthermore, horizons are always in motion, and whenever we investigate we
cannot disregard ourselves. This investigation, says Gadamer, is not primarily
empathy but the forming of "a higher universality" (p. 272), a fusion of horizons.
The search for truth, then, has to do with a dialogue between what is handed
down to us and our willingness to test and risk our prejudices as we examine it.

There must be an unending conversation with each thinker, while we hold
ourselves open to that thinker. It should also be kept in mind that for Gadamer
language contains its own concealment, a concept similar to Heidegger's conception of Being. This converting of the text into questions and answers based
on what interests the reader leads to a truth different from the truths talked about
in philosophy from Plato to Hegel. As Gadamer pointed out in *Hegel's Dialectic*
(1976), thought for Hegel is dialectical and self-unfolding, and his method is
grounded in the logical orientation of language. But for Hegel philosophical
consciousness is not conceivable without historical consciousness.

Gadamer disagrees with Schleiermacher and Dilthey because he does not
use hermeneutics for attaining "method" or "rules" for objective understanding
as parallel to the natural sciences. This use of hermeneutics Gadamer calls
"romantic hermeneutics." Gadamer attempts to establish "philosophical herme-

neutics," the conditions of the possibility of understanding that undermines both "method" and "objectivity." Thus, although we cannot overcome our prejudices by "method" and reach "objectivity," we can amend our prejudices in a dialogue with others and approach knowledge.

For Gadamer this "knowledge" can never be a whole, is always partial, and always involves a historical horizon since the historian is himself immersed in history. Even Dilthey feared the relativistic implications of this philosophy and attempted to reach "objective" knowledge; it is Heidegger who first insisted on a historicity that could not be overcome, a view developed by Gadamer.

For Gadamer (1982) as for Hegel, the truth in art is that "it presents man with himself" (p. 45). Art and history, like science, are vital modes of understanding based on a hermeneutic approach to man's relationship with the world. Later he (1977) claims that, "The work of art is the expression of a truth that cannot be reduced to what its creator actually thought in it" (pp. 95–96). The certainty provided by the scientific method does not guarantee truth, especially in the human sciences. The knower's involvement is the limit of method. Prejudices are revealed by dialectic and the concealed ideology in science is discovered. This is what Gadamer (1982) calls "the ontological prejudice, that is contained in the ideal of scientific objectivity" (p. 433).

Since it encompasses both the players and the audience, art, for Gadamer, challenges the way the audience lives its life. It attempts to present the truth and the tenuousness of the purposes and aspirations of the people in the audience, their historicity or prejudices. There is a fusion of horizons in art. But even a scientific approach to an object places it within a certain context and takes a certain attitude toward it. Thus the meaning of the object of study is codetermined by one's own circumstances and expectations. This is not subjectivism, says Gadamer, because prejudices are historically determined, not idiosyncratic in any given investigator. It is these historically and culturally determined prejudices that Gadamer is eager to expose.

By assuming that a text is coherent and a narrative has a truth to teach us—by adopting, as Bion later also advocated, a certain "good will" toward the text or narrative—Gadamer limits the arbitrariness of hermeneutic understanding. This crucial stance constitutes a defense of tradition even though tradition may be prejudiced, a standpoint for which Gadamer has frequently been criticized. Thus to a certain extent Gadamer advocates a conservative form of hermeneutics, in contrast to what Caputo (1987) calls "radical hermeneutics," carried to an extreme by Derrida, in which everything is deconstructed.

This conservatism of Gadamer also contrasts with Rorty's (1979) "edification," which leads more to a kind of cultural dilettantism. In contrast to Rorty, the crucial thesis of Gadamer, especially in his *Reason in the Age of Science* (1984), is that philosophy must integrate knowledge, get a consensus on the "good," develop aims and goals, and give direction to science. This is a reawakening of human solidarity. For Gadamer it can develop collectively through a dialogue with others, whereas Rorty does not think this is possible. Gadamer (1986) illustrates his method in the area of moral philosophy, investigating the idea of the good in Plato and Aristotle.

The enlightenment concept of an autonomous rational neutral subject is untenable. All subjects or investigators are situated and finite. Gadamer's position, as reviewed by Warnke (1987), is that knowledge is based on tradition and facts are based on contexts situated in history. He argues, however, that in a dialogue there can be a "consensus." This term consensus seems to have two meanings for Gadamer: (1) a common idea, and (2) a better meaning, consensus as a fusion of horizons with a consequent deepening, a less blind and one-sided view. Thus *Bildung* for Gadamer, a coming into one's own, acculturation, is a process through which individuals and cultures enter a more and more widely defined community. The cultured person is interested in issues and problems and ways of life quite distant, and which by being distant put one's own life in perspective.

In *Philosophical Hermeneutics* (1977) Gadamer opposes the neo-Kantians who do not recognize the historical position of the interpreter. This is the same argument that is used by Heidegger (1962) when he attacks "subject-ism." We are caught up and buoyed along with a text or a narrative and we can never stand beyond it. Thus understanding is dialectical and is a linguistic process that makes interpersonal communication the locus in which meaning is determined. Gadamer claims that this comes from Hegel and that knowledge is the consequence of a dialectic altering both parties. Weinsheimer (1985) describes the path of such a dialectic as "like the course of a tacking ship which proceeds forward by continually reversing its direction" (p. 250). In reviewing *Truth and Method* he emphasizes that prejudices, as Gadamer uses the concept, "which from the viewpoint of Enlightenment rationalism appear as obstacles to understanding" (p. 170), are indispensable and constitute history itself. But if we are actually interested in what a person says, rather than trusting to method and disinterested aloofness, then our prejudices will be challenged and the false ones sorted out. To illustrate, in *Dialogue and Dialectic* (1980), Gadamer presents us with eight hermeneutical studies on Plato. Here he points out that the interpretation of a Platonic dialogue demands that the interpreter be provoked into responding to the problem at issue. Thus the interpreter must become one of the interlocutors.

What makes this discussion so urgent today is the horror lurking in modern history, a horror that exhausts language. It peaked in the Holocaust, which lies beyond all hellenization, western values, and even Gadamer's "traditions." In spite of the media with their continual emphasis on material improvement and consumerism as the way to happiness, there exists a continuing malaise (Freud 1930) in western civilization, and an erosion of our politics and institutions that are the products of the Enlightenment with its faith in reason and progress and the values of science.

In *Philosophical Apprenticeships* (1985), Gadamer points out that Socrates in the Platonic dialogues had no objectivist philosophy. He really *was* ignorant and the discourse was what counted. He criticizes the Frankfurt school for their Marxist dogmatism, which he regards as a prejudice. He argues, "Man is nothing but his own possibilities. But what are his possibilities?" (p. 125). He reminds us of Heidegger's (1962a) "hermeneutics of facticity," that is to say, the self-interpretation of factual human existence rests on our forms of consciousness, which in turn are our inherited and acquired historical education, our aesthetic consciousness and historical consciousness, so, in Gadamer's phrase, "we are immersed in the educational game."

Gadamer argues that sciences conceal their ideology, especially the human sciences, but he reminds us that Kuhn (1962) has demonstrated this for the natural sciences also. For Gadamer, human wisdom is the knowledge of our own ignorance. Dialectic is critical and thinking points beyond itself. There needs to be an unending conversation with each thinker and the critical point is always to hold oneself open. An important corrective for the scientific method and a way of reminding ourself to hold ourselves open, for Gadamer, is art.

CONVERSATION WITH DR. GADAMER

The following conversation is reconstructed from my memory of a visit to Dr. Gadamer's home on October 12, 1991, in Heidelberg, during which he consented to briefly discuss philosophy with me. I have paraphrased the questions and answers, and these are not authentic, literal quotations, but just reflect the discussion as well as I remember it.

R. C.: I realize that you are now 92 years old, and I do not want to tire you out, so I will restrict my questions. The first is: How do you distinguish between productive prejudices that enable understanding and those prejudices that hinder it?

Dr. Gadamer: There is an intuitive knowledge that tells you that you are on the wrong track as you try to understand.

R. C.: I take it then you are a follower of Spinoza (who believed in intuitive knowledge).

Dr. Gadamer: Yes, but more a follower of Plato.

R. C.: But does Plato not imply an Absolute Truth outside of tradition and eternal, the very opposite of what you discuss in *Truth and Method?*

Dr. Gadamer: No, that is Platonism, not Plato. Plato believed that one can never reach the truth; it is always ineffable and only the gods can reach it. The deliberate ambiguity of the title of my book, *Truth and Method*, grabs attention and demonstrates this. No method reaches it, although many, including art, approach it.

R. C.: This seems to be an attitude that is different from your teacher Heidegger.

Dr. Gadamer: Heidegger had a nervous breakdown in his adolescence. For this reason he was rejected when he applied to be a seminarian leading toward becoming a priest. So he made his own religion out of Hölderlin. I personally am hopeful of the future more than Heidegger was; I think China will be the next industrial country. Like Heidegger, however, I wonder if the world will change track from the age of technicity. Perhaps the "dropout" movement in the United States will be the possible alternative to technology. I do not agree with the later mysticism of Heidegger, but I am a visionary, and I leave ambiguous which prejudices do and do not make sense.

R. C.: What did you retain from Heidegger?

Dr. Gadamer: He taught me that my acceptance and following of Husserl was incorrect, and that transcendentalism in Husserl is not feasible. Of course he was a great and inspiring teacher, but his interest in anxiety in *Being and Time* was due to his own instability. Heidegger's Nazism was simply due to his utter lack of courage. He was a bad soldier in World War I. But he quoted Schelling on how anxiety de-centers a person from himself, and I feel this is a better understanding of anxiety than is found in Hegel.

R. C.: What affinity do you feel to Hegel's method?

Dr. Gadamer: I dislike Hegel's dialectical method, which is too rigid and compartmentalized. My thought is closer to Rorty, although he is more extreme. I try to maintain a certain ambiguity throughout my writing, which I think is Plato's point. For in the "Seventh Letter," Plato claims that truth is impossible to express explicitly, and that is the difference between Plato and Platonism.

R. C.: Some authorities question the authenticity of Plato's "Seventh Letter."

Dr. Gadamer: It is surprising to meet a doctor from the United States who is knowledgeable about the humanities, is a humanist as we say. I think those authorities who accept the authenticity of Plato's "Seventh Letter" have the better and, for me, decisive argument. Do not mind our cat walking back and forth across your lap; that means it likes you.

R. C.: Thank you very much for taking the time to respond to my questions.

EXTENSIONS OF THE HERMENEUTIC APPROACH

The beneficial aspects of this approach come from the realization that humans are constituted by the shared world in which they live, and therefore in order to understand ourselves we must understand our culture, language, and history. On the other hand, we run the continual danger of relativism and nihilism if we deny the possibility of arriving at some kind of reliable truths and "facts." Are "facts," as, for example, Habermas (1971) argues, constituted by the particular economic or historical situation of a society, that is, produced and influenced by social and economic factors? Or is there the possibility of neutral objective information? For Habermas the natural sciences hide a technical interest directed toward control over natural phenomena; the historical sciences are shaped by a practical interest, and there needs to be a third form of cognitive interest, called by Habermas "empirical-critical," in which the ideological foundations of all the sciences are studied using methods such as Freud's psychoanalysis and Marx's theory of society. The methodology is primarily that of the self-reflection found in psychoanalysis, and Habermas argues that with the development of this third sphere of intellectual activity in a situation of free and uncoerced discussion, which he calls "the ideal speech situation," a rational consensus may be arrived at, which Habermas considers to be the closest possible approximation to truth.

Bernstein (1988a) points out that it is not possible "to state once and for all, in a rigorous, determinate, and nonvacuous manner, what are or ought to be the standards, criteria, or rules by which interpretations can be epistemically evaluated" (p. 89). This indeed is the central complaint made against those who would envision the psychoanalytic process, or the dialogue in any dyadic interchange such as psychotherapy, as generating meanings that can be best understood by the procedures of hermeneutics rather than approached by the standard methods of natural science.

In an effort to solve this problem, Ricoeur (1977, 1981) attempts to validate psychoanalytic interpretations not by the use of the observational sciences but by trying to apply certain criteria: that the interpretation must be consistent with the basic tenets of Freudian theory, must satisfy psychoanalytic rules for understanding the unconscious, must be "mutative" or therapeutically effective, and must be part of an intelligible narrative and not inconsistent with other aspects of the narrative. This is a very powerful argument, but many authors insist that it would be better to attempt empirical studies, for example, noting the patient's response to one or another kind of interpretation, with independent raters and so forth—a tracking procedure in the traditional natural sciences manner. Actually I think that Ricoeur's approach is what is customarily used in the day-to-day clinical practice of psychoanalytic psychotherapy. I will discuss his views in the next chapter.

Kohut's method of empathy as a data gathering procedure is viewed by Wakefield (1988) as falling under "epistemological versions of hermeneutics" (p. 139), a special procedure unique to the sciences of humans. It is not empirical by traditional standards because it cannot be publicly verified, and of course it depends greatly on the capacities of the investigator. Wakefield points out (p. 140) that this escapes the problem of relativism because an observer will be either correct or incorrect in that his or her empathy will either be accurate or inaccurate and the consequences from the clinical point of view are usually obvious. The problem, as I (1985) have discussed it elsewhere, comes of course in the definition of empathy and the arguments over the application of empathy, its curative value, and the suggestibility of patients as well as their need for compliance with a particular therapist's point of view. In that sense the same objections could be (and have been) raised against Freud's entire position unless empirical studies are employed to substantiate his interpretations and psychodynamic formulations. Hermeneuticists, it should now be obvious, would insist that such empirical verifications are in principle not possible.

HERMENEUTIC PSYCHIATRY

The hermeneutic approach is often confused with the so-called humanistic psychologies. Actually the work of Heidegger, Gadamer, and others is premised on what Heidegger called "a second Copernican revolution," that the isolated conscious subject is not the center of the experiential universe. It was this contention that brought Heidegger into direct opposition with his teacher Husserl. Humanistic psychologists and "third force" psychologists, as did Husserl, overestimate the role of the isolated conscious subject. According to Heidegger they are incorrect in conceiving of consciousness as something individual, private, and uniquely developed. Gadamer (1977, p. 243) reminds us that Heidegger called Husserl's work "objectivistic subjectivism" because Husserl incorrectly believed that the individual unique subject can be isolated and objectified, and constitutes a "transcendental" ego.

Heidegger's notion of horizons indicates that there can only be an approximate, tentative, and indirect way in which to access foundational data of human understanding. If Heidegger is correct, the customs and institutions of a given culture, not the idiosyncratic perspectives of isolated individuals, channel and constitute human experience. That is why even our own self-interpretations, self-understandings, and self-reflections are largely determined by our shared world, which provides us with the modes or templates of knowledge through which we know ourselves in any given culture at any given time. Above all, these authors stress the importance of language or what Gadamer (1982) calls "language as horizon of a hermeneutic ontology" (p. 397), an echo again of Bacon's "idols of the marketplace"; we are immersed in language that determines our experiences, our thought processes, and our understanding. Thus language is not simply an instrument for communication but has a constitutive role in our very experience itself.

If we follow Heidegger and Gadamer, the conclusion suggests itself that meaning in a dyadic relationship is generated by language and resides not in the mind of individual speakers or writers but in the dialogue itself. This suggests that we cannot valorize a private and inner realm in the mind of each individual speaker but must concentrate on the social dialogical meaning of the exchange. Here the interpreter's or the listener's "prejudices" could be understood to play a positive rather than a negative role because they help to produce the meaning. Similarly, clinical phenomena could be understood correctly only from the vantage point of a study of the input of both participants. A current example of this is the rather extreme concept of the "borderline patient" put forth by Atwood and Stolorow (1984), who view the "borderline patient" phenomenon as a consequence of the empathic failures of the therapist interacting with the patient's reactions to disappointment, rather than primarily as a function of psychopathology residing solely in the psychic structure of the patient, the so-called "borderline personality organization."

The question of the development of a hermeneutic psychiatry rests on the issue of whether Heidegger and Gadamer and Kohut have offered us a chance to develop a middle way between the humanist glorification of subjectivity and individuality, which contains hidden within it a narcissistic materialist economic ideology, and the poststructuralist denial of the self, in which the "I" is seen as solely constituted by the culture, a view that conceals an anarchist, nihilistic, and hopeless mentality. In another publication I (1988a) have discussed this issue in detail.

Following Heidegger, Merleau-Ponty (1962), who will be discussed in Chapter 10, attempts to resolve this problem by emphasis on the use of the bodily stance that we take toward people. Merleau-Ponty compares the clearing in which entities can show up for us (as described by Heidegger) with the illumination in a room. This illumination allows us to perceive objects but is not itself an object toward which the eye can be directed. For Merleau-Ponty this clearing correlates with our bodily skills, which in turn contain our own embodied understanding of what counts as real. If this background becomes overly generalized, it produces a situation in which one gets stuck in a certain way of having a sense of being, and so repeats his or her "solution" endlessly, leading to pathology. Unfortunately Merleau-Ponty died before he could work out this approach in detail, but it leads to what Dreyfus and Wakefield (1988) call, to contrast it with Freud, "breadth psychology" (p. 276), in which a certain atmosphere or context that has become embodied from the individual's childhood experience determines the way that individual experiences all relationships from that time on. This "generalization" is contrasted by Merleau-Ponty with the "repression" used by Freud in his depth psychology. Rather than representing the influence of unconscious childhood unresolved conflicts on current relationships, as Freud would have it, "breadth psychology" emphasizes the individual's incapacity to experience all people and all objects in any other way once generalization has taken place, which from that time on determines the future of the individual's efforts at perception and understanding. As Dreyfus and Wakefield point out, "Once such a way of taking people becomes a dimension of the background of all experience, a person is unlikely to experience anything that could cause him to change his one-sided way of relating to other people" (p. 277). In this sense, as Merleau-Ponty (1962) explains, "This past which remains our true present does not leave us but remains constantly hidden behind our gaze instead of being displayed before it" (p. 83).

Hermeneutics has been attacked from one direction by natural scientists and empirical philosophers such as Grünbaum (1984), and from another direction by authors like Spence (1982), who have emphasized the relativism that it can easily become. In addition there is a tendency on the part of hermeneuticists to write in a very difficult fashion, using a convoluted prose that is very unfamiliar to American audiences. In our pragmatic country we are used to and expect clear and lucid exposition, and we tend to react negatively to jargonistic and continental terminology, especially when it is not clearly defined. The existence of a whole variety of hermeneutic approaches further complicates the issue and often leads to a total rejection of the field by the impatient student of the topic. This is a mistake. For example, one of the finest works combining hermeneutics and the natural science approach is to be found in Ricoeur's (1970) *Freud and Philosophy* (to be discussed in the next chapter), a very difficult book to read, which, although it stresses the centrality of hermeneutics and interpretation in psychoanalysis, leaves the door open for the empirical study of what Ricoeur believes to be Freud's combination of praxis with interpretation.

The psychoanalytic process combines the development of meaning and interpretation in the dyadic situation with the appearance of transference reactions that can be observed and studied. The sequential unfolding of transference reactions in a well-conducted psychoanalysis appears at least to some extent independently of the personality or prejudices of the analyst (although to what extent remains hotly debated), and therefore psychoanalysis stands midway between a pure hermeneutic procedure and a pure natural science. I (1988b) believe that Ricoeur was trying to point this out in his book, although in subsequent writing he (1977) emphasized more explicitly the textual aspect of the psychoanalytic narrative, which led him into great difficulties with practicing clinicians.

Strenger (1991) has offered the best discussion to date on these problems. He suggests strengthening the hermeneutic approach by ruling out those theories that are hermeneutic in origin that are not consistent with accepted background knowledge embodied in other disciplines and/or do not cohere with such knowledge. This "criterion of external coherence" (p. 189) is helpful in reducing the danger of relativism in hermeneutics. He also supports the same pluralistic position that I (1989) have advocated for psychoanalytic listening, when he explains, "The pluralist position states that there could be many perspectives on human nature which need not be reducible to one another" (p. 191). He concludes that psychoanalysis should be regarded as "an overarching theoretical framework, which guides and suggests research in different areas like psychotherapy, psychodiagnostics, child development, perception, etc." (p. 196).

There is no reason why hermeneutic psychiatry cannot base itself on a combination of interpretive and natural science procedures. What is needed for this to happen is the willingness of empirical scientists and those trained in the United States pragmatic tradition to achieve a "fusion of horizons" with those continental thinkers and philosophers who are much more prone to reduce the distinction between the observing subject and the studied object. The student of hermeneutics will either be deeply impressed by the alternatives it opens up or will be utterly disgusted and turn away from thinking about the whole matter. We also must never forget the political implications that are involved, since power and money in our United States society are acquired much more easily by those who pursue the natural sciences than by artists, poets, dreamers, and hermeneuticists. But who ultimately will change the world?

4

RICOEUR

W E HAVE DISCUSSED HOW Gadamer, a pupil of Heidegger, separated out hermeneutics from phenomenology in Heidegger's work. Gadamer attempted to move entirely away from the natural sciences approach to understanding humans, by changing hermeneutic theory from meaning a subject without preconceptions studying a text—for example, the objective psychoanalytic authority studying a patient's dream—to realizing that "understanding" arises out of our preconceptions, our position in historical tradition. Thus to understand a "text" or a patient's narrative and associations we must merge our horizons with the author and his or her society, which always gives a new meaning.

For Gadamer, "horizons" are defined as limits to our vantage points, and limits of our empathy. The fusion of horizons with another person or a text leads to greater understanding of both the other and ourself; it is a linguistic process. Art and history, like science, says Gadamer, are modes of understanding our relation to the world and so also present truths.

Even a scientific approach to an object, and especially to a human as an "object" for study, places it within a certain context and takes a certain attitude toward it. Thus, in Gadamer's extension of this approach, "knowledge" is based on tradition, and facts are based on contexts, and everything is situated in history.

The concept of *Vorurteile*, which is usually translated as prejudgments or prejudices, is a crucial one to Gadamer's thought. These "prejudices" are inherited from tradition, constitute and determine what we now see, and have an anticipatory aspect. This anticipatory aspect consists of forestructures or foreknowledge with which we approach *any* new data in *any* science.

RICOEUR'S USE OF HERMENEUTICS

Paul Ricoeur, who was born in 1913, wrote, "Man is the only being who is subject to his childhood. He is that being whose childhood constantly draws him backwards" (1974, p. 113). Ricoeur was born a Protestant in France and became a professor of philosophy at Nanterre. In 1970, however, the student radicals got him removed and labeled him "an old clown." Humiliated, he moved away from social action to the scholarly study of what symbolic language conceals. He now commutes between the United States and France. Although he is a respected thinker, he is a very obscure writer.

The basic work of Paul Ricoeur is a search for methods for establishing Christian moral values (Kurzweil 1980). For him the unity and dignity of the human person is fundamental, and truth is intersubjective. It arises between human and human in communication and it resides in language. One of his most famous books is called *The Symbolism of Evil* (1969), essentially a theological work that attempts to search for first truths embodied in the symbols of salvation and creation by studying the symbols of evil. This hermeneutic interest in symbols is probably what led him to study Freud on symbols, to emphasize their importance in Freud's (1900) *The Interpretation of Dreams*, and then to examine the entire published work of Freud.

Ricoeur's own philosophy, which he refers to as "reflective," attempts to use what he considers to be a version of Hegelian dialectic. He examines all sides of a philosophical or psychological debate and, by shifting each view back and forth repeatedly, hopes to arrive at deeper and higher levels of understanding. He assumes a tremendous knowledge of other philosophers on his reader's part, and he tends to pick little phrases of numerous philosophers out of context and assume the reader's understanding and recognition, which is one of the reasons his works are so difficult to read.

For Ricoeur, all human sciences involve interpretation. There is no one Truth. The natural sciences study the nomothetic pole (see Chapter 1) of meaning, mathematical rules and laws. Using hermeneutics, Ricoeur studies the ideographic pole, in which ideas are represented by symbols, for example, symbols of evil, dream symbols, and so forth. He calls this "structural semantics," by which he means a field of communication dominated by the symbol. For Ricoeur, the symbol is a mystery that the philosopher has to ceaselessly open and decipher. He opposes all positivistic, logical-analytic, and empirical philosophy because he argues that those schools of philosophy simply reduce the natural, normal language of man to quasi-mathematical operations. This removes the mystery and the ambiguity from human communication, and as a result these philosophers end up working with something sterile, something that does not lead to anything beyond itself. Ricoeur argues that a study of symbols will lead philosophers to an increasingly mysterious beyond—the "wholly Other"—posited by Ricoeur on a desire for the beyond in every human being. His interest in symbols relates Ricoeur's thought to theology, and enables him to move away from the pessimism of Sartre and Camus, although Ricoeur overemphasizes the importance of symbols in Freud's dream theory.

By his "reflective" philosophy Ricoeur hopes to explore deeper and deeper levels of meaning in a given system of thought, such as that contained in the complete *Standard Edition* of the works of Sigmund Freud. Ricoeur's method as applied to Freud's thought consists of going over and over Freud's collected works; one is reminded of Kohut's famous advice to a student: When the student asked what he should read, Kohut answered, "Read Freud." When asked what to read after Freud, Kohut said, "Read Freud again." In this chapter I will discuss only Ricoeur's writings on Freud, which consist mainly of his (1970) book *Freud and Philosophy*, some of his (1974) hermeneutical essays, and his (1977) important discussion of proof in Freud's psychoanalytic writings. This is only a fraction of his numerous publications on many subjects.

Ricoeur describes his process of study as a "hermeneutical arch," moving from objective interpretation to subjective appropriation. Hermeneutics for Ricoeur brings to light an underlying coherence or sense in an apparently cloudy text or narrative. It deciphers or interprets. Something inaccessible becomes understood in terms of its transformations. In the instance of Freud, for example, he (1970) writes:

> By making dreams not only the first object of his investigation but a model of all the disguised, substitutive, and fictive expressions of human wishing or desire, Freud invites us to look to dreams themselves for the various relations between desire and language. . . . How do desires achieve speech? How do desires make speech fail, and why do they themselves fail to speak? This new approach to the whole of human speech, to the meaning of human desire, is what entitled psychoanalysis to its place in the general debate on language. [pp. 5–6]

For Ricoeur the latent dream text is what he calls the primitive speech of desire, and it is in Freud's work that he attempts to study the relationship between desire and language. Freud takes the text of the dream, which is language, and he works backward by the hermeneutic method, according to Ricoeur, and ends up with the primitive speech of desire. This is what Ricoeur calls the semantics of desire.

For Ricoeur (1970) there are two kinds of hermeneutics. The first of these he labels the "hermeneutics of suspicion." This was presented by Freud (1856–1939), Marx (1818–1883), and Nietzsche (1844–1900), to some extent Feuerbach (1804–1872), and, I would add, Foucault (1926–1984). All of these doubt the primacy of the sacred, says Ricoeur. Their task is demystification and a reduction of "illusions." A crisis of the philosophy of the subject is involved here; these authors point to the lie of consciousness and to consciousness as a lie. So for Freud consciousness expresses the unconscious and sexuality; for Marx the conscious is formed by economics. In 1888, Nietzsche's last good year, Freud was 32 years old and deeply immersed in psychoanalytic work on hysteria; he had not yet undertaken his self-analysis. In that year Nietzsche wrote, "All philosophy is 'interpretation,' a tearing off of masks" (Chessick 1983a).

For Ricoeur a sign points to univocal meaning, for example, a traffic "stop sign." A symbol, however, is "a region of double meaning." For Freud a symbol is a ready-at-hand cultural convention. Sex and aggression are the basic drives; his psychology is a psychology of appetition. For Ricoeur, a symbol unites the sacred with everyday life conventions, and the yearning for the sacred and is fundamental to human desire. Thus Ricoeur's philosophy, as he contrasts it to the hermeneutics of suspicion, is a hermeneutics of faith; Ricoeur insists that symbols through the use of hermeneutics can reveal the "beyond" and present a "kerygma," a proclamation of religious truth.

RICOEUR'S VIEW OF PSYCHOANALYSIS

In Ricoeur's opinion, psychoanalysis is not phenomenology, for it involves work ("analytic praxis") which is done against resistances. Resistances imply forces or energetics. Furthermore, Freud's psychoanalysis has the purpose of healing. It is a "technique." (Lacan, Ricoeur's contemporary, leaves out the energetics and focuses purely on the hermeneutics, as discussed in the next chapter.) For Ricoeur psychoanalysis is an archaeology of the subject, decentering the conscious ego. He defines "archaeological" in the following manner: Something is completely understood when a mental reconstruction is made of what was there before and why it left these and only these ruins.

Ricoeur (1977) emphasizes the narrative and downplays the nonverbal and interactional in psychoanalysis. He shifts our attention to the exegesis of the narrative, a decoding by hermeneutics, in which we look for hidden meanings in the narrative. Ricoeur implies that something hidden has power; a struggle goes on to keep it concealed, and the concept of energetics is therefore needed to understand and explain this aspect—justifying Freud's "economics" and "dynamics" in psychoanalytic metapsychology. But psychoanalytic questions are about meanings of the patient's narrative, not about natural science facts, argues Ricoeur. He continues by insisting that there are no facts in psychoanalysis, that it is a two-person dialogue, and that the narrative emerging from this two-person dialogue constitutes the "data" studied by psychoanalysis.

Ricoeur downplays the importance of transference, the crucial concept that establishes psychoanalysis as a natural science. Transference is the observable and repeatable aspect of psychoanalysis, and many psychoanalysts view it as the heart of psychoanalysis. Ricoeur agrees with this but says that through transference we plunge directly into the history of the patient's desire focusing on the patient's narrative. There is much influence of Lacan in Ricoeur's "semantics of desire."

In his difficult book *Freud and Philosophy* (1970), Ricoeur subjects Freud's entire written corpus to hermeneutic decoding. He points out what he considers to be Freud's error. Freud built a one-person or solipsistic metapsychological model, his "mental apparatus," out of a two-person dialogue that was dyadic and nonsolipsistic. Ricoeur's discussion places great emphasis on dreams as the key to the psychoanalytic focus on the relationship of desire to language. The text of a dream is the manifest dream; owing to repression it is a coded message. The latent dream Ricoeur calls the "primitive speech of desire." Freud uses hermeneutics to get from the text of the dream to the primitive speech of desire and this process is what Ricoeur labels the "semantics of desire." The same process is used for decoding neurotic symptoms.

Viewed in this fashion, Freud's crucial question is, "How does desire achieve speech?" Therefore, according to Ricoeur, Freud's view of the human is, "As a man of desire I go forth in speech." This approach, he contends, is found as early as in Freud's theory of aphasia. Freud's view of aphasia denies the standard brain location theory (Broca's area, for example) and instead conceives of aphasia as a nonlocalized neurological situation in which speech is cut off from the concepts signified by the words. This leads to Freud's (1914) later use of the connection or lack of connection of "thing-presentations" with "word-presentations" in his theories of neurosis and psychosis. Yet in Freud, says Ricoeur, there is a contradiction, for the human remains a "thing," a "psychic apparatus" in Freud's metapsychology, and this metapsychology is an attempt at a "scientific" set of quasi-neurological explanations.

RICOEUR'S GENERAL CONCLUSIONS

Ricoeur presents what he calls a hermeneutic decoding or "analytic" of Freud's writings. He argues that Freud engages in a kind of transcendental analysis of culture, moving from current cultural phenomena back to certain postulated primary or archaic concepts, for example, the primal horde, primal murder, primal love, primary process, and the like. This is a Kantian way of reasoning, in that one takes the apparent phenomenon as given and then asks, "What must there be in the historical past or underneath in the mind in order for the phenomenon to occur at all?" A very simple example is Freud's approach to slips of the tongue, the parapraxes that form part of "the psychopathology of everyday life." Freud asks, "In order for a slip of the tongue to be possible, what conditions *have* to be assumed?" He is led from this question to postulating dynamic forces interacting with each other behind and before occurrence of the slip.

Ricoeur, in his "analytic" reading of Freud's complete writings, studies the transition from a simple hydrodynamic model of parapraxis (unconscious motivation versus conscious motivation leading to compromise formation) to the famous topographic theory of Chapter 7 of *The Interpretation of Dreams* (1900), a much more complicated model in which the unconscious has vital infantile memories embedded in it. The application of this topographic model to a study of culture, says Ricoeur, led Freud then to the structural theory (id, ego, and superego), and finally to what Freud, in *Civilization and Its Discontents* (1930), calls (to the great pleasure of Ricoeur) "the battle of the giants": Eros versus Thanatos. At each step of this transition, Ricoeur notes, it was a characteristic combination of increased clinical experience and persistent philosophical restlessness that moved Freud on to the next model, so that his clinical experience and his constant attempts to understand more and more caused Freud to keep changing his models. Therefore each puzzling problematic was posed by increasing clinical experience and forced Freud to new postulates and new models.

So there exist three layers, each superimposed on the one before, to be found in Freud. The simple one-person topographic model borrowed from neurology fails because even coded dreams are communications to the other, and human desire is always for the other. Thus there can be no one-person or solipsistic natural science theory that explains a human. There exists at least a dyad of persons always involved in any narrative. For Ricoeur the core of psychoanalytic treatment is understanding the narrative that arises through this dyad which involves communication, and understanding through the transference of the patient's "semantics of desire." For Ricoeur self-understanding and not adaptation is the goal of psychoanalysis. All the thinkers covered in this book discard the concept of adaptation as the crucial goal of psychoanalytic treatment; some even attack it as a use of psychiatry for unethical purposes.

Ricoeur's unique and impressive method in the whole book (1970) is to confront Freud with Freud. In so doing, he attempts by the hermeneutic method to discover inconsistencies and to draw dialectical conclusions from these inconsistencies:

> the only way I can arrive at self understanding in my reading of Freud is to form the notion of an archeology of the subject . . . the only way to understand the notion of archeology is in its dialectical relationship to a teleology. And so I search in Freud's work—in analysis as analysis—for the reference to its dialectical contrary. I hope to show that such a reference actually does exist there and that analysis is inherently dialectical. Thus I do not pretend to complete Freud, but to understand him through understanding myself. [pp. 460–461]

He concludes:

> What I wish to demonstrate, then, is that if Freudianism is an explicit and thematized archeology, it relates of itself, by the dialectical nature of its concepts, to an implicit and unthematized teleology. [p. 461]

So Ricoeur's crucial thesis is that Freud's text, studied as a developmental whole and read many times, contains an "unthematized teleology." That is to say, it points to a "beyond," the creative and constructive aspects of art, religion, and language. Ricoeur says that there is more to language, art, and religion than simply a projection of the internal psychological conflicts of the human; there is a creative and constructive aspect to it that Freud, by using a teleological psychology, a psychology that works in terms of purposes, does not realize that he is actually implying and approaching in the evolution of his ideas over a long life.

Similarly, Ricoeur (1970) correctly points to what he calls Freud's hidden ethical standards. He renames the reality principle the prudence principle (p. 279). He says the prudence principle, the culmination of the reality principle, contains implicitly the ethics of psychoanalysis. This is really the crucial part of his argument. According to Ricoeur, love, art, religion, and culture contain factors that cannot be simply reduced to issues of prudence. They all contain higher values than prudence. So according to Ricoeur, Freud's world view is flawed and soured. For Freud and for the United States school of ego psychology, the healthy person is the person who is registering appropriately and adapting appropriately to reality. But according to Ricoeur, the head of this person is incorporeal; it is assumed by Freud in his late writings that there is incorporeally a little man within the man who is doing all this registering and deciding and figuring and so, in spite of Freud's effort to remove the mind–body split, he has ended up with the mind–body split all over again.

Ricoeur says that Freud projected his pessimism into the world. When Freud points to the dismal, neurotic, regressive, and projective aspects of art and religion only, he is actually projecting his own pessimism, his own blinders that allow him to see only the negative aspects, especially of religion. From this, Ricoeur correctly concludes that even code-breaking, even deciphering, even hermeneutics are permeated by one's own fundamental life attitudes. Thus there is no such thing as the study of truth that does not involve the person doing the study, according to Ricoeur. One's own life attitudes are hidden premises in whatever study one makes.

The oscillation between a humanistic and a mechanistic view of humans is a well-known example of the hidden tension in Freud's thought (Holt 1973). Even Freud's wish to decode symptoms and dreams implies a value system in its dedicated pursuit of meaning, coherence, and clarity. So Freud begins with a simple natural-sciences hydraulic model and ends with a mythology, according to Ricoeur. Let us turn now to the details of Ricoeur's study of Freud.

RICOEUR ON FREUD'S EARLY WRITINGS

Book II of *Freud and Philosophy* or "The Analytic" starts out with Ricoeur's claim that he will readjust and refine the traditional view of Freud. He points out that *on first reading* all the opposition appears to be "external": Freud and the Freudians against the disbelievers. But *on a second reading,* Ricoeur claims that there is an internal opposition within Freud, which appears when we study Freud himself and his writings as they change over the years. He says that in psychoanalysis this is true because theories and facts set each other up. They influence each other, and they are confirmed or are invalidated together. So each time we study something else in psychoanalysis or each time we apply psychoanalysis to another set of phenomena, we come up with material that leads to changes in the psychoanalytic experience-distant theories themselves. It is a circular kind of process.

He begins with Freud's original idea of psychoanalysis, which contains two aspects. The first of these involves explanations through the use of forces, or what Ricoeur calls *energetics*. These are the so-called economic explanations that are made, involving dynamic forces playing against each other. The second presents an exegesis of the apparent or manifest through the latent, the classical hermeneutic approach. But psychoanalysis has always to incorporate energetics into hermeneutics in order to make a psychoanalytic interpretation. This is because the distortions that take place when one goes from the latent to the manifest occur for a reason; there is a pressure that makes them occur, according to Freud. They are not random. There is a force at work that must be understood to explain why these particular sets of transformations take place. Because of the word "force," explanations must involve energetics, dynamics, and so on. The earliest conceptions of psychoanalysis, as in *The Interpretation of Dreams*, contain explanations using energetics and explanations using hermeneutics.

Historically, the next step came when Freud attempted to take these explanations and apply them to a study of religion, art, and culture. This attempt in turn, according to Ricoeur, led Freud to revise his original metapsychology, known as the topographic theory, which he had presented as adequate to the understanding of dreams. So we have a circular process whereby the application of the topographic theory in an attempt to study culture forces in turn a revision of the topographic theory into the structural theory. Next, according to Ricoeur, further studies of art, culture, and religion led Freud to posit the life and death instincts—which clearly upsets the entire mechanics that are presented in Chapter 7 of *The Interpretation of Dreams* and brings psychoanalysis back to mythological philosophy, a philosophy that is much more palatable to Ricoeur.

In Part I of Book II, entitled "Energetics and Hermeneutics," Ricoeur claims that there is an unavoidable ambiguity in psychoanalysis because the concept of energetics comes from classical natural science—the forces of Newtonian science—and yet the hard core of psychoanalysis, according to Ricoeur, is in hermeneutics, in dream interpretation. This ambiguity in the whole psychoanalytic method and fact-finding effort lifts us to a new kind of epistemological investigation. In other words, Freud has, without realizing it, introduced us to an entirely different field of human endeavor that cannot, as he thought, be simply based on old-fashioned classical sciences.

Chapter 1 of this Part I constitutes a review of Freud's "Project for a Scientific Psychology." This project is, as Ricoeur calls it, "Energetics without Hermeneutics"—Freud's only known effort to write a psychology based strictly on neurology and physiology without the use of the fictive model that he gives us in Chapter 7 of *The Interpretation of Dreams*—and it fails. It is an attempt to make a mental apparatus or machine based on neurology and physiology that somehow can deal with the transformations that we see in dreams. According to

Ricoeur, Freud developed over the years from trying to think of the human as a machine made up simply of neurons, toward concentrating on human roles and masks and purposes requiring deciphering; from the human as a machine to the human as a meaning-making creature.

Chapter 3 of Part I, Book II reviews the instinct theory and Freud's metapsychology. Ricoeur claims that when Freud began focusing on the concept of instinctual forces he made a subtle shift, in that the *aim* of the instincts becomes primary in his theory. In Ricoeur's phrase, topography becomes eclipsed by economics; the topographic descriptions now begin to become overshadowed by descriptions involving forces and energies.

RICOEUR ON FREUD'S LATER WRITINGS

When he shifts to Book II, Part II, called "Interpretation of Culture," Ricoeur describes what occurred when Freud applied the method of the interpretation of dreams to the study of culture. When Freud studied culture, he, like Nietzsche and Marx, thought he had both destroyed the sacred and demystified it. In approaching culture through the analogy to the interpretation of dreams and neuroses, the implication is that there is nothing primary in culture; culture, like dreams, consists of nothing but attempts to fulfill wishes. But according to Ricoeur the application of this interpretation-of-dreams technique to the study of culture forced Freud to revise the topographic theory and to adopt the structural theory.

The topographic and the structural theory are of entirely different orders. One is not an extension of the other, nor can we substitute on a one-to-one basis one for the other. Through the study of culture, according to Ricoeur, an entirely different order of theory in psychoanalysis was adopted, an important change in Freud's thinking. Even this was eclipsed by the final theory of the death instinct, which is really a mythological theory and goes far beyond the structural theory.

For example, in Chapter 2 of Part II, Book II, Ricoeur shows how Freud tried to apply dream interpretation to art and culture and how this attempt led to the notion of the superego; as evidence he reminds us that the transitional paper in which Freud first described the superego is entitled "Group Psychology and the Analysis of the Ego." Chapter 3 of this part of Ricoeur's book deals with religion. It is entitled "Illusion," and it describes how Freud tried to interpret religion entirely as coming from the wish for the father. The third part of Book II is entitled "Eros, Thanatos, and Ananke," forming a transitional section in Ricoeur's book, because he now begins to move away from the analytic to those elements of Freud's work that are more mythical, mystical, and symbolic. Freud's final instinct theory is the point at which he joins romantic speculation to science by introducing the death instinct, requiring a complete recasting of Freud's theories, which he never completed, a recasting which, says Ricoeur, contains implications negating his earlier explanations of culture, art, and religion that Freud did not recognize.

In a very interesting chapter (Book II, Part III, Ch. 3) entitled "Interrogations," Ricoeur personally confronts Freud. This is probably the psychological crux of the book, and it is written as if Ricoeur were directly asking Freud certain questions. Ricoeur claims that the death instinct represents a major methodological change in Freud's work because the death instinct is—as Freud wrote— based on philosophical speculation rather than clinical evidence. The death instinct is a "mythical metabiology," more myth than science, placing mythological philosophy within a scientific mold. Ricoeur maintains that the death instinct is an incongruous mixture involving inertia, compulsion, and destructiveness. Then Ricoeur asks the question of what *is* "beyond" the pleasure principle. He argues that Freud could never find the "beyond," and that this incongruous mixture of inertia, compulsion, and destructiveness represented Freud's failed efforts to find it. What is important to Ricoeur is that Freud was trying to get beyond the pleasure principle and he was, for reasons he himself did not understand, *impelled* to go beyond the pleasure principle. For Ricoeur what is really beyond the pleasure principle is Eros, the mythological Eros at this point, on which Freud was wrong. Freud thought that Eros simply represented the force to get pleasure by the discharge of tensions, but Ricoeur tries to argue, citing Plato, that Eros is a constructive force, a creative force that leads us to the sacred and the sublime.

For Freud enjoyment is not interesting, according to Ricoeur. It is very primitive and simply represents the discharge of dammed-up tensions. What Freud found interesting was the diversity of sufferings; Freud offers a never-ending catalog of the miseries and sufferings of life. Ricoeur points out that for Freud "reality" is the world without God, and that is why science is all that is applicable to it. The world without God is symbolized in Freud by a third mythical entity: Ananke. For Freud this mythological Ananke represents the harshness of life. It is for Freud, according to Ricoeur, a symbol of a world view— a very restricted, sour world view-in which life becomes harsh necessity and the reality principle is the application of scientific reasoning and thinking to somehow struggle with this harsh necessity and to survive and discharge tensions the best that one can. In the psychoanalysis of Freud there is a lack of reconciliation between *science*, in which life is simply the alternating of the reality and the pleasure principles, and *romance*, in which life is seen as a clash of giants—Eros and Thanatos. Freud died with these two world views or attitudes unreconciled to each other. Out of the lack of reconciliation of these world views springs, through Hegelian dialectic, Ricoeur's own philosophy, as described in Book III. Discussion of this is beyond the scope of the present book.

OBJECTIONS TO RICOEUR

For Ricoeur the methodological incorporation of hermeneutics and energetics was Freud's crucial epistemological discovery. It represents a new form of investigation, an alternative to investigating the data of clinical psychiatry and the narrative of psychotherapy by either natural sciences and empirical statistical study or by speculative subjective intuitions. Ricoeur has an important message to any mental health professional who feels there has to be an alternative to either the inhumane mechanism of hard science on the one hand or a purely speculative philosophy on the other.

The argument that hermeneutics combined with energetics begins a relevant and autonomous intellectual discipline with its own methodology gives the impression that it represents an important school of thought. But the problem with hermeneutics is that it does not generate any body of testable propositions. This runs the risk of its being an arcane source of wisdom that generates little evidence that we may proceed to study. Recognizing this objection, Ricoeur (1977) argues that something special happens in the analytic relationship, which he calls the analytic experience. It is *this* which is equivalent to what the epistemology of logical empiricism calls observables. For Ricoeur, in psychoanalysis there are not facts, there are only narrative reports. This view ignores our observed experience of the patient's nonverbal behavior and communications and the transference, and the possibility that psychoanalysts, like any group of trained scientists, could check and criticize each other's work. For Ricoeur the ultimate truth claim of psychoanalysis lies in its case histories, and the means of proof reside in the articulation of the entire network: theory, hermeneutics, therapeutics, and narration. What Ricoeur has attempted to do is to establish psychoanalysis as a discipline separate from the natural sciences, separate from hermeneutics, and separate from speculative philosophy, because it is based on a unique combination of energetics and hermeneutics.

In Ricoeur's study of Freud there is a flaw more fundamental than his overemphasis on symbols: In terms of the natural sciences, he overlooks the empirical implication of the phenomenon of transference and the observable and predictable unfolding of the psychoanalytic process. Although he (1970) clearly states that "psychoanalysis plunges *directly* into the history of desire" (p. 390), he seems not to be aware of the possibility that through the transference there is a link between Freudian conceptions and natural science so that one cannot—as Ricoeur does—conceive of psychoanalysis solely as a hermeneutics and energetics. There are *also* natural science phenomena involved in psychoanalysis, which show themselves in the observable and crucial phenomena of transference. On that point Ricoeur's philosophy has been the most severely criticized by psychoanalysts (Friedman 1976, Holt 1981, Modell 1978, Spence 1982). But Steele (1979) and Leavy (1980) support his conception of psychoanalysis as hermeneutics and energetics rather than as a natural science. Schafer (1983), "in sharp disagreement with Ricoeur (1977)," sees no reason to go beyond the "narrative framework into the one structured in terms of psychical forces" (p. 234).

Probably the most slashing and devastating attack on this weakness in Ricoeur's conception of psychoanalysis is presented by the philosopher Grünbaum (1983, 1984). This critic accuses Ricoeur of "truncating" psychoanalytic data, limiting it to texts and narratives, and tendentiously overlooking all the nonverbal and interactional phenomena of the psychoanalytic situation. He describes the hermeneutic approach as a "nihilistic, if not frivolous, trivialization of Freud's entire clinical theory" (1983, p. 24), referring to the disavowal of causal attributions in psychoanalysis and the hermeneutic shift of emphasis to exegesis. In a detailed examination of Ricoeur's work, Grünbaum (1984) also claims to expose many inconsistencies and contradictions, as well as misunderstanding of basic concepts.

In response to this it is possible to argue that Ricoeur's approach offers an important shift of attention from the naive Newtonian natural science conceptions that Freud worked with to a more sophisticated aspect of the psychoanalytic situation that involves communication theory and decoding. It is at least possible that a way out may be found from the collision among the minds of some of his supporters and critics by viewing the hermeneutic and the natural sciences approaches to the data of psychoanalysis as complementary.[1]

---

[1]I wish to thank Professor Ricoeur for reviewing the material in this chapter for accuracy. The opinions expressed are of course only my own.

5

LACAN

AMONG THE IMPORTANT theoretical developments of the century has been an emphasis upon the role of language and culture in shaping knowledge and truth. This development has been fundamentally interdisciplinary; focused on the nature and conditions of discourse and representation, it has broadened into every form of thought and expression, from the humanities to the sciences. Contributions to the discussions have come from different countries and different fields and specializations. Wherever these contributions have emerged, a common feature of the discussions is the reformulation of traditional issues in terms of the distinctive traits of the discourses in which they are expressed. Language, style, and interpretation become important for every form of expression. A second common feature is a concern with the historical and cultural conditions that define stylistic and rhetorical variations in discourse and even reason and truth themselves.

According to Hegel, human consciousness is limited by the social and cultural conditions of an individual's environment, and truth is not absolute or objective but only related to the historical or cultural horizon within which the individual thinkers live. So Fukuyama (1992) explains, "Human history must therefore be seen not only as a succession of different civilizations and levels of material accomplishment, but more importantly as a succession of different forms of consciousness . . . and since these perspectives were mutually contradictory, it follows that the vast majority of them were wrong, or forms of 'false consciousness' to be unmasked by subsequent history" (p. 62). It was also Hegel who pointed out that human nature is not permanent and the nature of human desire changes between historical periods and cultures, a point of view held before him only by Rousseau. This is discussed at length in Hegel's (1976) *Philosophy of Right*, especially in the remarkable paragraphs 190–195.

POSTMODERNISM

These discussions have frequently taken a political form. Involved is the question of who shall rule over an academic discipline. Who shall determine the interpretation of its tradition? What is implicit in such discussions are issues of desire and power. If knowledge is a function of desire, then it is implicated within lived historical and cultural experience. If knowledge is regarded as a form of power, then that it should be exercised over human beings has been thought by many to require legitimation. The modern form of epistemic legitimation is that of science, continuing a development begun in the Enlightenment, although Nietzsche and Heidegger extend that beginning back to the classical Greeks. Yet the questions that pertain to such legitimation stretch to include the disciplinary nature of discourse and the departmental structure of academic or psychoanalytic institutions. The question is whether there are forms of discourse and expression, of reason and truth, that command legitimate authority in virtue of their methods and structures, or whether truth and reason are to be found wherever discourse is present, regardless of the method or style employed.

There have been extensive discussions in almost every human science concerning the paradigmatic forms of expression that constitute its legitimacy — whether, for example, history is a science, whether its legitimacy is constituted by quantitative and statistical more than narrative styles, and whether there have been discourses systematically excluded from historical consideration. Closely related are questions concerning the ethical and political ramifications of a social theory, the extent to which any such theory is pervasively influenced by the social conditions inherent in its production.

Some of the more specific questions that generate discussion are the following:

1. Among the fundamental tenets defining "postmodernism" is the claim that the philosophic tradition — metaphysical and epistemological — has come to an end. To what extent can such a question be regarded as intelligible and important? To what extent can the Western tradition be regarded as unitary? To

what extent can any of that tradition's major forms be said to have reached fruition or exhaustion? To what extent do "metaphysical" discourses retain their legitimacy? What sense can be made of the claim that philosophy is to be replaced by science or, conversely, that the authority of science is the natural culmination of the Western metaphysical tradition? To what extent may other discourses—poetic, literary, narrative, historical, and also yet to be invented discourses—legitimately participate in what Rorty (1979) calls the "conversation of mankind"?

2. To what extent can a discourse that recognizes its own historicity think its future, especially if that future promises major changes and variations? To what extent can universality and objectivity be sustained in a strongly historistic context? What are the implications of these concerns for our understanding of language, the human sciences, and the natural sciences?

3. To what extent is every voice, every form of reason, entangled with desire and power? To what extent can a discourse or discipline claim legitimacy if every human voice is both subject to desire and an object of desire—that is, defines a site where human ends are implemented? To what extent can a discourse or discipline such as psychiatry or psychoanalysis claim legitimacy if every human voice is both manipulated by power and a site where power is exercised?

4. How can theory in the natural and especially in the human sciences either free itself from entanglements with power and desire or, within such entanglements, exercise a claim to truth? How can any theory, scientific or otherwise, understand its own linguisticality, including linguistics itself? It is to the credit of Lacan that, regardless of whether one can accept or reject his contentions, he brought these thorny postmodern issues to the foreground of current thinking in the mental health professions.

BACKGROUND FOR LACAN STUDY

The structuralism of Lévi-Strauss, who was born in 1908, was very popular in the early 1960s and replaced existentialism as the fashionable philosophy in France. It may be defined as a systematic attempt to uncover deep universal mental structures as they manifest themselves in kinship relations, larger social structures, and even in philosophy, literature, myths, and human behavior patterns in all cultures. These structures are built into the human mind. Sartre always opposed this idea, as it denies human freedom, and for Sartre, as it should be for all of us, human freedom was the highest value. Of course Sartre was inconsistent, since he later embraced Marxist determinism somewhat, in a kind of uneasy alliance; to what extent this vitiates and to what extent it represents an extension of his earlier thought remains controversial.

Structuralism is synchronic or ahistorical. It neglects the system out of which a system emerged. Compare this, for example, with the approach of Marx, which is diachronic or historicist. The method of structuralism is one of extrapolation from the rules and relations of grammar and speech to explore social phenomena in terms of linguistic oppositions and transformations. The key assumption of structuralism is the centrality of language to culture and culture to language.

Lévi-Strauss (1969) defines the unconscious as an aggregate of universal structural laws by which individual experiences are transformed into myths. Only a relatively few such universal structures exist. For structuralists the unconscious is not a reservoir of personal images, experiences, and so on. A clinical example of the application of structuralism to the interpretation of dreams may be found in an article by Kuper and Stone (1982). Also noteworthy is the dispute about the article, which appears in letters to *The American Journal of Psychiatry* (vol. 140, p. 662, 1983).

Lévi-Strauss distinguishes the "individual subject," which he disregards, from the "epistemic subject," a cognitive nucleus common to all at the same level of a culture. Therefore, says Lévi-Strauss, we must analyze each culture, especially its myths, its customs, and its language, to find *archetypal* human structures. This should be compared with Freud's quite different psychoanalytic approach, which analyzes free associations, dreams, and so on, to find the *unique* unconscious of the individual.

In May 1968, a political experiment in France began with a student revolt and spread to the entire culture. Government broke down and there was an attempt to substitute "action committees." The premise of this revolt was a romantic faith in man's reason. It lasted for about 2 months. The failure of the events of May, 1968 led to disappointment and disillusionment among scholars and other thinkers in France. An intellectually fashionable turn took place from voluntarism and humanism to structuralism, viewing man as determined by forces beyond his control. This turn was also a reaction to the "culture" of the United States and to the predominant school of ego psychology in United States psychoanalysis. So Lacan (1978) wrote, "It is the It that speaks" (*Ça parle*) not the ego. In Lacan's view the analyst needs to be sensitively attuned to multilayered and paradoxical human communication, and the result of this attunement reveals a linguistic structure that both conceals and expresses the patient's desire.

Behind this approach was what Nietzsche called the quest for anchors (and the conceptions of Heidegger, discussed in Chapter 1). Psychoanalysis in a media form became this "anchor" in France after Lacan (Turkle 1978). Even philosophy students practiced psychoanalysis and, after 1968, as is typical in failed revolutions, disenchanted intellectuals and deep thinkers such as Ricoeur (see Chapter 4) withdrew from praxis and revolution and social causes. The Lacan phenomenon and "pop" psychoanalysis in France was a product of the failed 1968 student revolt. In addition there was a great political role for Lacan's theories, as they enabled a bridging of the early Freud, as read by Lacan, with traditional Marxist views. After these events and theories emerged poststructuralism, which was even more hopeless and nihilistic, as, for example, in the "deconstruction" of Derrida, and Barthes's attempt to establish that there is no unity to a person at all. Curiously these extreme deconstructionist views gained the most recognition in certain academic departments in the United States, especially due to the efforts of an enigmatic Yale professor and Nazi collaborator, Paul de Man (1983; see also Lehman 1991).

LINGUISTICS

Saussure (1857–1913) distinguished language (la langue), a system of signs and social in nature, from speech (la parole), the individual's intellectual execution of language, his or her choice of words. For Saussure (1989) the important focus of study is the laws of language, not individual speech. Like Lévi-Strauss, he concentrates on the epistemic subject, not on the individual subject. The "sign" defined by Saussure is an arbitrary relationship that combines the "s" or signified (signifié), a mental concept and not a "thing," with the "S" or signifier (signifiant), a sound image: Sign $= \frac{s}{S}$. Each sign in a language is given a meaning by the other signs in the language. There is no essential meaning to signs. For example, if one draws a picture of a door on the blackboard, it signifies simply a door. But if one draws two doors on the blackboard and labels one "Ladies" and the other "Gentlemen," the signified is the same, a toilet, but the signifiers, "Ladies" and "Gentlemen," differ on the basis of their reference to chains of many other signifiers that history and culture and social mores have assigned to the implied sexual differentiation and the praxis involved in deciding which door one should enter in order to reach the toilet. And even this is rapidly changing in our culture as women who resent the inequity in public toilet facilities begin using those in the room marked "Gentlemen."

A "phoneme" is an elementary particle of language, a minimal unit. Language is structured by a combination of words, phrases, and clauses, and the selection of words, phrases, and clauses into a chain of signifiers (S) is determined by the culture. There are no hidden "essences" behind this selection. "Semiotics," developed by Peirce (1839–1914) in the United States, and "semiology" in France represent a study of signs, what constitutes them and what laws govern them. In the United States, Chomsky (1972) claimed that the general features of structures of grammar are the same for all languages and reflect certain fundamental properties of the mind. So he is also a structuralist. Structural linguistics, however, is inadequate because it deals only with the surface layer of utterances. Here Lacan enters the picture. He inverts Saussure's equation to put the signifier on top, and also includes symbols and symptoms with signs, introducing the signifier as a more general concept. For Lacan, Sign $= \frac{S}{s}$.

The great linguist Jakobson (1896–1982) studied the rules of how language is structured and how signifiers are related to each other. These ways of relating are first, *metonymy*, a principle of combination based on contiguity, for example "a good table," meaning good food. This, Lacan says, is the same as Freud's *displacement*. Another example of metonymy is synecdoche, in which the part is substituted for the whole, as "sails" for ships or "skirts" for women. The other basic way that signifiers relate, beside metonymy, according to Jakobson, is *metaphor*. Metaphor utilizes a selection principle based on similarity and substitution, for example, "a scepter" or "a crown" for a sovereign,, or employs one word or phrase to stand for a series of equivalents, for example, the ship "plows" the sea, or, a "volley" of oaths.

All languages have a similar fundamental structure, says Jakobson (1983). Synchronic linguistics studies language at a given moment in the evolution of it and focuses on the selection of substitutions in that culture at that time. Diachronic linguistics studies the evolution of language over time, focusing on the links, contexts, and combination of signifiers that develop. Lacan's term, the network of signifiers, refers to synchronic linguistics. What he calls "the diachronic whole of discourse" refers to diachronic linguistics. His point is that a person, although always immersed in the network of signifiers and the diachronic whole of discourse, is unaware of these in operation. As a result, signifier chains and meanings are unique to each person, and for Lacan the human is constituted by his or her language.

What this view contends is that the preverbal innate intuition of the self, also referred to by Kohut, is actualized and provided grammatical categories for individuality by language. Lacan says that language is a precondition for the act of becoming aware of one's self as a distinct entity, in contrast to Kohut, who emphasizes selfobject experiences as the precondition for this. But like Kohut he sees the patient's demand for recognition as a continuous force and emphasizes the patient's need to become aware of this. Therefore the therapist listens carefully for double meanings in the patient's discourse that both conceal and reveal desire (notice the influence of Heidegger), for the purpose of eventually reflecting this back to the patient.

LACAN'S APPROACH

Turning directly to Lacan (1901–1981), who died at age 80, one first comes up against his shocking literary style. He attempts to imitate the unconscious. He employs an allusive, elusive, illusive manner. So, for example, he uses rhetorical tropes, kaleidoscopic erudition, deliberate ambiguity, auditory echoes, irony, a disdain of logic, prankish playfulness, and sardonic and sarcastic humor (see Muller and Richardson 1982). His seminars were "happenings" attended by surrealists, literary figures, psychoanalysts, and members of all disciplines. His (1977) *Écrits* or essays defy translation and become almost gibberish, yet they are not. Lacan was a showman. He carefully cultivated an image. He wanted to show that truth is multilayered and paradoxical. The *écrit* must do something to the reader, break one's traditional mental set, as Joyce and the surrealists tried to do. Bowie (1991) notes the similarity in the thought of Lacan and Dali. Lacan attempts to integrate Hegel, Heidegger, Lévi-Strauss, the early Freud, Sartre, and others in his theories. His popular and controversial seminars (1988a, 1988b) were viewed by some as serious discourse and by others as an ongoing circus entertainment (Clément 1983, Schneiderman 1983). His outrageous play on words, known as Lacan's *languisterie* (Kurzweil 1980), has engendered great controversy (Macey 1988, Chapter 5).

Lacan was born in 1901 in Paris and he was an established psychiatrist when Lévi-Strauss developed structuralism in the 1930s and 1940s. He was also influenced by Foucault and the surrealists. His first work was his thesis for his medical degree, a case study on the paranoid style. He argued that no organic phenomenon can be considered independently of its relationship to the entire personality that engages in interaction with a social milieu. By 1939 he was an established psychoanalyst. In 1953 he left the French Psychoanalytic Society and founded a new one, announced in his (1968) famous "discourse in Rome." In the late 1950s he developed his ideas in his "seminars." From about 1960 to his death in 1981 his thought became more and more unorthodox and he began to express himself in abstract pseudo-mathematical formulas he called "mathemes" that are very difficult to understand. Some of his students have told me he became quite senile. This may or may not be true.

Lacan defined personality as a psychic synthesis that adapts the human to the milieu of society. It is formed first by the image in a mirror stage, an imaginary hallucinatory phase of development, and then by the milieu, which he calls "the name-of-the-father," or the symbolic order of society.

The mirror stage, which occurs from about 6 to 18 months, is one in which the infant jubilantly identifies with its reflection, a reflection that promises unity, mastery, and stature. This image is a rigid idealized totality. It begins the opposition of the ego versus the true self. Lacan (1978) calls this a *Spaltung*, a splitting of the subject, which is required before the entrance into the cultural milieu, so that when one enters the milieu there is something to label as "I" in discourse. There is no empirical evidence for such a stage, but Lacan at times seems to argue that the mirror stage is only a metaphor, so he would not expect evidence from infant research. The mirror stage for Lacan is a *misrecognition*. It is a form of bad faith, and it forms the ego, which is a false unity of the subject.

In the second stage, Lacan means by the name-of-the-father the social order or mapping of all human relationships and interchanges that the child enters through the acquisition of speech. Even this term, the name-of-the-father, is a typical Lacanian pun, for in French *nom* means name or law and *non* means no.

The potential consequences of this theory had great appeal to the Marxists because it bridges the thought of Freud and Marx. The implication is that if you change the culture (symbolic order) a different person will be produced after the infant enters it. But of course the infant must enter it, and this leads to Lacan's notion of the "parental metaphor." The father must be accepted by the mother, or the child remains subjected to her and cannot enter the symbolic order. This situation Lacan labels "foreclosure." So the mother's attitude to the father and child is crucial in the generation of mental illness. In the normal situation the identification with the father liberates the child and gives it a place in the family and culture. Otherwise foreclosure occurs, a total failure to enter the symbolic order, so the person remains in nondistinction between the self and the external world and dwells in the realm of the imaginary in a psychosis. The "hole" created by a lack of signifiers attracts a cascade of images; delusions attempt to make the real accessible, but there is a loss of consensually validated speech. In a less extreme situation, for Lacan a neurosis is a disturbed relationship between the imaginary and the symbolic order, so that speech and behavior become deformed. Here, in contrast to the psychotic and his imaginary world, we have what Lacan calls "a wish fulfilled but mutilated," the neurotic symptom (Lemaire 1981). For example, in the conversion disorders hysterical symptoms substitute for words and the body enters the conversation.

Freud used a nineteenth century hydrodynamic physics model. For example, Peterfreund (1971) explains that "If one reviews the psychoanalytic literature carefully it becomes clear that psychic energy is spoken of as though it were an imponderable fluid with identity, a fluid with directional properties, a fluid whose identity can be changed, a fluid that can be dammed up, discharged, transferred, and so on" (p. 53). Lacan used a human linguistics model. He wished to find the laws that explore and regulate the structures used in language. As an example, take the famous *Fort-Da* game of Freud's grandson at 18 months of age as reported by Freud (1920). For the *Fort-Da* or "gone-there" game, the little boy throwing the spool over the side of the crib (*Fort*, gone) and reeling it back by a string (*Da*, there), we have four different interpretations. For Freud it represents instinctual renunciation, allowing his mother to go away without protest, and a form of mastery that is "beyond the pleasure principle." As we shall see in later chapters, for R. D. Laing it is an attempt to establish ontological security. For Kohut it represents an effort to maintain control over a selfobject, and as it works it leads to a sense of cohesion of the self, triumph and joy. For Lacan it is an example of how the child is born into language. The desire for the mother and the frustration of this desire are expressed through verbal sounds, "gone" and "there." Thus man is constituted by his language, says Lacan, an idea he borrowed from Heidegger.

There is a little-noticed footnote in Freud's *Beyond the Pleasure Principle* (1920, p. 15n) in which Freud mentions the child looking at itself in the mirror and then under it (the mirror did not reach to the floor), thus making *itself* disappear. Here absence and presence are being verbalized (*Fort-Da*), not just the desire to control the mother, and this does seem related to Lacan's clever interpretation. Lacan studied Freud very carefully indeed.

LACAN'S READING OF FREUD

Lacan translates the early Freud of the topographic theory into linguistics. Free association, for Lacan, is the flow of signifiers (S). Each S refers not to an individual signified (s), but to another S, and meaning lies in the whole sequence of the signifiers (S) as they are related to each other. The premise here is that the subject, articulated with language, alienates his or her primary unconscious desire in the signifier chain, which reflects the desire in some way, and seeks to satisfy it with substitutes that are arranged according to the laws of metaphor and metonymy. For Lacan this represents the wanderings of true desire caught in the net of signifiers.

Symptoms and dream work produce for Lacan a personal code, and the patient is unaware of what they express. For Lacan, Freud's "condensation" becomes metaphor, and metaphor is also displayed in neurotic symptoms. Freud's "displacement" becomes metonymy and points to hidden desire. So the primary process in the unconscious follows the laws of !anguage, metaphor, and metonymy (condensation and displacement), from which Lacan concludes that the unconscious is structured like a language because it consists of repressed early signifiers of desire, connected by metaphor, and metonymy.

There is no room for biology in this theory. The so-called drives are explained as follows. Aggression, discussed in detail in the Epilogue to this book, is seen as a reaction to the mirror stage confusion and subsequent alienation of the chaotic self from the false ego. Sex is explained as coming out of a desire for the mother (more precisely, a desire to be what the mother most desires—the phallus), and desire becomes the driving force in humans, a concept Lacan borrowed from Hegel (see Smith and Kerrigan 1983).

There are three "orders" for Lacan—he refuses to call them stages of development because they overlap and all exist at the same time in the adult. After a prior primary narcissism or "inaugural unbounded" phase, there is from 6 to 18 months an imaginary order and mirror stage, which is preverbal and presymbolic. In this phase the mind is inhabited by images that are alienating, and a false ego solidifies. This inaugurates the unconscious realm by the first splitting of the subject. From about 6 to 30 months Lacan speaks of a phase called transitivism in which the child has difficulty distinguishing between himself or herself and another child. For example, if the other child falls down, the first child cries, and so forth. Then occurs a transitory period in which the child comes up against what Lacan calls the forbidden. This begins the entrance into the second major order, the symbolic order. This is the order of language, and a second splitting occurs, because at this point there develops a split between the inner and the outer world. The inner world now contains something that has emerged out of the misrecognition in the mirror stage labeled an "I" or the self, what the ego claims falsely to denote. This "I" identifies with the father's laws and cultural standards. The individual enters the symbolic order, requiring the quest for objects further and further removed from his or her desire. Progressively, splitting alienates the subject from his or her "true" (chaotic) self *and* from the meaning of his or her utterances. Both of these splits are to be undone in psychotherapy. The final order for Lacan is that of the "real," which represents ineffable brute fact, something outside of language that cannot be reached and is never clearly defined by Lacan. It is the "beyond" or the Other of Hegel; one cannot follow Lacan without a considerable acquaintance with Hegel's thought, and especially Kojève's (1969) quite controversial interpretation of Hegel, which greatly influenced Lacan.

There are three fundamental principles for Lacan. First, the human is constituted by language. There is no definitive nature or essence or center to the human. The unconscious consists only of the earliest signifiers, and it is structured like a language. There are no drives and no unconscious before one enters the symbolic order. Second, discourse embodies society. A politics is embedded in our language, and we are all caught in it, since the human is an individual subject only on the condition of being a speaking being and a member of society. Third, there is no autonomous ego. This is a false notion, an *ex post facto* explanation, like explaining why the stocks went up or down yesterday by saying, "The market is nervous about interest rates."

The concept of desire is taken from Lacan's understanding of Hegel. Desire for Lacan is to be the desired of the other, and desire, not Freud's libido, is the driving force of humans. In animals there exists only "the demand of the brute," and this is true of humans also up to the mirror stage. The infant is first in a dual symbiosis with the mother in the realm of primary narcissism, according to Lacan. As this ruptures it realizes that it is not the mother, and human want appears, the human form of desire. This represents a desire for the lost paradise of fusion with the mother.

For Lacan the "phallus" is the signifier (S) of human desire for this perfect union with the mother, and he states that a "primordial castration" has occurred when this union is ruptured. Here Lacan is again influenced by Heidegger. For Heidegger the first experience of human limits or finitude and the first experience of being-towards-death occurs when this union with the mother has been ruptured. For Lacan the developmental aspects of this are the same for both sexes up through the entrance into the symbolic stage (see Mitchell and Rose 1982).

A "dialectic of desire" occurs because of this rupture. Another Lacanian play on words appears here, because his phrase *désir de l'Autre* can be translated as either "the Other's desire" or "desire for the Other." The ultimate quest is to be recognized and desired by the desired; this is the "gleam in the mother's eye" of Kohut. The child wants to be the desired of its mother, her fullness, her phallus, but must end up expressing only culturally legitimate desires, which it does through endless substitutions and multiple displacements. This is so because, alas, it is impossible to achieve this desire—the father, who has the phallus, is there. In considering the triadic relationship, one must remember that the father, for Lacan, represents (a) the real father, (b) the imaginary father, and (c) the law of the father, the symbolic cultural order structuring all human relationships. Thus, for Lacan, the father is a spoilsport. To the infant he says, "Thou shalt not sleep with thy mother," and to the mother he says, "Thou shalt not reappropriate thy product."

For Lacan the oedipal struggle represents foregoing this original desire and channeling it through the symbolic order, expressing it in some way through words. The child identifies with the father and finds legitimate signifiers. In so doing it accepts finitude and the limits and restrictions of culture and life, and it accepts the laws of the father and his culture. This is known as "oedipization," which for Lacan represents entering the social order. When it is accomplished, the oedipal struggle is resolved. From then on, in one's language, a chain of signifiers in which "the signified incessantly slides under the signifier" occurs.

Here is the reason that Lacan inverts Saussure's $\frac{s}{S}$ to $\frac{S}{s}$, in order to emphasize the primacy of the signifier.

Lacan's example is from the short story by Edgar Allen Poe called "The Purloined Letter" (see Muller and Richardson 1988). In this story we never read the letter, so its message is a signifier, a migratory signifier which attracts different meanings, mediates power relationships, and determines subjects in what they do and see. In my opinion this is a rather extreme reading of Poe's story, but Lacan's use of it has become famous. The example I like is from a poem by Ezra Pound (1949):

ΊΜΕΙΡΩ

Thy soul
Grown delicate with satieties,
Atthis.
O Atthis,
I long for thy lips.
I long for thy narrow breasts,
Thou restless, ungathered.

The Greek title means "I desire." But what is it that the poet desires? The poem centers about Sappho's beloved Atthis at the end of the seventh century B.C. Who was Atthis, the object of Sappho's desire? Little is known about Sappho. Was she, as she is often called, really a lesbian? She married and had children. Atthis in this poem would be, for Lacan, a narrow phallus, a restless, ungathered signifier, inexpressible directly. What Nietzsche called "an unsettling groundlessness" is in this poem by a flawed genius with many similarities to Lacan both in his personality and poetic works.

LACANIAN PSYCHOANALYSIS

Lacan (1990) opposes all authoritarianism and bureaucratic attitudes of psycho-analytic leaders, institutes, and hierarchies. He opposes the structural theory of Freud and the United States' psychoanalytic ego psychology with its goal of adaptation. Lowenstein, of the famous triad of psychoanalysts (Hartmann, Kris, and Lowenstein) who developed this ego psychology, was Lacan's analyst, and so Lacan has been accused of having an unanalyzed negative transference. Psychoanalysis, says Lacan, should simply return the message of the "it" to the subject, as it did in the years before the 1920s (see Chessick 1987a).

Putting aside the *ad hominem* issue of his unanalyzed negative transference, Lacan's explanation for his repeated oppositions and challenges is that the
establishment represents middle-class values of the culture that psychoanalytic
theory and treatment must take apart in order to clarify and reveal the demand
of the analysand, which is pure primitive desire hidden in the very symbolic or
cultural order. The result is a paradox in institutionalized psychoanalysis and
psychiatry, for surely some rules are necessary. Thus in some ways Lacan ends
with a cult, as one might expect (for example, see Gallop 1985). Yet Lacan
correctly recognized the great danger in the institutionalization of psychoanalysis and psychiatry, the collusion to hide inequity, to adjust to iniquity, and to
adapt to the culture. Both the political implications of this and the disadvantages of such collusion for the practice of intensive psychotherapy are apparent,
especially after our study of the authors in the previous chapters.

Lacan flouts all the rules. There are no diagnoses. Instead he uses styles.
His notorious "5-minute hour" and the self-proclaimed readiness to do psychoanalysis, the so-called pass in his institutes, and his own frequent change of
institutes, as well as teaching psychoanalysis in a university, are further examples. Along with many rule infractions and confrontations, he instigated many
broken allegiances and violated many friendships (Turkle 1978).

To summarize, for Lacan psychoanalysis is hermeneutics. It brings out
underlying contexts and structures from the unconscious and reveals a personal
code. The past is hidden by linguistic transformations owing to the necessity to
fit into the symbolic order, the process of oedipization. Psychoanalysis is
primarily a study of the discourse with the Other, and historical reconstruction
is unimportant. Psychoanalysis brings to light the desires hidden in metaphors
and tropes used by the patient (see Figure 5-1). The human subject or self is
endlessly displaced and reconstituted by the symbolic order of desire through
which language passes. Thus a study of your language can guide you back to
your own unconscious desires—which are insatiable. In contrast to Ricoeur, no
energetics are needed in this process. Repression consists of transformations that
have been required for the infant to fit into the symbolic order. For Lacan (1968)
the human is a marionette of his or her culture, and the formation of the self,
contra Kohut, is a betrayal leading to "paranoiac alienation."

The enemy of the "true" (chaotic) self is the ego, born in the mirror phase,
a false notion that the individual has of himself or herself as a coherent entity.
For Lacan this is a misrecognition. Lacan decenters the self (Ragland-Sullivan
1986). We all have divided selves, he says, and we all are alienated from our
"true" self. There is no autonomous ego and no center to a person. He changes
the focus from biology and instincts to language, and from mechanisms to tropes
or figures of speech. Lacan was militantly antibiological and conceived of
psychoanalysis as an interpretive discipline.

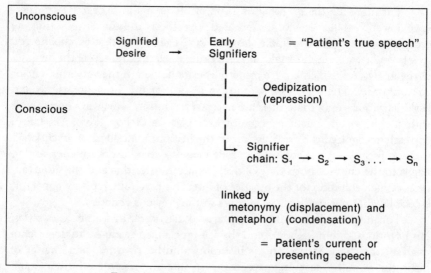

Figure 5-1. Lacan: A Summary Diagram

For Lacan transference was a misrecognition of the other in the dialogue based on the desire for the other, a misrecognition that substitutes for the desire for fusion with the mother. There is no case history by Lacan published in English so far, except one interview (Schneiderman 1980); in another publication I (1989a) devote much of an entire chapter to going over this single interview Lacan offers with a psychotic patient.

For Lacan there is no original instinctual unconscious, just chains of signifiers. As a result of the fitting in to the symbolic order, the link between the signifiers and the signified, as well as to the early signifiers, is broken. This is repression. The signifiers float, connected by tropes. The person loses his or her grip on what his or her signifiers mean and the analyst "must restore discourse to its owner." Lacan's theories and readings of Freud cannot be established by any evidence or research. Psychiatric labels are useless and what is crucial is each person's unique narrative.

Psychoanalysis for Lacan (1977) is a reversal owing to the silence, what he calls the dummy (le mort), of the analyst. Because of this silence a twofold regression takes place. First, there is a regression backwards among the signifiers, what Lacan calls "undoing the secret knots" to the unconscious primal signifiers of desire that constitute the unconscious. Second, there is a regression to the loss of narcissistic images by which the ego is constituted in the mirror stage. The frustration of the patient's demand sets this in motion. Silence, or the dummy of the analyst, produces this, and through the transference reaches the truth of the patient's desire. It restores full speech to the patient.

Leavy (1980) presents an excellent clinical example, in which the patient manifests a complaint of the intrusiveness of the analyst under which is her desire to be intruded upon by the analyst-father. The real question that the patient asks is, "Why do you ignore my attractiveness?" It represents her demand to be recognized, and it is also a very similar phenomenon to that outlined by Kohut. Leavy concludes:

> To speak at all is to express the desire to be recognized and heard, whether the speech is in the form of a demand or not. The act of interpretation has accordingly a threefold revelatory purpose: to disclose the message hidden in the manifest statements, to disclose the desire implicit in the message, and to disclose the identity of the person or persons on whom the demand is made. . . . For example, the situation has to be imagined that the patient referred to earlier (by way of her series of statements that add up to a complaint about intrusiveness and a confession of her own) also is inviting the intrusive attention of the analyst, saying, in fact, "Why do you ignore my attractiveness?" in which question the second person of the dialogue stands for the actually intrusive, but also frustrating, father. [p. 80]

Notice the similarity of Lacan's effort to restore "full speech" to the patient (Figure 5-1) to Heidegger's concept of discourse (Rede) contrasted to idle chatter, described in Chapter 1.

LACAN'S THEORY IN PERSPECTIVE

For Ricoeur, psychoanalysis is an archaeology of the subject, an unburying of the unconscious and a disclosing of the life lived in unconscious fantasies. Energetics are used to "explain" the burial. For Lacan, desire is never really buried. Repression is not burial in the sense that Vesuvius buried Pompeii; rather, the unconscious consists of reversible linguistic transformations, which occur because of the need to fit into the symbolic order as one learns to speak. There are no separate energetics needed; just understand linguistics and one can understand the unconscious, which is structured like a language.

Psychoanalytic theories vary. Some are centered on the here-and-now and its effect on the transference. Some offer nurturing repair of structural damage. Some stress remodeling or reinforcing the ego. Some offer the therapist for identification or for a new object relation. Lacan says that persons come into their own by allowing the signifiers in their unconscious to have free speech. The other theories, he says, just reinforce alienation for the purpose of adaptation.

To compare Lacan with Freud (see Vergote 1983), Lacan's unconscious made up of signifiers more closely resembles Freud's preconscious than his unconscious. Freud's unconscious consists of id energies and thing presentations and primary process, governed not by the laws of language but by the laws of wish fulfillment. Lacan substitutes primordial signifiers for the wild energy of Freud's id, which is not at all like a language.

Kohut's baby is a joyful baby, born with a rudimentary sense of self. Lacan's baby is resigned and lacking and torn from the mother with a yearning for fusion. The sense of self that is formed when the person enters the symbolic order is for Lacan a betrayal; therefore Lacan does not really resemble Freud or Kohut in style, presentation, or method.

Furthermore, Lacan differs in a major fashion from all other psychoanalytic theorists. His heresy is that the mirror stage begins the hiding of part of the self from itself. The child constructs itself in language as it wishes itself to be seen. For Lacan the "true self" (infantile chaos) has to bow to this procedure and allow masks, that is to say, the ego, to proliferate so that one can fit into the symbolic order. This is the same as Sartre's bad faith, and it decenters the self. The result is an alienation from the hidden "true" self, which, for Lacan only, is thought of as chaotic, amorphous, and inchoate. So for Lacan there is no "true self." All this is asserted by Lacan without evidence, and definitively separates his views from those of the psychoanalytic establishment.

As an example of the enormous difficulty of understanding Lacan (especially in translation from his very sophisticated French), there are no fewer than five ways he uses the term "other" (Lemaire 1977). "Other" can mean language, the site of the symbolic order. It can mean the psychoanalytic dialogue, that is to say, the dialogue with the other, the I who speaks with him who hears, as Lacan puts it. Then there is the subject's other, the unconscious, the subject's forgotten message. Slips of the tongue, for example, represent the bursting through of unconscious signifiers, and this is the discourse of the other when the "it" speaks. The other can also guarantee the analyst's good faith. It is used in that fashion to indicate the professional third party aspect to psychoanalysis when it raises the issue of formulating truth. Finally, the other for Lacan can mean the father or the mother.

The biggest flaw in Lacan's work is his neglect of the nonverbal phase of development, in the imaginary order, as a direct influence on the psychoanalytic process, with its production of preoedipal or archaic transference demands and behavior. Superego lacunae and fundamental ego deficits are ignored, along with much that has been learned about ego functions and self psychology since the 1920s. Furthermore, the famous 5-minute hour, the silence or "dummy" of the analyst, and so forth, may often represent manipulation of the transference. It is this kind of technique that produces wholesale introjections, "allegiances," controversies, and so forth, destroys certification, and removes psychoanalysis as a medical specialty in France entirely (for details see Roudinesco 1990).

The greatest advantage of Lacan's work is his concept of the informed physician who relates to patients as people and tunes in to what the patient is uniquely saying. He correctly emphasizes the importance for the therapist to be immersed in a study of literature and the arts in order to attain a full understanding of the patient's speech (see also Chessick 1983b). He warns us that thinking of the patient as having a "weak ego" may cause us to talk to the patient in a condescending manner. The analyst's first task, he says, is to listen and hear what is beyond the spoken discourse.

Lacan emphasizes the transaction between the individual and society. Like Foucault, he points toward the study of society to explain the individual, because the human is constituted by a language in which a politics is already embedded; language or discourse embodies society, and we enter society when we develop language. For Lacan there exists no center in humans, no autonomous ego.

In approaching Lacan's publications, I suggest beginning with the excellent overview article by Bowie (1979). Books by Benvenuto and Kennedy (1986) and Lemaire (1977) are the best among many introductory texts, and Muller and Richardson (1982) offer an indispensible guide to be read along with a number of Lacan's essays. Schneiderman (1986) provides an interesting and informative Lacanian reading of Freud's (1909) case of the "Rat-man" for comparative purposes.

Psychotherapists will be especially interested in Lacan's concept of "dehiscence" (called *béance* in Lacan 1968). This represents the empty center, a rent or gap that constitutes a basic fault penetrating human existence. This gap between the false unity of the ego and the infant's chaos produces a tension, an alienation, and a splitting that generate aggression. This alienation from the "true" self (for Lacan an infantile chaos) is what Freud called the "death instinct" (see Chapter 11). It generates a pulsion (Lacan's word for "drive") to return to chaotic fragmented pre-ego states, the "beyond" of desire, which for Lacan is represented by death and also by his concept of *jouissance*. The latter term sometimes is referred to by Lacan, a notorious womanizer, either as the female orgasm or some sort of ecstatic state.

The fragmentation dreams described by Kohut occur, according to Lacan, when the ego is in danger of being dismantled in psychotherapy and the patient is slipping back into the pre-ego chaotic state. Similarly, the archaic transfer-ences for Lacan represent attempts to enforce the illusion of coherence and mastery, an attempt that leads to aggression so frequently observed in these kinds of transferences. For Lacan, the human is always fundamentally in conflict with its own truth, with nature, and with society.

For Lacan (Benvenuto and Kennedy 1986, Mitchell and Rose 1982) the female enters the symbolic order as "not-all," devalued, and therefore the definition of femininity is always negative and implies a lack. Her sexual enjoyment or *jouissance* is an "extra," an "encore," not describable in language. This is surely a mystical view in which the curves and bikini of the female hide the darkness of the subject's origins. So feminine psychology for Lacan is "beyond phallic parameters," which make it poorly understood and in a way beyond the edge of psychoanalysis (see also Chessick 1983d, 1987b).

QUESTIONS

The following are some questions an ordinary psychotherapist might wish to ask of the Lacanians:

1. What is a psychoanalyst? How is he or she to be trained and certified?

2. What is a Lacanian psychoanalyst? How is he or she to be trained and certified? How does Lacanian psychoanalysis differ from traditional psychoanal-ysis in actual clinical practice? From psychotherapy?

3. If the "ego" and the "true self" are false images, exactly what *is* true about the individual subject? How is this "truth" to be established? How does this relate to Lacan's important notion about *béance?* Where does the *objet à* fit into clinical practice?

4. The literary critic Lionel Trilling (1965) writes, "And there is no reality about which the modern person is more uncertain and more anxious than the reality of himself" (p. 41) and, in his discussion of Jane Austen's novel *Emma,* he praises her for "the hope she expresses when she begins to understand her mistakes, that she will become 'more acquainted with herself' " (p. 41). What help can Lacanians give us with this ubiquitous clinical problem? How would they answer Trilling (and Kohut)?

5. How can the fashionable French hostility to the United States be kept out of the interchange between Lacanians and American psychiatrists and psychoanalysts so that a sober assessment of points of view becomes possible?

6. How can United States psychiatrists read the English translations of the extremely difficult Lacan (to say nothing about the arguments and disputes

among his followers), when after much study they are told that all sorts of other writings of Lacan, which contradict those available in English, also exist? Does this not also raise the question of whether it is at this time possible to present Lacan in the United States?

7. Is it possible to overcome the widespread continental fashion of deliberate obscurity among intellectual writers in order to present to pragmatic Americans a clear picture of Lacan's views? Even though Lacan probably would not have approved of this? Is a clear picture of his views even possible?

8. How are we to separate those individuals, medically and psychologically untrained in the customary sense, who are practicing authentic Lacanian analysis, from those who are claiming to be Lacanians but only practicing wild analysis and acting out their own personal narcissistic problems?

9. On what criteria are we to decide whether the entire Lacanian movement is a serious attempt to "return to Freud" and improve on the clinical practice of psychoanalysis or a surrealist attempt to joyfully obscure and confuse or even destroy the field out of some need, conscious or unconscious, for example, perhaps out of unresolved negative transference from a previous failed traditional analysis (e.g., Lacan's analysis with Loewenstein)?

10. Gallop (1985) wrote a book about Lacan's views. In it (pp. 111–113) she admits that she quit a traditional analysis after two months because of some sort of bizarre breakdown that involved her envy of the analyst's money and so on. Then she decides not to be an analyst and begins "therapy . . . for three months with a woman psychologist who is neither a physician nor a psychoanalyst" (p. 113). Later (p. 187) she dreams of Lacan "approving" of her work. Is this not a postpsychotic defensive reintegration in a person who is not analyzable? How can such individuals be weeded out as undesirable self-styled experts on Lacan? Do you wish to do this? If not, why not?

11. Lacan does not give a clear understanding of the stages or phases of psychological development in their relationship to the "Borromean knot" of the imaginary, symbolic, and real "orders," and in his later work the whole idea of such stages is suspect. Lacan apparently contradicts himself on this. How is one to compare Lacan's developmental metapsychology with those of other psychoanalytic schools if no such clear exposition is available?

12. There is a great paucity of Lacanian clinical material. In the one published example in English of Lacan interviewing a psychotic (in Schneiderman 1980) there is a desperate need for a clear exegesis of what Lacan was proposing to do, or even why he was interviewing the patient at all (see Chessick 1989a). We are told by various sources that Lacan was a great clinician. What is the evidence for this? Bowie (1991) notes that "Lacan's own work, considered as a whole, does not seem to offer a satisfactory correlation between theory and clinical practice" (p. 201).

13. Lacan's concepts of "gaps," "lack of being," "holes," and "nothingness" are hopelessly vague for a United States reader. Even a knowledge of Hegel and Sartre does not help much because their notions, besides being muddled on this subject, are metaphysical. But the concretization of these notions in clinical work with psychotics by Lacanians, besides involving a massive epistemological jump, carries no identifiable content for the average clinician. Again, exegesis is desperately needed.

14. Gedo, an American psychoanalyst who is not afraid to be critical of traditional views, considers his approach the diametric opposite of Lacan. For example, he (1986) argues:

    a) Lacan's work "utterly disregards" the empirical foundations of psychoanalysis. Psychoanalytic ideas in Lacan "dissolve into literary conceits and the psychoanalytic situation loses its therapeutic aim" (p. 206). Here Gedo means *all* therapeutic aim, not just that of adaptation.

    b) "In the psychoanalytic situation, where the observer is simultaneously participant in the dyad, the relative importance of processing the lexical meaning of the verbal interchange is even smaller than it is during a dramatic performance. I would compare it to my experience at the opera; if I am provided with a synopsis of the action, I seldom miss having a precise understanding of the words; when I read the libretto without hearing the music, I find the text to be without interest and fail to respond in any way" (p. 199).

    c) Lacan ignores entirely the vast preverbal area of human experience, such as the building of preverbal tension-regulation structure by the mother–infant dyad as it fluctuates in action, or the self/selfobject relation described by Kohut in the preverbal period. For Gedo and many others this is a fatal flaw in Lacan's work.

How would Lacanians answer these charges? And by what criteria or data is the ordinary practicing psychiatrist to choose between these polar opposite theories? What is the role of clinical experience in making these choices?

15. Lacan's famous abbreviation of the psychoanalytic hour is often downplayed by Lacanians in English writing. If this is abandoned, what effect will it have on the whole of Lacanian treatment? If not, how can it be practically instituted?

16. In general, violations of the therapy frame, whether by shifting the lengths of the various hours, allowing telephone calls, and so forth, have profound effects on the nature of the analytic material produced by the patient. By what criteria are we to: a) assess patient material as reactive to frame

violations rather than as signifiers of desire? b) decide if a frame violation represents countertransference acting out by the analyst?

17. Lacan's views on feminine psychology appear to be contradicted by a massive and growing body of experimental and observational research that establishes inborn gender differences appearing at birth and increasingly developing during the preverbal period. They are also very offensive to many women, and one wonders if they are manifestations of his personal psychopathology or have simply been misunderstood. His mystical concept of *jouissance* (which seems for him to have as many metaphysical meanings as the Λόγος of Heraclitus) suggests the former explanation. All this needs much clarification in order to be presented to United States psychiatrists. What are we to do about the confusion in Lacan between Phallus as Signifier of primal desire and the real phallus (Muller and Richardson 1982, p. 337)?

18. What is considered validation in the clinical material to indicate that effective Lacanian therapy is being carried out? To put it another way, how is a psychoanalytic session carried out by a well-analyzed Lacanian analyst to be distinguished from that carried out by somebody who is a self-styled Lacanian analyst but is actually doing a narcissistic form of wild analysis?

19. More generally, what are we to regard as empirical data to form the basis of a psychoanalytic science for Lacan? For example, on what data are we to justify his pseudo-mathematical formulations? Are these "mathemes" of any value at all? If so, what?

20. I feel that Lacan has put forward some important ideas, but they are — perhaps deliberately — in such a metaphorical form as to suggest a hopeless ambiguity. Is one left only, as I suspect Lacan narcissistically had in mind, with making a "leap of faith" into his system, or is there any way in which his work can be compared with other systems of thought and tested in the clinical process? How are contradictions to be resolved? What could legitimately lead to change or modification of this system? Much serious discussion of Lacan's ideas is still needed and would be very worthwhile. The transference love (Clément 1983) of his followers surrounding the charismatic Lacan must be worked through, and his work still needs to be evaluated in a sober fashion.

6

SARTRE

JEAN-PAUL SARTRE WAS BORN in Paris in 1905 and died there in 1980 at age 74. Albert Schweitzer was his uncle. His father died when he was 15 months old, which he (1964b) said, "sent my mother into chains and me to freedom." He was raised by his mother and grandmother and grandfather, and he (1964b) claimed that his writing from the age of 7 years defined him against his imposing grandfather, who was a teacher and a very eloquent man. In 1928 he met Simone de Beauvoir (1908–1986) and formed what was probably the only lasting human commitment of his life. In 1933 he discovered the phenomenology of Husserl, which set him on the road to his life's work. Table 6–1 gives an orienting overview to the phases and titles of some of Sartre's voluminous publications of special significance to mental health professionals.

Sartre's (1964a) novel *Nausea* (published in 1938) justly made him famous. He was a German prisoner from 1940 to 1941 in World War II and spent considerable time in the prison camp studying Heidegger and generating his (1984) *War Diaries*. In 1943 his play *The Flies* and his philosophical work *Being and Nothingness* appeared, followed closely by his play *No Exit* and the first two volumes of his novel *Roads to Freedom* in 1944. In 1946 his (1947) most famous essay, "Existentialism is a Humanism" was published in an attempt to try to explain more simply the very difficult philosophical peregrinations in *Being and Nothingness*; this popular essay made Sartre a world figure. In 1960 his views

Table 6-1. Sartre

Central theme: Passionate interest in the human condition.

Central defect: Grossly metaphorical character of his leading ideas; hard to integrate with philosophical tradition and to clarify.

Phases of his work:

1. Phenomenological psychologist

    Transcendence of the Ego (1936*)—Objects are independent of consciousness, not products of the transcendental ego as Husserl thought (Sartre 1957).

    The Imaginary (1936*)—Imagination is an activity of consciousness to set up an unreal state of affairs. It constitutes, negates, and isolates the actual world.

    Nausea (1938*)—Considers this novel his best work; phenomenology (Sartre 1964a).

    The Wall (1939*)—Stories that focus on the vivid lived world (Sartre 1948b).

    Essay on Theory of Emotions (1939*)—Emotions are escape strategies (Sartre 1948a).

2. Ontology of human existence

    Being and Nothingness (1943*)—Subtitled "phenomenological ontology," which is a misphrase, since traditionally ontology deals with Being and phenomenology deals with appearances, that is the "ontic" (Heidegger). Yet for Sartre ontology is superior generality. Typical of Sartre's idiosyncratic use of terminology (Sartre 1973b).

    The Flies (1943*)—Written against German occupation (Sartre 1949).

    No Exit (1944*)—"Hell is other people" (Sartre 1949). Other illustrations of his theory are the novels *Roads to Freedom* (first two volumes in 1944) (Sartre 1973a, 1973c, 1973d); *Existentialism is a Humanism* (1946*), the essay that made him famous and led to a whole amorphous popular movement (Sartre 1947) (compare Lacan in France in the 1980s); *Baudelaire* (1947*); *Anti-Semite and Jew* (1946*) (Sartre 1965); and *Saint Genet* (1952*), the first detailed demonstration of his regressive/progressive method, his "existential psychoanalysis" (Sartre 1953, 1963a).

3. Restatement of Marxism

    Critique of Dialectical Reason (1960*)—Emphasis on praxis, and the practico-inert, defined as the organization of the world by human praxis that ironically ends up interfering with individual praxis, projects, and creativity (Sartre 1968).

    The Family Idiot (1971-1972*)—his overwhelming biography of Flaubert, written under the influence of amphetamines (Sartre 1981, 1987, 1989).

    Preface to Fanon's *Wretched of the Earth* (1961*)—Advocates violence, with a cry to be on the side of the Algerian fighters and an emphasis on helping the third world to throw off oppression. Not to assist this violence is to choose to assist the oppressors. A demand for intellectuals to be active (Sartre 1963b).

*Year of original publication.

shifted toward Marxism and he published the first volume of a *Critique of Dialectical Reason*. In this work he moved from pure existentialism to Marxism, and from using analytical reason to advocating dialectical reason, which he defined as requiring the thinker to be a participant in human affairs, not just an ivory tower observer. The introduction to this volume, published separately (Sartre 1968), is one of his most original and exciting works.

In 1964 he refused the Nobel prize for literature. In 1968 he became involved in radical causes and was a rather isolated intellectual maverick; it caused him considerable humiliation but he insisted that commitment is an act and not a word. He became scorned and out of favor with the French intelligentsia as his rhetoric became more and more extreme. From 1971 to 1972 he published his remarkable *The Family Idiot*, a three-volume, 2000-page work on Flaubert. During this time he was on alcohol and amphetamines and he remained on such drugs heavily for the last 20 years of his life (De Beauvoir 1984).

There is a remarkable superficial similarity of Sartre's thought to that of Heidegger, whose work, as he studied it in the prison camp, catalyzed his ideas. Sartre made Heidegger popular outside Germany through his novels and plays, but Sartre was primarily a literary man, not a philosopher. There are actually profound differences between the philosophy of Sartre and that of Heidegger (Fell 1979), and the philosophy of the latter is far more sophisticated and more likely to exert a lasting influence. On the other hand, Sartre was the greater writer, and a reassessment of his contribution to improving the human condition is yet to come (Aronson 1980, Detmer 1988, Gerassi 1989).

EXISTENTIAL PSYCHOANALYSIS

Sartre also developed what he called "existential psychoanalysis." The basic premises of this are as follows. In his 1938 novel *Nausea* he (1964a) defined "being-in-itself" as brutal, absurd, and nauseating. He described our relationship to "being-in-itself" as gloomy and viscous, although he never says why this is so. In *Nausea* he argued that creativity gives meaning to life, a concept not far from that of Kohut, but much less carefully worked out. In his (1957) monograph *The Transcendence of the Ego*, published in 1936, he insisted that the ego was a fleeting construct and not a primary aspect of personality. This is an opposite point of view from that of Husserl (1913), and the monograph was written against Husserl's "transcendental ego," discussed in Chapter 10. It also was certainly opposite from Freud's emphasis on and conception of the ego, and closer to Lacan (who came later).

Sartre based his philosophy and psychology on his concept of the "reflective self." This concept was developed in *Being and Nothingness*, his (1973b) major philosophical work published in 1943. Here he described two forms of consciousness, both of which he calls "nothingness," as opposed to "being." These two forms of consciousness are first, the "prereflective consciousness" in which, for example, I see a table or run after a taxi. That is to say, awareness of one's self is a side issue while one is busy with things and activities. This is to be distinguished from what he calls the "reflective consciousness," which arises when we think about ourselves as an object; it is a secondary form of consciousness. Therefore the self or ego is a derivative notion that arises from the reflective consciousness, for example, when I think of myself as looking at a table, or I imagine myself running after a taxi.

In Sartre's philosophy, in some mysterious way, "prereflective consciousness" arises from "being-in-itself" (Copleston 1977). It is not clear where "being-in-itself" comes from; it is just "there." Humans alone have "reflective consciousness," and so the being of humans is different from all else in the world. This being of humans that has reflective consciousness, Sartre calls "being-for-itself" to distinguish it from "being-in-itself." Being-for-itself causes the human alone of all creatures to impose a meaning on existence. The human makes his or her own essence. There is no God, no soul, and no permanent "human nature," and therefore there are no objective eternal or divine values or meanings or purposes for humanity.

A third form of being, called "being-for-others," is also found in humans alone. It connects the human immediately with others. His famous example of this comes from the immediate shame one feels when one is gazed at in a compromising situation, such as being caught peeping through a keyhole. Suddenly we are transformed from a subject to an object for another subject. This, he says, is how we are certain there *are* other subjects; it decisively negates solipsism.

Sartre's early philosophy was an anathema to Marxists because Sartre in his early work viewed the human as primarily nonhistorical and nonsocial in his or her being. Focus is wholly on the individual and his or her unique choices or projects, and so the individual in Sartre's early philosophy is not seen as in any way historically or socially determined. Our awareness of our being "condemned" to be totally free to make choices (within our situation of course—we cannot "choose" to fly), Sartre says, leads to anguish (*angoisse*), the sense of standing on the edge of a precipice both attracted and repelled by the abyss. To escape this anguish we can blame God, circumstances, the unconscious, emotions, our childhood, and so forth, but all of this is what Sartre calls bad faith (*mauvaise foi*). For Sartre each person is responsible for what he or she is. There are no excuses.

Our original choice or basic project reveals our ideal self and values through our actions, and is understandable only through a retroactive study of our life. Sartre is unclear (McInerney 1979) as to whether secondary choices later in life can affect our basic project, but he does agree that the basic project can be changed in extraordinary circumstances. Therefore, all there is to a person is the sum of his or her actions and purposes. There is no unconscious and no internal mental apparatus as postulated by Freud. Sartre (1947) writes that the human is a process, not an entity. The human is "condemned to be free" (p. 27).

For Sartre, Freud's censor and psychic agencies and the unconscious all are agents of bad faith (*mauvaise foi*). Sartre is closer to Kohut's (1977) "psychology of the self in the broad sense." The unity of the psyche is crucial and it is driven by its basic project, which is not much different from what Kohut (1977) calls the basic program of the nuclear self. For Sartre this basic program or project is preconscious, not unconscious; there is no realm of the unconscious. Sartre's denial of the unconscious was based on a misunderstanding of Freud (see Chessick 1984), and toward the end of his life, in his (1981) work on Flaubert and his (1985) movie script on Freud, he came quite close to utilizing the concept of the unconscious, without admitting it.

The goal of existential psychoanalysis for Sartre is to undo bad faith. Bad faith is not much different than Kohut's notion of disavowal or the vertical split, but for Sartre existential psychoanalysis should reveal one's basic project by the method of retrospective study. It is a literary task and says nothing about how to remove resistances to uncovering.

SARTRE'S LATER PSYCHOLOGICAL VIEWS

Sartre changed his opinions many times in a long life. His final psychological views may be found in the crucial example of his (1981, 1987, 1989) study of Flaubert, which took the last 10 years of his life to write. One must remember that he was primarily a literary writer, not a psychologist or a philosopher, and so he was not technically careful. He expressed himself best in novels and plays and he argued that philosophy changes with the times, but literature reveals the absolute. He thought of himself as a writer (Sartre 1955, 1988).

The crucial question that Sartre raises in his study of Flaubert is, "Where did Flaubert's ambition to be a writer come from?" This was Flaubert's (and Sartre's) basic project despite the fact that his parents wanted Flaubert to be a doctor. And, indeed, his younger brother became a doctor, an obscure rural general practitioner. Sartre's method in this work is a sort of literary psychoanalysis, with a careful total documentation of the person's life. It is based on the following developmental theory: First, there exists in each individual, according to Sartre, what he calls a basic constitution. This is formed by two factors. The first is the individual's *prehistory*, the structure of the family: their social situation, the sibling order, the character of the parents, and so on. The second factor that goes into forming the basic constitution is what Sartre calls the *protohistory*. The protohistory represents the early life events, whether truly or falsely constructed by the child: the preverbal relationships, especially with the mother.

Love for the infant is crucial. Sartre (1981) writes, "The baby must be given a mandate to live. He is here for something" (p. 133). The mother's love gives the baby this mandate, just as Kohut emphasizes how the mother has to respond to the baby's emerging self. Sartre's reason for this need for mother's love, however, is much different than that of Kohut. He says, in the famous ending of *Being and Nothingness*, that man is a useless passion; man alone makes himself and creates his values and is a giver of meanings and then dies. In *The Age of Reason* he (1973a) writes, "A child: another consciousness, a little center-point of light that would flutter round and round, dashing against the walls, and never be able to escape" (p. 57). For Sartre one's parents engender a sense of meaning and mission in life, and society supports it or opposes it, a view developed later by Lacan.

If there is no parental love, the result, says Sartre, is that one experiences an empty, passive, boring self and life, a description similar to that of Kohut's (1977) empty, depleted self. A low self-esteem results. Such "unloved ones," both Sartre and Lacan would say, tend to dwell in the imaginary realm. One solution to this problem, as Sartre found in the case of Flaubert, is that if one has talent, one may recreate the world in the arts from one's imagination (Sartre [1964b] applies this also to himself in *The Words*, his unfinished autobiography).

In addition to one's basic constitution, a person's development depends on what Sartre calls *personalization*. In childhood the individual forms a basic choice or project that culminates, although it may be disavowed, in an identity appearing in late adolescence. For example, Sartre calls attention to Flaubert's "nervous crisis" in which he decided to be a writer and not a physician. Even the quality of a person's sex life, says Sartre, is a manifestation of the basic project — again, quite similar to a contention of Kohut's (1984): that the so-called sex drive is actually a disintegration product and that adolescent sex, for example, is often more for the purpose of raising self-esteem than for releasing a drive. So there are superficial resemblances here to Kohut's (1977) program of the nuclear self, when Sartre writes that to live is to project oneself toward one kind of future rather than another.

Along with basic constitution and personalization, the third factor in development for Sartre is society and cultural tradition, which influence, by enhancing or opposing, our basic project. Here (1968) he introduces the concept of the "practico-inert," both a material scarcity and a bureaucratic set of conditions of society. This takes the place of "being-in-itself" from Sartre's earlier *Being and Nothingness*. The practico-inert, the material situation of our society and the bureaucratic apparatus, resists our projects and limits our knowledge but is the only instrument we have for living together. Sartre introduces the family as a mediator between the universal and the individual. This new view is of course much more acceptable to Marxists, because it postulates that a wrong culture can alienate us from our own basic project and our own struggle to choose and realize ourselves (Poster 1982). This leads Sartre to rail against capitalism and its cooperative United States' psychiatry of adaptation, as he calls it. More significantly, Sartre moves from an earlier lone human theory of freedom to great focus on social problems, for to be free, he asserts, others around you must be free: "We must act upon our history." This shift begins in his seventh play in 1951. Up to that time he seems to have seriously believed that any situation can be transcended by subjective effort. In *The Devil and the Good Lord* he argues that individual salvation is only possible in the collective struggle, and he attempts to deal with his own isolation and lack of warmth.

Sartre presents an atheistic materialism. Ethics arise from "What is good is useful to human freedom." Thus one cannot avoid the political life. Freedom for oneself and others is the supreme value to be achieved by anyone who wants humans to approach their potential, such as philosophers and psychiatrists (Detmer 1988). For we must allow each person to carve out freely his or her project and meaning in between birth and inevitable death. The emphasis on freedom endures throughout Sartre's writing; even in his (1965) early work *Anti-Semite and Jew*, published in 1946, he bases his analysis of anti-semitism on the fear of being free and alone. This is one of Sartre's best psychological studies, concluding that if Jews did not exist we would have to invent them as a needed object of hatred.

All existentialists emphasize basic conscious choices as the key to our lives and oppose breaking down the human into parts or "agencies" such as the id, ego, and superego of Freud. More akin to Kohut's psychology of the self, the human is seen not as an entity but as a process. Whereas Heidegger emphasizes the importance of death, Sartre emphasizes human life (existence), moving in his thought from a focus on individuals to social problems, from concern over individual despair to the calamitous consequences of "scarcity," as he called it, especially in the third world. So Gerassi (1989) labels him "the hated conscience of his century." He was most hated by those he called "*salauds*": anti-Semites, capitalists, and others in bad faith and parasitic on their victims (Caws 1977).

OBJECTIONS TO SARTRE

Sartre's is a basically pessimistic philosophy and psychology. We do not know what our basic project is except retrospectively. It is, however, preconscious and not unconscious. We are alone in the universe, and our struggle is a useless passion because we are condemned to die. We cannot predict our future choices or how they will affect our basic project. Everything depends on what Sartre calls "contingency," a very famous term he used throughout his work, referring to chance and the unexpected in life. We are usually in bad faith and fooling ourselves. Sartre, in a view similar to that of Nietzsche and Kierkegaard, calls average adults "swine." Kierkegaard calls them "shut up," Nietzsche calls them "disgusting," "finished," and "the last man." Between children and parents there is only, says Sartre, "the dialogue of the deaf." For Sartre the universe is "allergic to man." We do, however, have the potential to revise our basic project at any time, although, as stated previously, he never makes it clear how that happens. He does imply that bad faith can be undone at any time, and here he seems very much to resemble Kierkegaard and Heidegger.

Standing between the Marxists, who claim that the person is entirely the product of socio-economic historical forces, and Sartre's early view in *Being and Nothingness* that the person alone chooses without the influence of history, Sartre develops his final view. He now sees choices as constricted much more by the practico-inert, which brings him closer to the drive/defense/conflict/compromise view of Freud.

However, Sartre's approach was a nonbiological, non-Freudian method of treatment, and his existential psychotherapy is based on this. For Sartre explanations based on the Oedipus complex represent bad faith, and to become free one must believe one is free. Freedom is key to keeping the future open, and to health. Neuroses are seen as an escape from freedom, and so Flaubert's neurosis was suddenly resolved at age 21 when he made a basic choice. The symptoms of Flaubert's neurosis were agony, malaise, boredom, emptiness, hypochondriasis, passivity, apparent retardation, and daydreaming. Thus Flaubert the "under-loved" came to be called "the family idiot."

What is remarkable in the life story and early philosophy of Sartre is his lack of empathy for individual humans (Cohen-Solal 1987, Danto 1975, Hayman 1987). His is a world without empathy, a world of void where the individual must go it alone. Yet Simone de Beauvoir was for 50 years a mirroring, long-suffering, and subservient companion to him, to the very end. Moreover, can Sartre's existential psychoanalysis without the unconscious explain anything? His retrospective approach gives an apparent unity to a life, but are we referring to conscious or even prereflective choice, or to the best possible compromise at any given moment made by the ego to satisfy its three harsh masters—the id, the superego, and reality? Cannon (1991) makes a serious effort to replace Freud's metapsychology with Sartre's existential psychoanalysis and apply it to clinical work.

Sartre confuses the ego of the structural theory with the conscious of the topographic theory (Soll 1981, Brown and Hausman 1981). He forgets about the preconscious, and in *Being and Nothingness*, where he first propounds "existential psychoanalysis," he is actually arguing with the topographic theory described in Freud's *General Introduction to Psychoanalysis*, which Freud himself came to recognize as inadequate. The censor does not have to be in any way conscious of the drive it represses. It is the preconscious that is duped. For this reason Freud moved to the structural theory, in which part of the ego is unconscious. So there is more in the unconscious than just the repressed. The ego requires no knowing consciousness in order to operate. The crucial difference between Sartre and Freud is really in Freud's strict determinism as compared with Sartre's early thesis of radical freedom and responsibility, as well as in Sartre's determination always to approach the psyche as a whole, rather than as made up of agencies (Brown and Hausman 1981).

Sartre seems to be always looking for an overthrow of existing institutions and gives no suggestions on how to make existing institutions better. His was a kind of mindless activism with little appreciation for parliamentary democracy. In later life he accepted Marxism without even critically examining it.

SARTRE'S CONCLUSIONS IN PSYCHOLOGY

Influenced by Dostoevsky's novels, Sartre believed that philosophy and psychology were indistinguishable. A writer, he thought, should be a philosopher and unveil the truth about the world. He or she should offer new insights and ideas. Art's unreality makes it a source of change through reflection and self-knowledge. People make themselves in order to live in a network of internal and external conditions, but also, to go beyond Freud, there is a dialectic. They go a bit further than their situation and they create themselves. This is in contrast to Freud's strict determinism. For Sartre humans act on situations that place them in new situations, and so a dialectic takes place, in which humans constitute and reconstitute themselves throughout life.

The superficial comparison between Heidegger and Sartre is fairly obvious. Heidegger's *Dasein* becomes "being-for-itself" (*pour soi*). Heidegger's "inauthentic" becomes Sartre's "bad faith." Heidegger's "facticity" or "throwness" becomes Sartre's "contingency," defined in *Nausea* (1964a) as "every existing thing is born without reason, prolongs itself out of weakness, and dies by chance" (p. 180). But Heidegger is Being-centered (ontological) and Sartre is human-centered (ontic), a crucial difference.

For Sartre bad faith and choices reveal the true person. Actions count. The basic project is chosen by the prereflective consciousness and thus whatever we consciously desire is the concretization of a prereflective choice, a choice based on the early object relations with the "other." Therefore the prereflective choice that we make is a function of our relationship with others and is based on the internalization of parental attitudes. Our adult desire is a concretization of this prereflective choice of project. Our first desire is the need to be loved, the urge to exist for another. Sartre says that when there is no mirroring or no primary other to recognize the child, the child concludes with the belief that the world is hostile. Therefore the manner of the child's self-regard, and the later self one experiences, is always based on the self as first seen and constituted by others.

But for Sartre childhood does not unilaterally produce the adult! The process is dialectical, and one constantly remakes one's personality, incessantly taking up the process of childhood drama with the other as a guiding motif of one's life. So for Sartre Marxism is not enough, because it begins with the human as a wage earner. Psychoanalysis calls attention to the history of the person, and the existentialists introduce the family as the mediator between the culture and the individual.

He often calls his method the regressive/progressive method. He uses the times to explain the person and his or her work, and the person and his or her work to reveal the times. The regressive aspect of his method is analytic reconstruction of the underlying character and its roots, the starting conditions. The progressive method is synthetic—to identify the individual's basic project and how it was created in the family situation. This is the link between Sartre and R. D. Laing, which we will discuss in the next chapter. An excellent review of Sartre's mature method and developmental theory as he applies it to the life of Flaubert is presented by Barnes (1981).

For Sartre (1948a), emotions are a way of relating to the world, not just passively experienced. Emotions avoid a rational dealing with the world. They are subtle escape behavior, strategies to prevent action, and a way to avoid situations by a "magical transformation." For Sartre emotions represent an abrupt drop of consciousness into a magical world, an unrealistic response to external pressure. Out of bad faith we pretend that emotions happen to us, says Sartre.

He (1968) distinguishes between analytical reason, which is understanding something by watching or dissecting it, and dialectical reason, which is understanding through participation, by being part of what you are trying to understand. Sartre attempts to present us with what he calls the "new intellectual" who unites with the masses, stands for humanity, and espouses universal values. He compares this with the "classic intellectual" who stands only for the values and interests of the bourgeoisie, which are not those of humanity in general. For Sartre, the task of the intellectual is to criticize the powerful and defend the voiceless. To criticize, oppose, and denounce leads to the fate of being solitary and tormented. This is Sartre's notion of literature as praxis (Gerassi 1989). He goes to an extreme in his advocacy of violence in politics, found in his (1963b) preface to the famous book by the psychoanalyst Franz Fanon, *The Wretched of the Earth*. Sartre encourages violence in politics because, he says, to eschew it is to let others have their way by violence, in a sense to be an accomplice to the violence of others (see also Sartre 1978). This argument seems to reach a repellent solution but is not easy to refute.

SARTRE'S PHILOSOPHY: RECAPITULATION

Let us briefly review Sartre's philosophical position upon which his psychology is based. An excellent commentary to read along with *Being and Nothingness* is by Catalano (1980). In *Being and Nothingness*, Sartre avoids the problem of Descartes, whose philosophy forced him to distinguish the thinking subject from the objects of thought. Sartre, in the tradition of Brentano (see Introduction), says that all consciousness is consciousness *of* something. As Brentano explained, it is intentional. It posits the object toward which it reaches. The prereflective consciousness intends or reaches or emotes toward an object that it posits. The reflective consciousness intends toward the ego, the "me," just as the prereflective consciousness tends toward an object. So, for reflective consciousness the subject and object both arise, they are posited together, when the reflective consciousness reflects on the prereflective consciousness. Therefore the "self" or the "ego" is derivative and fleeting. There is no need, as in the philosophy of Descartes, to prove a separate existence of the external world, because the external world conception arises pari passu with the conception of the subject when the reflective consciousness operates.

For Sartre being-in-itself just is. Consciousness bestows meaning on it through "negation," that is to say, consciousness makes an entity appear by differentiating it from its background, by negating its background. *L'en-soi*, being-in-itself or contingency, is called by Sartre "gratuitous." It is described in *Nausea* as *de trop*—"just there," uncreated and without reason. Therefore to ask the Being the question, "Why is there something rather than nothing at all?" as Heidegger does, has no meaning, since it presupposes being-in-itself already.

Being-in-itself, or Being in Sartre's sense of the term, is dense, massive, and full, claims Sartre. This is in contrast to *le pour-soi*, or being-for-itself, or consciousness. Consciousness is other than Being. It is not-being, and it arises through a negation or nihilation of being-in-itself. Consciousness introduces nothingness. It is not-being and its activity is a process of nihilation, that is, consciousness brings beings into being by temporarily nihilating other aspects of being-in-itself.

For Sartre consciousness comes from the continuous process of the diremption of itself by being-in-itself. This allows consciousness to arise, but Being can never take the form of consciousness except when being-for-itself collapses into the being-in-itself, at which point one dies and consciousness ceases. The result of this is that consciousness or being-for-itself is free. It is not determined by Being although it arises from Being. Thus consciousness first exists and *then* makes its essence. It creates itself in each person. One's operative ideal is revealed in one's actions and may be quite different from one's stated goals and ideals. One's past is given meaning by the self in the present and does not, as Freud thought, determine the self, argues Sartre. The human is a useless passion. He or she strives towards realizing a unique basic project but ends in death.

The keyhole example mentioned before in explaining being-for-others establishes the other as an evident presence—a subject for which I am the object. Sartre insists that conflict is the meaning of being-for-others. For examples, (1) in love, as Sartre views it, the lover tries to absorb the other's freedom; (2) in indifference, lust, or sadism, one tries to reduce the other to an object. Neither can be done successfully, and therefore Sartre writes, "Hell is other people" (although what he meant by this is disputed).

THE INTELLECTUAL AND THE ARTIST

For most of the authors discussed so far, theory is a political practice and a struggle with power. For the Marxists the role of the intellectual is to represent the working class. Marxists believe that the intellectual should form working-class consciousness and lead the praxis of the masses. Those intellectuals who do it from the inside, as members of the proletarian class, are what Gramsci (1985) calls "organic intellectuals," and those who lead it from the outside are representatives of Lenin's "vanguard party intellectual." In contrast stands the traditional bourgeois intellectual, the detached thinker, or, in Sartre's term, the classic intellectual.

As discussed in Chapter 2, there is also a "concrete" or "specific intellectual" described by Foucault, who is an "expert in specialized scientific fields and speaks through science." An example of this would be Oppenheimer. This type of intellectual is contrasted by Foucault with the "universal intellectual," who speaks for the conscience of the collectivity and transcends science. Examples of such intellectuals are Sartre and Bertrand Russell (in his later years).

A third type of intellectual described by Foucault is the so-called social thinker, such as Marx and Freud. These are "founders of discursivity" and they are found only in the human sciences. One returns repeatedly to their texts even if there are errors in them, and each reexamination of their texts modifies their field. For example, the restudy of Freud, or the restudy of Marx by later intellectuals, will lead to modifications of Marxism and Freud's psychoanalysis, respectively, and this has indeed repeatedly occurred.

The second type of intellectual mentioned by Foucault, the "universal intellectual," is very similar to Sartre's "new intellectual." This type of intellectual unites with the masses, and stands for humanity and universal values, in contrast to the "classic intellectual" who stands for the values and interests of only the bourgeoisie and not for that of humanity in general. Sartre insisted that one must always attempt to situate his or her own individual thought within the context of historical development.

The "mad" artists and poets such as Goya, Nietzsche, Van Gogh, Rilke, Artaud, Sade, and Hölderlin create outside the discourse of "normal" people and herald a new episteme, says Foucault. The lightning flashes of these artists force the world to question itself; even psychoanalysis cannot comprehend such creativity. In Freud's (1928) words, "Before the problem of the creative artist analysis must, alas, lay down its arms" (p. 177). In this sense all these thinkers agree the artist has a role as an "intellectual" also, and an extremely important function, often overlooked in our age of technology.

7

R. D. LAING

R. D. LAING WAS BORN IN Glasgow in 1927 and died in 1989. He received his M.D. in Glasgow in 1951 and specialized in psychiatry; his views on psychiatry became increasingly radical over the 1960s. Descombes (1980), in his *Modern French Philosophy*, argues that psychiatry has ignored the speech of the madman. In many ways this is true, except for a few, such as H. S. Sullivan, Fromm-Reichmann, Lacan, Laing, and Foucault. Elsewhere I (1989a) discussed, for example, a case presentation by Kraepelin which is analyzed by Laing. The case presentation turns out to be a power struggle, very much in the tradition described by Nietzsche, Foucault, and Laing, between the patient and Kraepelin. What appeared to be unintelligible gibberish on the part of the patient actually turns out to have a very dramatic message.

Laing's seminal book was *The Divided Self* (1969a), first published in 1959. It is based on the cases that he studied as a psychiatrist in Glasgow. He said that he wrote it at the age of 28 at the end of his training in 1955. It represents an inspired fusion of psychiatric and psychoanalytic knowledge with Paul Tillich's concept of ontological insecurity, and with the thought of Heidegger, Sartre, and Kierkegaard. Laing borrows certain of his principal themes from Kierkegaard's *Sickness unto Death* and *The Concept of Dread*, Kierkegaard's (1946, 1954) basic psychological works (see Chessick 1987b for discussion).

Laing's basic principles in *The Divided Self* are first, as Sartre claimed, that the human is free to choose his or her style and form of commitment. In sharp contrast to Sartre, however, Laing sees "choices" and splitting of the self as induced by family power struggles and forces outside the subject's control from his or her childhood. Sartre, on the other hand, originally recognizes no pre-intentional causal origins, although, as we have seen, he pays more attention to these in his later work on Flaubert. For the most part, Sartre emphasizes conscious intention (Hunter 1977). Second, the human experiences this freedom in dread. Kierkegaard's Danish term for this is *angest*. Some authors use *angst*, the German term for anxiety, or *angoisse*, the French term for anguish. All of these terms have the same meaning in this context. Third, owing to *angest*, the human hides freedom by absorption in a conventional life. This is also from Kierkegaard and Heidegger, but Laing differs from them because he does not consider this to be the universal condition, only the schizoid condition. So Laing uses existential terms only when he talks about patients.

In *The Divided Self* Laing recognizes genetic and biologic factors in schizophrenia; in his later work he does not. He never explains why some "schizoids" go on to schizophrenia and some do not. His crucial and lasting clinical contribution is his delineation of what he calls the schizoid style, a matter of great importance often overlooked or given short shrift in textbooks. He tried his theories out in Kingsley Hall, which he founded in 1965, and he wrote a number of other books, which may be classified as follows:

The first group of these books could be labeled "social phenomenology." They include *Self and Others* (1962*) – in this excellent book (Laing 1969b) there is much theory and elaboration of the family power struggle; *Sanity, Madness and the Family* (with A. Esterson in 1964*), consisting (Laing and Esterson 1971) of eleven cases; and two essay collections, *The Politics of Experience* (1967*) and *The Politics of the Family* (1969*) (Laing 1967, 1972). In the latter two books, which became quite popular on college campuses, Laing maintains that cultural institutions direct human lives in ways that fail to maximize human potential, and deliberately restrain the emergence of fully autonomous selves. There is an echo here of Sartre's practico-inert. Laing believes, in disagreement with Freud, that this flaw is not inherent in all culture and that we can change culture to diminish its alienating force. Today Laing's sociological views are largely ignored by college students who seem more interested in football, adapting to the culture, and making money (Bloom 1987).

Laing's ideas took a mystical turn in his book *Knots* (Laing 1971), written after his trip to the Himalayas and Ceylon (Sri Lanka). *Reason and Violence*, written with David Cooper in 1964 (Laing and Cooper 1971), is an attempt to explain Sartre's *Critique of Dialectical Reason* and is a very complicated work, although

---

*Date of first publication

Sartre himself praised it in his preface to their book. As Laing developed his views he became more and more extremely radical, anti-psychiatry, and pro-schizophrenia in a mad civilization, espousing a philosophy somewhat similar to the well-known movie *King of Hearts*. The mental health professional who reads his (1976, 1985) later work may tend to get exasperated and unfortunately to ignore his valuable basic contributions. At one early point (Boyers and Orrill 1971, Evans 1976) he was psychoanalyzed by Charles Rycroft, a non-Kleinian analyst in the British Institute for Psychoanalysis, London.

OVERVIEW OF LAING'S CONCEPTS

What are these basic contributions? Laing argues that psychiatric assessment, such as the history or mental status examination, especially if taken at length at the beginning of the treatment, not only does not help but may harm the patient because, as far as he is concerned, the diagnosis of psychopathology is a reciprocally reinforced projection system and says more about the psychiatrist than the patient.

For Laing the authenticity of the therapist, the genuine encounter with the patient, and the therapist's empathy are crucial (Friedenberg 1974, pp. 21–22). He (Laing 1969a, p. 36) quotes Fromm-Reichmann's well-known saying that if one cannot understand the patient, the fault is with the psychiatrist, not the patient. The treatment goal is not adaptation as in United States ego psychology, but is for the patient to actualize his or her unique potential. We do not tell patients what to do even though they want us to do so; we rely instead on their freedom and autonomy, released by the treatment, to carry them to their own projects.

Diagnosis for Laing is a "political act" (Friedenberg 1973, p. 46), and terms like schizophrenia and narcissism are pejorative labels. Laing unfortunately comes to view psychiatry as having an evil purpose, as an agent of an oppressive culture and undertaken in bad faith; he becomes very extreme in some of his later generalizations, confusing stupidity with malevolence.

He moves away from a focus on the patient's contribution to the illness and he emphasizes instead the person developing as a reaction to the power situation in the family and society. The constitutive elements in the patient or subject must always be described and understood, as Hegel originally said, in relation to others. For example, the patient's behavior in the hospital, according to Laing, is primarily a function of the particular institution, the personnel, and the psychiatrist, as in the popular novel and movie *One Flew Over the Cuckoo's Nest*.

Laing practiced his version of "counterculturalism." Here he borrowed Nietzsche's concept of *ressentiment* of the oppressed in society, such as women and minorities. For Nietzsche, as for Laing, the alienated enraged individual is conceived of as a product of modern industrial civilization; perhaps the most famous literary example is in Dostoevsky's novella *Notes from Underground*. Laing, like Sartre, insists that this situation can be changed—in contrast to Freud—and that freedom in civilization can be found for all.

Laing reaches the conclusion that since the concepts of sanity and madness are socially relative, medical illness is an unsatisfactory model for mental disorder. Psychotic phenomena are intelligible and there are no criteria for the diagnosis of schizophrenia; it is an unsound concept. To understand madness, Laing says, one must study the family, not only the individual. Dissident members of the family and the culture often are incorrectly labeled as "mad" (or "bad"). The purpose of this, he claims, is oppression. Statistical normality in our civilization, he argues, is not preferable to madness. Madness, if uninterrupted by drugs or electric shock treatment, can be naturally curative, according to Laing; perhaps a temporarily needed radical regression is necessary to give the individual refuge, and it may lead to a psychological rebirth. In these cases one must simply protect the patient and not interrupt the process, waiting as long as necessary. Try that view out on the insurance company or a peer review committee! Yet I believe it embodies much wisdom and fits clinical experience in certain cases in my experience.

There are, therefore, three R. D. Laings. First, there is Laing the scientist, who studies the family and group interaction and who has a keen eye for the effect of the reality situation in childhood producing a schizoid turn—which may or may not lead to schizophrenia. Then there is Laing the philosopher, an existentialist and idealist. He makes sweeping statements deliberately shocking, such as that 95 percent of United States psychiatrists are schizophrenics (Evans 1976). He prescribes madness for the individual in our culture, and his rhetoric often resembles that of Nietzsche's last year of writing. Later he becomes a mystic, viewing schizophrenia and the regression in schizophrenia as a trip back in human evolution toward a rebirth, and something that is fundamentally desirable. The third R. D. Laing is the political radical who opposes adaptation as the aim of psychiatry, since he sees it as adaptation to a culture that is oppressive and itself in need of radical change.

I will focus only on Laing the scientist and clinician. His scientific contributions are found especially in *The Divided Self*, which was the work of a young creative genius; his *Self and Others*; eleven cases in *Sanity, Madness and the Family*; and scattered remarks in *The Politics of the Family*.

Laing labels his method "existential phenomenological foundations for a science of persons." He wishes to return to the patients themselves without preconceptions, an approach reminiscent of Husserl's method. He attempts to study the being-in-the-world of schizoid and schizophrenic persons (in this early work he still uses the diagnosis of schizophrenia). This being-in-the-world of the schizoid person is discovered by study of the patient's way of being with the therapist. One must articulate what the patient's world is, avoiding technical or scientific terms and not postulating "apparatus" or "machinery," as this dehumanizes the patient. Laing directly attacks the reifying medical model, used by contemporary U.S. psychiatry to a greater and greater extent.

There is a curious double figure of the human, says Laing, in terms resembling those of Foucault. One can study the human as a person, as a self-acting agent with intents and purposes, or alternatively as an organic thing, depending on the investigator's orientation. *Thus the intention of the investigator determines the direction and results of the investigation.*

For Laing the patient's speech and actions are a form of hieroglyphics. One must use empathy and hermeneutics to understand what the patient tries to communicate. Focus on the symptoms of disease or the *DSM-III-R* approach makes this impossible. Actually, a technical vocabulary may conceal the reality of the patient's plight, for it is not neutral and it already implies a stance. Looking for symptoms in psychopathology, says Laing, prejudices us and depersonalizes the patient. In our culture "objective and scientific" is reputable and "subjective and intuitive" is disreputable; this prejudice, as Gadamer (see Chapter 3) would call it, inhibits our capacities to understand and treat our patients. As Sartre and Laing explain, one cannot scientifically study the human without the human disappearing.

THE SCHIZOID PATIENT

According to Laing, the schizoid individual is split in two ways. With respect to the world, he or she is not at home in the world, but rather alienated, split off, and alone. The second split is within the patient's own self. The true self is split from the false self; the latter remains also associated with the body. Such a patient often speaks of his or her body in the third person, a clue that this split has taken place. For Laing this is "tragic man" and represents a double alienation, as he calls it. These concepts are modeled after Heidegger.

Laing (1969a) defined psychosis as "the degree of conjunction or disjunction between two persons where one is sane by common consent" (p. 37). If there is a disjunction, then the person is sent to receive drugs and given laboratory tests and perhaps even placed in the hospital.

He borrows the term "ontological insecurity" from the theologian Paul

Tillich, for whom it was the universal human condition. For Laing it is the special problem of the schizoid. In the state of ontological insecurity there is no sense of continuity and no cohesion of the self in time, as illustrated, for example, in the literary works of Beckett. The problem the schizoid patient has is to preserve the self, as compared with neurotics and normal individuals, who wish to gratify the self.

The cause of ontological insecurity, according to Laing, is the lack of mirroring of the true self, the absence of the smiling notice and appreciation of the patient's self as a child. He (1969a) writes that the development of a self requires "the loving eye of the mother" (p. 125). This is required for ontological autonomy, Laing says. Such patients, however, do not suffer from unconscious conflicts. Their problem is "beyond the pleasure principle." He gives a case example of agoraphobia based on the well-known unconscious fantasy of being a prostitute. But the patient's sexual fantasy used sex as a way of recognition, to create the illusion of being looked at and desired. It was not based primarily on repressed infantile incestuous desires. Gratification is not the issue for patients with ontological insecurity, says Laing. This closely resembles what Kohut (1984) states in his later version of self psychology, although the terminology is quite different.

There are three forms of anxiety that manifest themselves in ontological insecurity. The first of these is of *engulfment*, the fears of being overwhelmed and of the loss of self in a merger with the other. This is prevented by isolation from people and a deliberate effort to confuse others and to be misunderstood. The second is labeled *implosion*. This is a sense of persecution by reality, a fear that it will crash in and obliterate the person who already feels empty. A third form of anxiety in ontological insecurity is of *petrifaction*. This represents becoming a thing or a robot, and is not far from Sartre's concept of being-for-others. To defend against petrifaction the patient uses depersonalization, that is, he or she stops responding when the other individual is tiresome or disturbing. This destroys the other person's subjectivity. It "petrifies the other," but it leads to more ontological insecurity, since one's ontological security depends on an enlivened reaction from the other. So a vicious circle becomes activated.

In patients with ontological insecurity, dependency on the other is substituted for genuine mutuality. The schizoid patient oscillates between merger and isolation, not, as in the normal person, between relatedness and separation. The patient splits into a secret true self, and a body associated with a false self. All of us reversibly do this under stress, for example, at a boring party, during a painful or embarrassing medical examination, during painful dental work or under torture; but in the schizoid individual a definitive split occurs between the true self and a false self system, in which the false self system becomes the manifest personality. Laing borrowed this from Kierkegaard's

(1946) concept of "shut-up-ness." For Kierkegaard the "shut-up" is the mute; he or she does not wish to communicate and feels dread if required to do so. This unfreedom to communicate with others makes a prisoner of one's self, says Kierkegaard. He (see Poole and Strangerup 1989) writes, "what the shut-up keeps hidden in his close reserve may be so terrible that he dare not utter it even in his own hearing, because it seems to him as though by this very utterance he were committing a new sin, or as though it would tempt him again" (p. 61).

This definitive split becomes a basic and irreversible schizoid style. The patient, in a common clinical picture, tries to do everything for himself or herself in isolation. The advantage of this is that it protects the patient from ontological insecurity and the anxieties described above as associated with ontological insecurity. The disadvantage is that it is impossible to succeed, since we all need other people; isolation of one's self leads to despair and a sense of emptiness and alienation from the world. The common schizoid "existential" complaint of the futility and meaninglessness of life arises from this. The patient longs to get into life and experiences a dread of the increased emptiness and dissolution that develops as the patient feels more and more isolated and vulnerable. This is a problem, says Laing, which begins in infancy. He (1969a) writes, "The more the self is defended this way, the more it is cut off and destroyed" (pp. 80–81). There is no exit for this mode of being-in-the-world, similar to Sartre's concept of "no exit," hell as an eternal trap with no way out.

The true self is never revealed by the schizoid individual. It is hidden by compliance, which, as Kohut (1984) pointed out, is the hardest resistance of all to deal with in any treatment. In the famous terms of Martin Buber (1958), there is for the healthy person an I-Thou or creative relationship, in which the mutual potentiation of ourselves with the world around us and others takes place. Laing compares this with the Quasi-it (compliant false self) –It (petrified or depersonalized other) relationship, a sterile relationship in which both the person and surrounding individuals are impoverished. As Laing (1969a) writes, if you don't live in the world with people, "something dies inside" (p. 144).

In these patients the inner true self breaks up into subsystems or fragments. It hates itself and becomes preoccupied with fantasies and memories that get more and more unrealistic, since the individual is not in contact with others and the world for correction. Clinically the patient complains of a world in ruins, and the self as dead, impoverished, and empty. There is no frantic activity that can bring it to life again, although the patient may try everything. All of these concepts were taken up later by Kohut.

Such a person never really marries. He or she is perpetually alone, and never commits himself or herself fully to anything in the world, as this would reveal the true self (As Hegel said, acts are definitive). The patient is filled with longing, envy, and hatred of the self and the world, and is guilty over duplicity, fearing at the same time his or her own destructiveness or fragmentation, which Laing calls "going crazy."

THE FALSE SELF SYSTEM AND PSYCHOSIS

To get a better understanding of Laing's concept, it is worth comparing the three different types of false self systems. In the *normal* individual some behavior is mechanical, but the person is not compelled to it, and there is no encroachment on spontaneity and no feeling of being lived in contrast to living. In the *neurotic* individual, such as the hysteric, there is bad faith, as Sartre calls it. This is a way of life aimed at taboo gratification. This individual "pretends" to himself or herself and to others; a famous example is Sartre's character Matthieu in his (1973a, 1973c, 1973d) novel *Roads to Freedom*. The *schizoid* false self system, however, is aimed not at gratification but at preservation. It involves being compulsively compliant, being good, not making trouble, and it hides fear and hatred.

The typical clinical problem of the schizoid patient is a morbid self-consciousness. This assures the patient that he or she exists, and the patient is apprehensive and hypervigilant, sensing a danger that is felt everywhere as a consequence of the patient's ontological insecurity. This poses a dilemma because the patient wishes to be seen and to have his or her self confirmed but at the same time wishes to be invisible, since it is a threat to the self if the patient is seen.

Persecutory delusions or ideas of reference represent an attempt to mirror one's self. They represent some form of imagined responding, says Laing. The cold gaze of the mother now becomes inside and is projected in an attempt at self-mirroring. Laing (1969a) presents the case of Peter, who was always treated by his family literally as not being there. As a less dramatic example, I had a patient whose mother he remembered always strangely stared past him and never looked at him. This patient was overwhelmed with chronic anxiety and ontological insecurity. In Laing's (1969a) concept of "genetic ontology," Being depends on the mother's presence. Elsewhere I (1991) have applied this to our clinical work with psychotic and borderline patients.

To compare R. D. Laing's views with those of Freud let us return to Freud's *Fort-Da* game, "gone-there," discussed in Chapter 5. For Laing the 18-month-old grandson of Freud is playing at making himself disappear in an attempt to master ontological insecurity. Children often do this with their reflection in the mirror (as in Freud's footnote) as well as with a toy. The danger that the child faces, according to Laing, is of not being seen by the mother. Her loving eye confirms the child's self, and only in her loving, responding presence can the child have a self. In contrast to this, for Freud, his grandson is attempting to master a danger situation of the loss of the mother, the object of his instinctual gratification. This is a behavior "beyond the pleasure principle," since it deliberately reenacts the painful separation and loss. For Laing, however, gratification is not involved. The intactness or fragmentation of the self is the danger that must be mastered, or ontological insecurity becomes the permanent result. There are no instincts involved and no gratification.

Psychosis develops from this situation of a false self system in a certain way, according to Laing in his (1969a) early work. The schizoid solution fails, anxiety increases, and more desperate measures are needed. The inner world becomes more and more unreal; deadness and hate increase. The false self system expands and becomes autonomous, and the individual gets the feeling that he or she has a mechanical body that belongs to others. The patient tries magic, to touch, to feel, or even to steal, somehow to fill the emptiness; this dynamic is found these days in many cases of bulimia. Their last hope may be in such extreme activities as child molestation, promiscuity, homosexuality, or perversions to somehow magically regain cohesiveness and a sense of self. Again there is a great similarity to Kohut's description of fragmentation of the self.

The true self may suddenly emerge, manifesting all its unrealistic fantasies, and we discover, says Laing, that our carefully recorded "psychiatric history" has been the history of the false self system. This is similar to Kierkegaard's contention that "shut-upness" is a lie. The cure here, using drugs and so forth, would be to get the patient back to manifesting the false self system. The patient either decides to go back to the false self system or murders the self in such activities as self-mutilation, suicide, or homicide (killing the projected "bad" part of the self). This preserves any sense of being alive and reduces anxiety because the patient says, paradoxically, "If I am dead I cannot be killed." In chronic schizophrenia the self breaks up into fragments or "archetypal agencies," to use Laing's term. The final result is the disintegrated, dilapidated hebephrenic.

In treatment we must always remember that a true self exists somewhere in every patient. We try to contact this. When we do, the patient feels understood and schizophrenia ends. Thus for Laing schizophrenia is a smoke screen for protection, and the physician must fight to get through it to the true self. Diagnosis is based on the "praecox feeling," that is to say, the physician is in the presence of another person, yet feels that nobody is there. It is a life-in-death existence.

MYSTIFICATION

One of the most important clinical contributions made by Laing (1969b) is the concept of "mystification" (pp. 122–124), also discussed by him at length in a little-known article (Laing 1965), which should be a classic for study by all mental health professionals. Driving a person crazy means to make it impossible for the person to tell who he or she is, who the other is, and what situation they are in. A common example would be a parent with a child or a therapist with a patient who is in a situation where it is forbidden to gratify aroused sexual desire but the parent or therapist subtly stimulates the child or patient sexually.

What keeps the patient in the mess is the shared ideology or fantasy system of the family, or of the therapist–patient dyad, which makes it impossible for the patient to see the problem clearly. Furthermore, as Laing says, the more untenable a position is, the more difficult it is to get out of it. An untenable position (1969b, p. 124) is a situation in which feelings are denuded of validity, acts are stripped of motives, and the situation itself is robbed of meaning. Emergence from a shared fantasy system with the parents is felt as murder, bad, evil, and selfish, and this is the answer to the question of Confucius that Laing (1969b) quotes ("The way out is via the door. Why is it that no-one will use this method?") at the beginning of Self and Others.

Mental illness is seen as the way out that the free organism in its total unity invents in order to be able to live through this intolerable situation. Laing points out that every preschizophrenic was in a highly mystified state before a breakdown.

In The Politics of Experience (Laing 1967, p. 57), mystification is illustrated by the work of Franz Fanon (1963), also mentioned in Chapter 6. Exploitation of third world countries is presented by the exploiting imperialists as benevolence, in which the Europeans view themselves and present themselves as God's gift to the third world. Our violence is described in the rhetoric of morality, as are the rationalizations currently in use today for the military-industrial complex. The media abound with such platitudes, making an ever-increasing contribution to the mystification of our citizens; the result, as Laing would predict, is burgeoning voter apathy and withdrawal from the political process. So Sartre (1988) writes that mystification is "characteristic of our age" (p. 229) and the writer's duty is to demystify the public and oppose injustice. The concept of mystification actually comes from Marx, for whom it means "plausible" misrepresentation of what is going on in the service of the interests of one socio-economic class over another. So, when exploitation is made to seem benevolent, it appears to be bad or mad to think of rebellion.

Laing carries this further, because in the politics of the family or society to mystify means to befuddle, cloud over, or confuse what is going on by substituting false for true constructions of what is being experienced, done, or occurring, and by the substitution of false issues for actual issues. The purpose of mystification is to maintain stereotyped roles, such as political ideology, family roles, and "pseudomutuality" (Wynne et al. 1958) in the family. The state of mystification is one of being muddled and confused, but a mystified person may not consciously feel confused. A mystified person can be falsely calm, or conflicted over false issues. The therapist must decide what is the central issue, even if this (as is often the case) is disjunctive with the perceptions of family members.

Laing (1969b) also introduces the clinically important related concept of "attributions and injunctions." By assigning a person to a particular position in the family, attributions "put him in his place" and have in effect the force of injunctions. An outstanding clinical example is given in *Self and Others* (1969a):

> Joan's mother sent her a blouse for her twentieth birthday. The blouse had interesting characteristics. It was two sizes too big for Joan. It was not the sort of blouse she would have chosen for herself. It was very plain. It cost more than her mother could afford. It could not be changed in the shop in which it was purchased. One might expect Joan to be disappointed or angry. Instead, she felt ashamed and guilty. She did not know what to do with herself because *she* was not the right size for the blouse. She ought to have fitted the blouse, not the blouse fit her. She ought to have been able to like it. She ought to have fitted her mother's idea of who she was. In this case her mother confirmed the girl in the fact that she had a body with breasts, but did not endorse the actual breasts that she had. During puberty her mother had the habit of making remarks like: "How are your titties coming along, dear?" Joan would feel her body going to pieces when her mother spoke to her like that. Presenting her with a sexless blouse too big for her was ambiguous and confusing. This girl was physically frozen and dared not be attractive and vital if her mother said in effect that she was not. The blouse, being unattractive, implied an attribution: "You are an unattractive young woman." This attribution implied an injunction: "Be unattractive." At the same time she was mocked for being unattractive. Joan ended wearing the blouse, feeling helpless, despairing, and confused. [pp. 133–134]

8

HISTORICAL

BACKGROUND: THE SELF

SOME BACKGROUND CONCEPTIONS THAT will aid the reader in understanding these various authors, help to place them in perspective, and also prepare the reader for an appreciation of Kohut's theories will now be briefly presented. It is important to remember that Kohut received a classical education in Vienna and was undoubtedly quite familiar with the main themes of German literature and philosophy.

Goethe (1749–1832) and Hegel (1770–1831) initiated a revolt against "mechanisms" as models of explanation, reliance on which they called a failure of nerve. They emphasized self-feeling in contrast to objectified nature and mechanics. Goethe argued that the "communal spirit" is the highest value, a value that is ethical and not economic; his goal, he said, was to make humanistic values prevail throughout the world.

Hegel (1807) insisted that human beings were not just clever animals but were also spiritual; that they aspire to freedom and have values and destiny. The human for Hegel is the series of his or her deeds. There is no internal "other," and Sartre followed Hegel closely in this. On a metaphysical plane, however, Hegel claimed that through individual human consciousness, Spirit produces itself, and, in a philosophy quite unlike that of Sartre, Hegel maintained that it cannot choose a different direction. The human, according to Sartre, can never reach his or her goals, whereas for Hegel, Spirit does reach a final goal—that of self-knowledge found in the philosophy of Hegel! Hegel also insisted that the individual's sense of self comes into being only through being acknowledged. It is a precondition for the "I" of Descartes, which is not, as Descartes thought, an immediate intuition. The self or "I" is an interpersonal construction; an individual subject is what society makes out of the human.

R. D. Laing made use of Hegel's thought in clinical work. Laing describes the person who is denied recognition by others. For example, actions and speech expressing this person's true self are ignored or misinterpreted, while others ascribe to this person experiences and intentions conflicting with his or her true self. In a closed system like the family, the person's identity disintegrates under these conditions, setting the stage, as we have seen, for mystification, injunctions, attributions, and ultimately escape by adopting a schizoid style.

Heidegger, as we have learned, used Hegel's concept of authentic awareness as constituted by a return out of forgetfulness and error, but he opposed Hegel's notion of a rational culmination of self-aware Spirit, mentioned above. He argued that Hegel's Spirit represented an extreme "objectification" of metaphysics, an ultimate separation of the knowing individual human subject from metaphysical absolutes or forms. The poet Hölderlin (1770–1843), a contemporary of Goethe and Hegel, pointed out how humans draw their goals from primitive chaos through the power of poetry and song. Nature is not an emanation of Spirit, argues Hölderlin, but it is an unfathomable and inexhaustible invitation to creative activity. The philosopher Fichte (1762–1814) around the same time introduced his concept of "the absolute ego," which, years before Freud, he proposed as a metaphysical entity. He described it presciently in a Freudian sense as a power not our own that determines our moods, ambitions, and the direction of our lives. Fichte's "ego" was a metaphysical concept in German idealist philosophy, but it does represent the pre-Freudian concentration, on the continent of Europe, on the role of irrational powers in constituting the human subject.

LUKÁCS

Georg Lukács (1885–1971) is known as a major figure of western Marxism, a term coined by Merleau-Ponty to designate a philosophical position that hopes to refurbish and improve on the reductionistic vision of the proletarian revolution as a historical necessity. The book that gave Lukács his reputation, *History and Class Consciousness* (1982), was actually repudiated by him, and the work he regarded as his greatest intellectual work, the volumes on *Ontology*, are almost completely unread and unreadable. Lukács changed his mind many times, often under the rule of political oppressors in order to save his life, and he wrote in an unimaginably obscure and unnecessary Marxist jargon. It is my contention that if one can tolerate this multiple recantation problem and the obscure jargon there are some valuable contemporary ideas in Lukács's work, and the problems he struggled with all his life are still with us.

Lukács sought to reinstate the Hegelian mode of thinking, with his emphasis on the word *totality*. But, as Bell (1991) explains, "In a kind of travesty of Hegel's metaphysics, for Lukács the historical subject, the agent of the world-historical spirit, was not the world-historical figure—Alexander, Caesar, Napoleon—who breaks the structures of old societies, but the proletariat."

Lukács's concept of "totality" is a metaphysical concept related to Hegel's Absolute Spirit. In *The Theory of the Novel* he offers a Foucault-like historical description of how in literature the epic, in which the hero is the community, was replaced by the novel, in which the hero is the seeker, the problematic individual who seeks self-knowledge. The epic and the novel are described by Lukács as "extensive totality" and set off by him against drama, which is supposed to express "intensive totality," or the essence of soul. The concepts of "totality" and "totalization," which run from Lukács to Sartre and many western Marxists, remain obscure (Jay 1984).

The young Lukács (Congdon 1983) agreed with Ibsen that the dramatist must compel the audience to rethink basic principles, focus on the human condition, and challenge social abuses. He saw Ibsen as a solitary, lonely figure expressing the tragedy of human alienation as an inevitable curse. In *History and Class Consciousness* he focused on Marx as a humanist who was concerned with the problem of alienation, and this was written a decade before the Paris manuscripts were discovered. He emphasized the influence of Hegel on Marx but disagreed with Marx in that he saw class consciousness as not simply due to the economic base but cultural in origin and reciprocally influencing the economic base. It should be noted that *History and Class Consciousness* was published in 1923, the same year as Freud's *The Ego and the Id*, with its implications of inevitable human malaise and conflict. But Lukács's book, sometimes called "a blueprint for tyranny" (Congdon 1983, p. 186) would have been an anathema to Freud.

Lukács argued that philosophers have to change not only their fields but also their life-styles. He insisted that the academic horizon distorts the struggle and the suffering of the masses and misleads philosophers to focus on irrelevant issues. It is also true that he was insensitive to democratic values, that when in political power he urged an unfortunate kind of censorship, and that he did not have at all a compassionate or desirable personality (see Kadarkay 1991). Some recently published material from the Lukács archives (Lukács 1991) indicates that after the 1968 Soviet repression of the Czechoslovakian reform movement he recognized the dangers of Stalinist tyranny privately at least for 3 or 4 years.

One of the greatest weaknesses of Lukács's thought is that he tends to politicize every issue and wrap it in Marxist jargon, which makes reading him painful. Part of this, I believe, is because Lukács, perhaps like Mikhail Gorbachev, to whom he has been compared, was constantly torn between liberalization and holding on to absolute orthodoxy, and uncertain of where he himself stood. I agree with Steiner (1982) that "Lukács's Marxism is, in essence, a refusal of the world's incoherence, of the murderous stupidities whereby men and women misconduct their lives" (p. 67).

The debate between Lukács and Sartre was very important and has contemporary value. Certainly Lukács was correct in opposing Sartre's early philosophy of absolute existential freedom. It is clear that no one has absolute freedom and no choices are independent of their social context, including the unconscious influences that arise developmentally in the milieu of the family. A big complaint by Lukács about the existentialism-influenced person is that he or she is discouraged in Sartre's early philosophy from trying to help and improve the life of others through politics. "Freedom" for the existentialist is an empty ideal. Of course Sartre changed his view on such freedom as in his later philosophy he moved closer to Lukács's point of view. One of the most memorable epigrams of Lukács is that in Sartre's existentialism, which Lukács claimed is based on the philosophy of Kierkegaard, Husserl, and Heidegger, these thinkers created a permanent carnival of fetishized inwardness, a carnival that continues to mesmerize and mislead bourgeois intellectuals.

Lukács (1982) developed the concept of reification—the way objects and persons are made into "things" and thus lose their identity. Reification for Lukács became the major mode of alienation, a term that was very important in the Paris manuscripts of Marx (1844) but which became replaced by the term exploitation in his later work. Reification represents the human becoming an object like a commodity, and can be thought of as an extension of the famous description of commodity fetishism by Marx (1818–1883) in Volume 1 of *Capital* (1867, pp. 163–177). In reification, human social relations take on characteristics of the relation between things. Lukács differs fundamentally from Heidegger because for Lukács progress in human relations is possible and crucial, whereas for Heidegger progress is an ontic concept irrelevant to the Being-question (Goldmann 1979). According to Lukács (1982), only Marx explains how we get from one of Foucault's epistemes to another, but Foucault would not agree with this, since he came to regard Marx's work itself as based on the outmoded nineteenth century episteme, as discussed in Chapter 2.

Lukács (1982) argues that what philosophy does and does not find problematic in any given era is a function of the historically predominant cultural basis of existence from which these problems spring. For Lukács, as for Sartre, the human is dialectical and not simply formed by the economic base of society. There is *praxis*, especially including the modes of production, which leads to the formation of ideology or Marx's "superstructure," that then in turn has an effect on the *praxis* from which it comes. The conclusion from this is that there is no such thing as an objectively frozen human or fixed human essence; human beings are constantly shaped and reshaped in each era. Neglect of this possibility, above all, was the crucial mistake of classical philosophy, the Enlightenment, and of philosophical anthropology.

Lukács found to be simplistic Marx's view that the entire ideology of a culture was based on the prevailing means of production. To Lukács and many western Marxists (McLellan 1979) it seemed possible that there was an interaction between Marx's base (means of production) and superstructure (ideology), although he felt that the economic motive was dominant; still, this allows ideology to be a driving force of history even though it is based on the prevalent economic practice of a given culture. This theory represents a significant improvement over orthodox Marxism, but Lukács was severely persecuted for it.

In Nietzsche's early work *The Birth of Tragedy* and in Lukács's early work *The Theory of the Novel*, both authors look to art for salvation, although Lukács historicizes aesthetic categories whereas Nietzsche does not. Both stress the fact that the modern human is not at home in the world and endures a gulf between the self and the world. For Lukács, Dostoevsky's art will lead us to a utopian solution. It is clear that even in his pre-Marxist days Lukács was struggling with the issue of alienation and the problems dramatically raised in Marx's (1844) 1844 manuscripts—what Lukács then called "estrangement" (Gluck 1983). These early writings of Marx (1844) appealed also to the psychoanalyst Erich Fromm (1969, 1989), although Fromm's work has fallen into neglect by clinical psychoanalysts because it is so reductionistic, too theoretical, and unfortunately devoid of clinical applications. Lukács (1982) implies that the lasting essence of Marx is his method rather than his conclusions, since the kind of "science" that the later Marx (1867) labels his doctrine of historical materialism is no more a form of traditional natural science than is Freud's psychoanalysis. This brought Lukács endless persecution and vilification from Leninist-Stalinist Communists.

Lukács's concept of "irrationalism" in his books *The Young Hegel* (1976*) and *The Destruction of Reason* (1980) is also very important. He calls attention to "the aristocracy of knowledge" in our culture, "knowledge" as something superrational and in possession of an elite few. His description of the creation by bourgeois society of myths to present these superrational truths as constituting

---

*First published in 1948.

a false consciousness in philosophy is quite relevant and controversial today (Bloom 1987). His explanation of the line of development from the early hermeneuticists like Dilthey to thinkers like Heidegger is important; he traces and deplores a turning away from social activity in Schopenhauer and then in Kierkegaard and reaching its apogee in Heidegger, a turning accompanied by a despair that cried out for relief in a strong man and a fascist regime.

His (1969) article "On the Responsibility of Intellectuals" was originally written in 1948 and is a sort of footnote to his (1980) book on *The Destruction of Reason*, published in 1953. In the book he traces the course of irrationalism from Schelling to Heidegger, arguing that the antirational tendencies of the philosophers discussed paved the theoretical path for the rise of Hitler. In the article he warns intellectuals that they must become cognizant of the social consequences of their teachings and intellectually prepared to fight the antihumanist, irrational, life-threatening social forces struggling for domination today. He writes, "One cannot find in Hitler one word which had not [*sic*] already stated by Nietzsche or Bergson, Spengler or Ortega y Gasset" (p. 124). He continues, "It is, therefore, absolutely necessary and a great task of the progressive intelligentsia to unmask this entire ideology, even in its most refined representatives" (p. 124). He makes the astonishingly correct prediction that the world is moving in the direction of a *pax Americana* and he concludes:

> The intelligentsia stands at a dividing point. Should we, like the intellectuals of France in the 18th century, or those in Russia in the 19th, become path-breakers and champions of a progressive turn in world history; or, like the German intellectuals of the first half of the 20th century, should we become helpless victims, will-less helpers of a barbaric reaction? It is obvious which course is worthy of the essence, knowledge, and culture of intellectuals and which is unworthy. [p. 131]

Lukács made a fascinating transition from his messianic phase (1919–1923), which concluded with his *History of Class Consciousness*, to a new phase from 1923 to 1928, in which he adopted the "Blum (his pseudonym) theses": one had to aim at a democratic republic and use persuasion and gradual change in order to develop the will of the proletariat to make further changes. In other words, he contradicted Marx's "scientific" contention that change to socialism was inevitable, and he left it possible that unless the proper consciousness could be developed, such change may not occur at all. After that new phase, from 1929 on, Lukács was mainly preoccupied with survival during the time he was living in the Soviet Union and afterwards in communist Hungary, until his death in 1971. The outstanding general book reviewing the life and thought of Lukács is by Parkinson (1977); for a brief introduction see Lichtheim (1979). A deeper understanding of Lukács's formative years is provided by Congdon (1983) and by Gluck (1985).

The chief difference between Heidegger and Lukács is that Heidegger sees alienation as eternal or ontological, whereas Lukács (like Marx) attributes it to the capitalist economic system. Lukács maintains that the artist, like the scientist, selects from phenomena and has an attitude toward the objects that he or she portrays in the art work that is also evoked in the audience, with the goal of leading the audience to an awareness of its "prejudices" or preconscious attitudes. He quotes from Rilke's (1984) poem "Archaic Torso of Apollo." At the end of the poem the statue says to the reader, "You must change your life" (p. 61). In this sense art for Lukács functions very much like psychoanalysis, in that it leads to a heightened awareness of preconscious attitudes that have been determined by one's family and the culture in which one lives; freedom from such attitudes enables the individual to make choices that would otherwise not be possible.

For Lukács (1982), in the case of workers (as perhaps today in the case of women), the emergence of class consciousness (or feminist consciousness) by itself overthrows the bourgeois assumptions of reification and enables a free human practice, releasing the meaningful process of change and creativity. His notion of dissolving frozen reification in order to release the creative process and make meaningful choices possible is very close to some psychoanalytic object relations theories (Giovacchini 1967), viewing treatment as bringing about the release of frozen introjects and their replacement with healthier and more benign intrapsychic structures. One might argue that the psychoanalyst who is properly trained and has a correct ideological approach functions with a patient in a way similar to those philosophers and political leaders who enable the actualization of class consciousness and feminist consciousness in groups of individuals; in each case there is a liberation and a chance to make changes where it was once thought that no changes were possible.

Lukács emphasizes Hegel's prophetic vision of the contradictions in society and the fatal alienation of humans in a society where production for production's sake — one might say power for the sake of power — has no reason for its moderation. This alienation, in which the individual becomes alien to himself or herself, Hegel identifies with objectification, or the externalization of the human through labor, a new concept that enables Hegel to raise the human problem in all its complexity. Lukács explains that although an individual can work more by lengthening the hours of work or increasing the intensity of one's labor in order to produce more, the value of his or her work begins to diminish. Intelligent integral labor becomes transformed into stupefying drudgery and dehumanization of the laborer. The movement of production and distribution as a system leads to a restless search for machines and new markets without any limit. This thinking can already be found in Hegel (Hyppolite 1969).

Lukács claimed that according to Marx, Hegel confused objectification or the externalization of humans and nature in society with alienation, and this is why his social analysis was inadequate. In objectification the human makes his or her self as an object and expresses or externalizes the self in nature through labor and work. In alienation the human, once having externalized one's self, finds it alien, and sees one's self in one's work as "other than one's self," or fails to find or recognize one's self. This lost recognition or loss of self-identity in the externalization of the self is the great misfortune of the human, both on the level of objects and the social or intersubjective level. The individual is unable to recognize himself or herself, either in his or her work or in another person. One is overwhelmed by one's product, and thus is unable to see one's self reflected in another's soul. This is the unhappy consciousness for which Hegel offers the prescription of dialectical philosophy (Hyppolite 1969, p. 82).

Marx explains this calamity in terms of history and insists that objectification becomes alienation as a result of certain historical circumstances that are destined to disappear in history. But Hegel was the more subtle of the two, because in his view by objectifying one's self in culture, the state, and human labor in general, one at the same time alienates one's self, becomes other than one's self, and discovers in this objectification an insurmountable degeneration that one must nevertheless try to overcome. This tension is inseparable from human existence, says Hegel, and stands at the center of human self-consciousness. It is an oversimplification by Marx to assume that such tension can be reduced to a superstructure of the economic world. Hegel is more sophisticated to insist that objectification and alienation are inseparable, and their union is the expression of the dialectical tension observed in the very movement of history. Lukács's use of Marxism to attempt to refute Hegel's notions, as he did in his (1976) book *The Young Hegel*, is open to critical debate.

The influence of Fichte is also very strong in Lukács. For Lukács the proletariat is a quasi-transcendental subject of history roughly equivalent to Fichte's "absolute ego." Social class is the acting subject of reality, and history is the process that emanates from it as from a ground. By understanding history as the spontaneous stepping forward of human practice, Lukács emphasizes the present moment as a site of revolutionary decision, the point at which human freedom becomes concrete. The most important contemporary contribution in this line of Lukács's discussion is that the act of becoming conscious overthrows the reified form of the object, enabling free human practice to enter again into the world of things, releasing humans from reification and the petrified rigidity of capitalism as well as from the domination of the past over the present, and opening them into a meaningful process of change and creativity.

There is a weakness in Lukács's argument in his polemic against philosophical contemplation, because he never really clarifies what he means by an authentic level of practice as contrasted with contemplation. I believe this can be understood by changing the terminology, which in reading Lukács would be a welcome relief. What he is getting at is that the process of understanding is itself the first step toward revolutionary change. The simple fact of understanding that a given group, such as workers, are alienating a part of themselves automatically leads to a revolutionary change in the practices of that group, as the young Marx believed. Practice becomes revolutionary when it is joined by self-consciousness. By raising consciousness, the spark of critical self-awareness ignites revolutionary praxis, and through this, critical theory sheds its contemplative philosophical aspect. Consciousness at a crucial moment thus transforms the historical thought in which it is embedded and acts like a material force.

This is the crossroads where the thought of Lukács and the thought of psychoanalysis meet, because it is our clinical experience in psychoanalysis that understanding disrupts previous rigid compromise formations, allows previously unconscious conflicts to emerge into consciousness, and leads automatically to a form of psychological practice in which new compromises and solutions are formed. The behavior that results from this psychological change inevitably is in sharp contrast with the individual's previous behavior, and outside observers often experience what they call a revolutionary change in the individual. These "revolutionary changes" are often unwelcome to persons in the individual's environment who have adapted to the individual as he or she formerly was and have benefitted from that adaptation. It is for this reason that having an important member of one's family or group in psychoanalysis poses a threat to the rest of the family and the rest of the group, no matter how much they may consciously advocate the need of the individual to have treatment. This often leads to an actual undermining and destruction of the treatment, or at least a powerful reactionary force to maintain the status quo. I am suggesting that there is a parallel in the way Lukács describes the raising of class consciousness and the automatic change in history that this produces, to a properly conducted psychoanalysis that allows the individual to understand himself or herself and automatically leads to a change in behavior.

The great weakness in Lukács's position is his idealization of the proletariat, insisting that their needs should be the dominant ethical demand and that the proletarian class is the ground of history. This is just as arbitrary as advocating dominance of the law of the bourgeoisie, and the answer usually is resolved by the most powerful group. But this is not a philosophical resolution of a problem, and from the philosophical point of view there is no good argument for Lukács to install the proletariat as the "subject of history" akin to Fichte's absolute ego. Lukács attempted to address this problem, but he never managed a satisfactory solution. Arguments about the importance of any one class or group are interminable and displace one's energies from the important issue, namely, that all classes and all groups should have equal justice and equal freedom. There is a great danger in advocating the dictatorship of any group whatsoever, and here is a great weakness in Lukács's thought because, although he at times advocated a form of democracy for socialist countries, he was unable to tolerate the notion of a genuine democratic socialism. Perhaps this is because he was born a Hungarian aristocrat! Congden (1983) explains Lukács's intense preoccupation with alienation on the basis of his estrangement from his family and Hungarian society. He concludes, "Lukács's tragedy was that he . . . hated injustice more than [he] loved human beings" (p. 108).

The bottom line of Lukács's thought is actually a "faith" in the organic growth of proletarian consciousness. He never really says how this is going to happen. For Lukács it is dogma that the subject and object of history become one in the proletariat. Regardless of the difficulties in Lukács's argument, the basic concept of *History and Class Consciousness*, that the raising of class consciousness leads automatically to a revision of history, and the conclusion that socialism has the potential to overcome estrangement or alienation of humans and make humans whole instead of the fragmented beings that capitalism has made of them, is an important contemporary conclusion. The weakness in Lukács resides in his misunderstanding of the nature of democracy and the dangers of tyranny.

There is a general consistency between Lukács's political ideas and his aesthetic ideas. For him a work of art evokes the experience of a totality, of a world. This knowledge enables self-consciousness. As mentioned earlier, the artist, like the scientist, selects from phenomena, and the artist has an attitude toward the object portrayed that is also evoked in the audience. Thus the audience is led to an awareness of its attitudes; this is the goal of art. In Lukács's thinking the line between art and science is blurred, for, as he writes in *History and Class Consciousness*, every "fact" is already an interpretation. The whole thrust of art and politics for Lukács is to try to salvage the human from the deadening effect of reification, a problem even more pressing today than it was at the time Lukács was writing.

For Marx and Lukács (Feenberg 1981) philosophy is the raising of the operative horizon of everyday life to consciousness and subjecting it to rational criticism. Even the paradoxes studied by philosophy are symptoms of cultural contradictions in society and can only be transcended through resolving these in social life. Roberts (1988) emphasizes that *History and Class Consciousness* assaults the inhumanity of capitalism. For Lukács "contemplation" in bourgeois philosophy is a response to a world that is presupposed to be unalterable by the individual. The mechanism of factory labor abolishes creativity and reinforces this view, which is essentially an outgrowth of commodity fetishism. History is a change of structural forms by means of which the human interacts with the environment, a sequence of massively discontinuous wholes, a totality. It emanates from a social class, and a moment of revolutionary decision can change it. He argues that workers must become self-conscious of our prevalent commodity fetishism; they must realize that they are commodities under the capitalistic system. The act of becoming conscious of this by itself overthrows the reified form of the object and, according to Lukács, free human practice can then enter the world, releasing a meaningful process of change and creativity.

Gluck (1985) points out that the "Sunday Circle" led by the young Lukács broke up over the argument about whether there should be an individualistic solution or a communal solution to the human dilemma of alienation at the turn of the century. An individualistic solution implies social democracy and a deepening of the human's inner life, whereas a communal solution implies communism and an abdication of the autonomy of the self. This debate remains a contemporary unresolved issue even today, even with the disintegration of Soviet communism. One must confront Lukács's (1980) hostile description of Heidegger's philosophy: the inner life of a modern philistine frightened to death of nothing, a nonentity in himself, and gradually becoming aware of his nothingness. It seems to me that a basic choice is involved here as to what sort of a person and what sort of a philosopher the individual wishes to be.

One also cannot ignore the disastrous relationship that Lukács had with his mother, which can only be described as real cruelty toward her throughout her life (Kadarkay 1991). A standard explanation would blame the partiality that she showed to his older brother. Much of the young Lukács's aesthetic thought, which emphasizes ascetic raptures as escapism from the banality of everyday life, can be explained as his narcissistic withdrawal from wholesome personal relationships. Many authors have commented on his tendency to spurn human decency and seek transfiguration and the pursuit of metaphysical ideals. In the debate as to who had the more disturbed and pathological personality, Lukács or Heidegger, there are strong arguments on both sides. One also must keep in mind that Lukács blamed himself for the suicide of a young woman early in his career, which was indeed a function of his cruelty towards her.

A psychoanalyst is also intrigued by the strange attraction that the young Lukács had to religious mystics and the thought of Dostoevsky (Congden 1983, Kadarkay 1991), and his later capacity to fool himself into seeing first Béla Kun and later Stalin as the embodiment of "totality," but perhaps he had to do this in order to survive during the time he was living in Moscow. Or is this his need for a strong dominant father, in contrast to his real father, who always supported and gave in to him and was apparently in awe of and even perhaps afraid of his son? It was during his Moscow years (1930–1945) that Lukács wrote *The Young Hegel*, which shows the continuity of Marxism with Hegelianism, but which at the same time uses Hegel to justify tyranny. In all fairness, other authors have used or abused Hegel for the same purpose.

Lukács's insistence on the limitations of freedom in his debate with the early work of Sartre seems especially correct in the light of Kohut's (1978) recent work on the importance of empathy and an empathic matrix. His concept of estrangement, before the discovery of Marx's 1884 manuscripts and before Kohut's work, was prescient, as were his criticisms of later Marxist theory and of Nietzsche in the light of current events. His complaints about the turning inwards and away from social concerns in modern philosophy, a trend he says was initiated by Kierkegaard and Schopenhauer, has important implications both for philosophers and for the concept of mental health implied in psychoanalytic treatment, as well as for the practice of psychiatry. To conclude with Steiner (1982), "No member of the intelligentsia since Rousseau had experienced more acutely, nearer his nerve-ends, than Lukács, the menace of alienation" (p. 67).

PATOČKA

Jan Patočka, although he was not one of the world's greatest philosophers, is certainly one of the most heroic philosophers who ever lived. His life and thought form a welcome antidote to the excesses of Lukács. As a retired professor of philosophy at Charles University in Prague and one of central Europe's most respected scholars, he died on March 13, 1977, just short of his 70th birthday, of a massive brain hemorrhage suffered under police interrogation by the repressive communist regime in Czechoslovakia. Over the preceding 2 months he had been interrogated repeatedly, the last interrogation lasting over 11 hours. This was because along with Václav Havel (1988, 1990), the present president of Czechoslovakia, he was one of the three main spokesmen and sponsors of Chartra 77, literally sacrificing his life to it. This charter, as is well known, led to a series of events that eventually liberated Czechoslovakia, at least for the time being.

In this brief review I hope to mention some of what I consider to be the most important contributions of Jan Patočka from the point of view of the practicing psychoanalytic psychotherapist and teacher of philosophy. I believe

Patočka to have been quite influenced by Husserl, Heidegger, Jaspers, and indirectly by Masaryk, the first president of Czechoslovakia's new republic. Everyone at the time of course was worried about the political crisis in Europe. At first Patočka took seriously his teacher Husserl's (1970) unfinished work on *The Crisis of the European Sciences* (written between 1934–1937). In this work Husserl complained that perhaps beginning with Galileo there had been a "mathematization" of nature, and as a result very important aspects of the lived world were ignored. Furthermore this mathematization of nature led to the treatment of humans as mechanical objects and the study of humans as objects subject to natural laws, losing sight of the value of the unique human being.

Patočka, about 10 years later in 1946, was more influenced by his studies with Heidegger, whose (1962a) account was much more radical than that of Husserl, and who blamed the current European crisis situation on the development of metaphysics from Plato's metaphysics of Ideas to Nietzsche's exaltation of the will to power. At one stage Heidegger labeled Nietzsche the last metaphysician of the West and emphasized the inevitable rise of technology and nihilism from the standpoint of the development of metaphysics. The technocratic nihilism that Heidegger, Husserl, Masaryk, and Patočka all saw as a threat to the modern world was traced to Plato's effort to appeal to a realm beyond time, history, and power, and to give that realm a sort of objectivity, separating it from the human subject who aspired to know about it.

Patočka maintained, however, that Heidegger emphasized the wrong aspect of Plato's thought. Patočka argued that Plato was not propounding a doctrine about the nature of Being or looking for scientific certainty but rather presenting a vision without "substance" behind it. So Patočka emphasized the poetical aspect of Plato's philosophy, what the Greeks called εἰχὼς μῦθος, a likely story. Patočka claimed what a philosopher can do is project a vision of a community where all are happy and harmonious. Living in a state of working towards such a community is for Patočka the experience of transcendence, which he equates with the experience of freedom. It is not surprising that a man who lived so many years under cruel political oppression, first from the Nazis and then from the Stalinists, would find freedom to be the central transcendent concept for humans.

Patočka agreed with Heidegger that Being is not a being, and the effort of metaphysics to become a science of the absolute object ends up with no object at all. Patočka knew this and maintained that the active effort to understand and actualize eternal Ideas is what matters to the philosopher, not the arrival at some heavenly realm of eternal Forms. This allows Patočka to argue that to label a theory that calls for activity in the name of a freer and happier human community either a historical product, or a remnant of bourgeois thinking, or of no account because it is part of quantitative (calculative) thinking, or a remnant of metaphysics, cannot justify our rejection of such a call. The pressure to act in a morally obligated way to obtain everyone's freedom is an absolute, although it does not have an objective absolute existence in some supernal realm. His (1989) most important philosophical essay, I believe, is "Negative Platonism," written in 1953, in which he argues there is a contradiction in our relation to the whole that cannot be expressed in words, as even Plato maintained in his "Seventh Letter." All we can do is try to live like Socrates.

Heidegger lumps Husserl, pragmatism, and Marx together as "metaphysical" in their search for power instead of what they should be doing—freeing themselves from the need for mastery and investigating Being. But Patočka's philosophy is a philosophy of hope and social action, based on conscience, not metaphysical principles. For Patočka there are no metaphysical "facts" or "objects," and he thinks that the substantive nature of these metaphysical entities has been overly stressed by commentators on Plato.

Kant argued that shared human dignity is intrinsic to rationality, universal, and not dependent on social conditions. Hegel, on the other hand, insisted that it is a product of special historical circumstances. Patočka was against both naturalism and historicism in this matter and viewed the human as transcending his or her context by understanding and acting within it, rendering the human context meaningful in an act of freedom and sacrifice. Thus for Patočka, like Frankl (1962), one gives meaning to one's life by active moral doing, and Patočka wrote about it a number of years before Frankl.

One of the problems with Patočka's point of view, as I see it, is a certain mystical quality. He tries to straddle the fence, agreeing with Plato that there are Ideals above the historical and natural world but disagreeing with Husserl that any absolute science or definitive knowledge of these Ideals can be obtained. His basic principle seems to have more to do with the call of conscience than with philosophical reasoning. The influence of Heidegger continuously shows itself here; in *Being and Time* Heidegger (1962a) speaks of the call of conscience as bringing the person from inauthenticity to authenticity (see Chapter 1). But Patočka particularizes and concretizes this generalization of Heidegger's in his own unique fashion. So although one is moved by moral considerations to feel that Patočka is right, one cannot demonstrate the correctness of his position by any kind of metaphysical or rational chains of reasoning.

Rorty (1991) also concludes that although Patočka's conscience led him to do the right thing, he could not supply good philosophical reasons for doing what he did. This is used by Rorty to justify his (1979) own view that philosophy does not reach for truth but merely is a form of "edification." For Rorty there are no metaphysical foundations for moral or political choice. For Patočka there are certain moral principles that have validity beyond convenience, circumstances, advantage, or historicity, and these are required for the functioning of any society. Rorty maintains that this is a leap in the dark, and Kohák, in his introduction to Patočka's (1989) writings, compares Patočka with Kierkegaard, who also advocated a leap of faith (although in Kierkegaard's thought it is religious faith).

For both Heidegger and Patočka there is an autonomy to reality both prior to humans and more than humans, and paradoxically both concealed and revealed. The Socratic question is, "What can ground and guarantee the moral significance of human life or the moral order of the cosmos?" Husserl tried to answer this through phenomenology in an effort to reach a transcendental subject, but Patočka argues cogently, as did many other critics of Husserl, that this results in the Cartesian split between subject and object all over again. It is this Cartesian split that eventually led to the treatment of and attitude towards humans as "things" or mechanical apparatuses and produced the current "darkening of the world," as Heidegger called it. It separates humans from each other and from the biosphere in which we are inextricably immersed.

For Patočka the philosopher's actions precipitate out the vision of the Good; the vision of the Good stands out in reality only with the philosopher's act. This is what he considered to be a "negative" answer to the Socratic question, a question that one must grapple with continuously in order to answer it. For Patočka it is not the fixed product but the ongoing process that gives meaning to metaphysical "entities," and behind that there is no "substance."

From his phenomenological investigations Patočka stressed three basic movements that constituted being human. He found these to be parallel to Aristotle's three functions of the soul. The first of these, comparable to Aristotle's vegetative function of the soul, consists of sinking roots in the world, active movement, the spontaneous gestures and movements of a baby and child. The second of these, comparable to Aristotle's animal function of the soul, is to prolong our stay in the world by the movements of self-defense, sustenance, and work, movements coerced by needs rather than spontaneous. The third of these, comparable to Aristotle's rational function of the soul, Patočka labeled self-transcendence. This is an active reaching up to the vision of the ideal.

He insisted that reality or Being is irreducible and prior to subjectivity, but that our lived experience has always a constitutive role in it. For Patočka the genius of European culture is a drive to moral transcendence in the vision of the Good, True, and Beautiful. This is what captures the deep sense of being human, and he considered the drive to culture to be a primordial human thrust. This is quite an original set of concepts in Patočka's philosophy. Patočka contrasts self-preoccupied inauthenticity with human authenticity, that affirming of freedom and responsibility in contrast to the mindless anonymity of the world.

It is quite interesting to compare Patočka's point of view with that of

Rescher (1973). In Rescher's "conceptual idealism" there is a limited form of philosophical idealism expressed, in which the individual constructs reality through the use of certain historically determined mental sets, without which no experience of reality would be possible. This differs from absolute idealism because in the latter these mental sets are seen as eternal and have a more generative function, whereas in Rescher's view it is a combination of external stimuli and culturally determined mental sets that leads to the construction of what we experience as reality. Patočka's view might be thought of as the alloplastic version of Rescher's autoplastic conceptual idealism. For Patočka it is not through internal mental constructions that the reality of Being is actualized but through activity, more specifically, sacrifice in the service of obtaining human freedom.

Patočka's negative Platonism denies second-level entities, but claims particulars are importantly related to the whole. The Idea of the Good is a transparent symbol, and here the influence of Jaspers's (1932) philosophy is very strong, because such Ideas in Patočka are like Jaspers's ciphers, pointing to the beyond itself (Chessick 1987b). Patočka carefully studied Jaspers, the influential psychiatrist and philosopher, and contemporary of Heidegger.

Patočka, in contrast to Husserl, insists that Being is not reducible to some sort of transcendental consciousness. This is his important criticism of Husserl. Patočka is convinced of the irreducible hardness of reality. He insists that reality is genuinely autonomous, and presupposed by consciousness. Our encounter with this irreducible hardness of reality is central to Patočka's arguments, because he claims that it is our collision with this Being as an irreducible hardness that jars us out of our preoccupation with particular purposes and raises the question of the whole. Thus one might say that Patočka is a phenomenologist who wants to be a metaphysician. Following Husserl, the natural world is contrasted by Patočka to the mechanistic-material world. But the latter world view assumes an objective pretheoretical world, subject to objective theory-free observation; it forms the fundamental bedrock of traditional science. Patočka's phenomenology attempts to grasp what is presupposed in being human and what is presupposed in the assumptions of science.

Kohák (in Patočka 1989) writes,

> What, though, does it mean to focus on the "natural" world? Essentially, it is an attempt to grasp that about humans that is independent of particular historical contingencies, what is common to all humans, everywhere and at all times, what is presupposed in all being human. Here the first trait is precisely that a human being is always a being in the world, a world understood not as a sum of particular objects but as a constant horizon which is there as the

pregiven context of all particular perceptions. It is this presence as a whole that frees humans of their exclusive preoccupations with particulars and leads to raising the philosophical question. [p. 98]

Probably following Hegel, Patočka argues that such a struggle with the world in which we are immersed alerts us to the otherness of the other. Kohák (Patočka 1989) asks, Why cannot love do this? But for Patočka, however, struggle comes first, and considering the conditions under which he had to live, that is not surprising. Even under such terrible oppressive conditions Patočka saw philosophy as a counterpole to everydayness, as a freedom from bondage to everydayness that was won by the pursuit of the vision of the Good and sacrifice for human transcendence or freedom.

For Patočka, in his essay on "Negative Platonism," the experience of freedom is the same as the experience of the whole or transcendence, but it has a negative character in the sense that there is no substrate, "if by a substrate we understand some finite and positive content, some subject, some predicate, or some complex of predicates" (1989, p. 196). This is why the human spirit keeps returning to metaphysics, "ever again, in spite of its putative emptiness and invalidity, demonstrated a hundred times, in spite of its being indefensible, even meaningless from the standpoint of objective rationality, returning to realms in which it can make not a step forward as it becomes accustomed to measuring that under the guidance of the positive" (p. 197). Patočka managed to give transcendent value to Plato's realm of eternal Ideas, even though it is not possible to defend Plato's realm as containing any sort of objective reality or rationality. His negative Platonism preserves for humans the possibility of trusting in a truth that is not relative, even though it cannot be formulated positively with objective contents, and in spite of the historicity of man and the relativity of his orientation in the world.

Clearly the contributions of Patočka deserve worldwide attention, and although his claims are not amenable to precise scientific reasoning, Patočka may have hit on an asymptotic situation that approaches the limits of human transcendence as closely as the mind of the human is able to go. One might argue that he is offering a viable solution to the paradox posed by our having, until now, to choose between the nihilism implied in much of postmodern philosophy on the one hand, and the apparently indefensible claim for absolute scientific knowledge in metaphysics, which was Husserl's goal, on the other.

But Patočka goes even further in his philosophizing, at times approaching almost a religious sentiment:

The idea of human rights is nothing other than the conviction that even states, even society as a whole, are subject to the sovereignty of

moral sentiment; that they recognize something unconditional that
is higher than they are, something that is binding even on them,
sacred, inviolable, and that in their power to establish and maintain
a rule of law they seek to express this recognition. [p. 341]

Clearly no metaphysical or philosophical arguments can support this leap of
faith on the part of Patočka; those who are skeptical of it must ask themselves
what alternatives we have, we who in our brief lives are surrounded by perpetual
darkness. Rather than to curse this darkness, the lives and philosophies of
Socrates and of Jan Patočka represent at least the flickering of a match.

Patočka's sacrifice of his life for Charta 77 shows that he lived his
philosophy, one in which he insisted that moral sentiment is higher than the
state or society, that we have in us a conscience that leads us without objective
metaphysical reasons in a primordial thrust toward the vision of the Good. Who
has a greater right than Patočka to insist that under all conditions we should
maintain "a demeanor dignified, truthful, and unafraid in all circumstances" (p.
344). A living example of this is presented by Havel (1988) in his prison letters,
which also serve as a dramatic introduction to Patočka's thought, making up in
poignancy for what they lack in philosophical rigor.

UNAVOIDABLE PHILOSOPHICAL PREMISES

Jaspers (1883–1969) insists that one must immerse oneself totally in a few
thinkers to experience their struggle rather than read superficial textbooks, and
he (1962, 1966) illustrates this thesis in one of his major works. To understand a
philosopher one must sense his or her active philosophizing, not just read the
theories presented. This requires a form of empathy. Powerful minds disagree.
Hegel claims that philosophy progresses by way of a dialectic to culmination and
fulfillment. Nietzsche views philosophers as merely correcting each other's
systems and leading to no truth or fulfillment. For Heidegger philosophy is
retrogressive; it leads away from the crucial question with which it began,
namely, the human's relationship to Being. Philosophy, according to Heidegger,
has moved toward the technical and away from openness to being.

Notice, as we turn to discuss Kohut, that he is Hegelian on the subject of
ethics. Hegel (1976) introduced the concept of *Sittlichkeit*, the moral obligations
one has in a given community of which one is a part, based on established
customs and norms and practices of that community. He contrasts this with
Moralität, Kant's absolute categorical imperatives, which Hegel claims are empty
and cannot be practically applied in a specific situation. For Kohut ethics must

address the needs of each unique generation; they are grounded in human experience and so they change. They fortify the individual in weak or uncertain areas of his or her time. For example, Freud, who was a scientist fighting obscurantism, made his highest professional values independence and clear sight. Today, claims Kohut, the need is for a selfobject matrix throughout life, and the highest value is to stay empathically in tune with this matrix and with the rapidly changing generations.

Foucault's and Laing's ideas are related to Heidegger's thought because for them mental illness is not an intrapsychic entity within the patient. They follow instead the Heideggerian notion that humans are always constituted by being-in-the-world, and so mental illness is a societal event that occurs between people who may in fact have conflicting values and goals; this results in the changing history of madness and society, patients and doctors.

One may choose the levels of interest that one wishes to study, but each level or area of interest depends on the postulates above it. One cannot escape from preconceptions. There is no such thing as self-contained positivism or empiricism; where does the naive nineteenth century natural-sciences postulate to depend only on experience for truth come from? The highest level or order for study is the question of Being, as pointed to by Heidegger and others, if one accepts this question as meaningful. If one does not, then one must study the premises on which one rejects the question! Hegel showed such questions of ontology to be inextricable from one's epistemology, or theory of knowledge. There is no absolute objective reality "out there," and Plato was wrong in his concept of eternal Forms existing separately in heaven (even Plato began to question his own theory, as in his obscure dialogue *Parmenides*[1]).

A specifically chosen combination of ontology and epistemology leads one to certain abstract ethical theories or to a philosophy of science that immediately delimits one's field of study. So, for Freud, in *ethics* the highest value is truth, based on cognition, scientific progress, and independence. In his *philosophy of science* he repeatedly insists psychoanalysis is a "natural science." For Kohut, in *ethics* the highest value is the expansion of empathy between people and nations, and one needs a selfobject matrix all one's life. In his *philosophy of science* he posits psychoanalysis as resting on empathic observation, which makes its mode and data different from other sciences and delineates the field.

Another way to describe this is Toulmin's (1986) distinction between *modern science* of the nineteenth century, in which the scientist is "detached" and studies phenomena "objectively" with no effect on his or her observations, and *postmodern science* of the 20th century. Postmodern science accepts an admitted

---

[1]For a careful review of *Parmenides* and an interpretation of what it means and explains, see Miller (1991).

inevitable human participation of the scientist in phenomena that he or she tries to study and explain. There are no value-free investigations and no nonsubjective investigations; one could argue that hermeneutics are necessary to uncover this, a necessary component of all scientific investigation.

A lower order, which I (1983c) have labeled elsewhere "metapsychiatry," is the application of all this to the uses of psychiatry. So, for example, in the now defunct Soviet Union psychiatry was used to convince dissidents that they must go back to the rules of the Marxist-Leninist state. In the United States psychiatry is becoming increasingly used to provide fast-fast-fast relief for the discomfort of mental symptoms, with stress on cost efficiency so that everyone can get back to the serious business of life, which seems to be making money, as much as possible, as fast as possible, and in any way possible (Wolf 1987).

These higher-level principles also determine our meaning of the term "research." For Freud psychoanalysis was primarily research. Currently in the United States brain study is the fashionable research in psychiatry. Freud's "metapsychology" was an imagined mental apparatus, an intermediate between philosophy and science, based on certain—now known to be erroneous—ideas about neurophysiology and evolution. The subject of metapsychology at present is in a state of chaos; it is debatable whether any improvements have been made in it since Freud's time (Gill 1978).

At the lowest level are the clinical applications of all this. But the common claim that we clinicians are simply working with "experience-near" concepts has been realized recently to be quite false. All data are approached with certain "experience-distant" ordering assumptions such as those described by Foucault, and all clinicians are assuming premises from the higher levels just described.

LANGUAGE

Hegel gets the credit in philosophy for pointing out the central importance of language, and Heidegger developed this emphasis to a great extent. The importance of language to psychoanalysis was given its greatest clinical application in the work of Lacan. All knowledge is mediated by language, and there are two crucial types of language in the field of psychotherapy and psychoanalysis, as shown in Table 8-1.

Freud in his writing often mixes these languages up, owing to an inner tension between his humanistic background based on his study of Goethe and Brentano, and his obsession with being a scientist and acceptable to the medical community. Even the *Standard Edition* translation of Freud by Strachey shows this. In a current controversy, Bettelheim (1982) claims Strachey translated

Table 8-1.   Contrasting Languages

The Scientific Chain of Meaning (The language of the understanding)	The Humanistic Complex (The language of the imagination)
True and false propositions	Reality and appearance
The problem of error	The problem of illusion
Causality and scientific law	Destiny and human purpose
Prediction and chance	Fate and fortune
Fact, matter of fact	Drama, the dramatic event
Competition, biological growth	Tragedy and comedy
The stasis or equilibrium of systems	Peace and freedom

Freud in such a way as to sound scientific and acceptable to the United States' physicians; Bettelheim pointed out that many of the German terms used by Freud have a much more humanistic connotation.

In *Why Psychotherapists Fail*, I (1983b) made an effort to combine these two types of scientific and humanistic languages and urged therapists to consider the patient from both points of view. Kohut comes the closest to this with his notion of a complementary theory. Traditional Freudians employ scientific-sounding languages, and Lacan stays very much with an obscure humanistic language. But the problem with Kohut's descriptions, and especially with those of Lacan and others who use the humanistic language, is that such language tends to deemphasize energetics, the power or forces in the unconscious mind and their conflict with repressing forces. Ricoeur tried to get around this, but still remained with the humanistic language by viewing psychoanalysis as a combination of hermeneutics and energetics.

PRECURSORS OF KOHUT'S IDEAS

The psychoanalyst Federn (1952) pointed out that the ego was more than simply the sum total of the usual ego functions that psychoanalysts talk about. He wrote, "The ego, however, is more inclusive; more especially it includes the subjective psychic experience of these functions with a characteristic sensation" (p. 61). We may label this subjective experience the ego has of its own function the ego-experience (*Icherlebnis*), the ego's experience of itself.

This phenomenon of the ego's experience of itself cannot be clearly explained. As long as the ego functions normally, one may ignore or be unaware of its functioning. To use Federn's (p. 5) metaphor, normally there is no more awareness of the ego than there is of the air one breathes; only when respiration becomes burdensome is the lack of air recognized. The subjective ego experience, as Federn's editor Weiss (Federn 1952) explains, includes "the feeling of unity, in continuity, contiguity, and causality, in the experiences of the individual" (p. 6). In waking life the sensation of one's own ego is omnipresent, but it undergoes continuous changes in quality and intensity.

Federn attempts to distinguish within the subjective ego experience between ego feeling (*Ichgefühl*) and ego consciousness (*Ichbewusstsein*). Ego consciousness represents an enduring consciousness and knowledge that our ego is continuous and persistent, despite interruptions by sleep or unconsciousness, because we "know" intuitively that internal processes, even though they may be interrupted by forgetting or unconsciousness, have a persistent origin within us, and that our body and psyche belong permanently to our ego. Ego consciousness involves our conviction of the continuity of our person in respect to time, space, and causality. Thus our sense of ego consciousness plays a central role in the argument of Kant's *Critique of Pure Reason*. Ego consciousness in the pure state remains only when there is a deficiency in ego feeling. Thus the mere empty knowledge of oneself is already a pathological state known as estrangement or depersonalization.

Ego feeling, in contrast,

> is the totality of feeling which one has of one's own living person. It is the residual experience which persists after the subtraction of all ideational contents—a state which, in practice, occurs only for a very brief time. . . . Ego feeling, therefore, is the simplest and yet the most comprehensive psychic state which is produced in the personality by the fact of its own existence, even in the absence of external or internal stimuli. [pp. 62–63]

Ego feeling is the constantly present sensation of one's own person, the ego's own perception of itself.

Federn maintained that ego feeling is quite different from mere knowledge of one's self or of consciousness of the ego at work; it is primarily a *feeling* or *sensation*, normally taken for granted. This seems parallel to Heidegger's (1962a) contention that the Being of beings is the most apparent; and yet, we normally do not see it—and if we do, only with difficulty. Remarkably, Federn pointed out, and he certainly had not read Heidegger, that the classical Greek language, in contrast, for example, to English, is necessary in order to get an intuitive verbal concept of ego feeling. This is because in the classical Greek language there is a middle voice, a neutral objectless form. In English the middle voice is expressed by certain intransitive phrases such as I grow, I drive, I live, I prosper, I develop, I perish, I age, I die. The middle voice implies action involving one's self and not passing over to other objects.

Our intuitive conviction or grasp or foreknowledge of the Being of humans comes from our inner ego-feeling. Our inner sense of existence, of being alive, our capacity to develop a state of relatedness to both the human and nonhuman environment, and of life having some sense of meaningfulness, requires a healthy development of ego feeling. This in turn requires what Winnicott has described as good-enough mothering. To avoid confusion I should mention that Freud in 1917 used the same term, ego-feeling (*Ichgefühl*) in "Mourning and Melancholia," but he used it to mean something akin to self-esteem, which is of course quite different. There is an overlap between Federn's concept of ego feeling and Kohut's (1971) "sense of self," although they are not employed in compatible theoretical systems.

Winnicott (1968), as I will discuss in Chapter 10, had a similar notion to that of Federn, in which he said that good-enough holding for the infant leads to a sense of Being, a sense of being "real." Heidegger (1962b) claims that Kant retreated away from the notion of ego feeling in the second edition of his *Critique of Pure Reason*. For Heidegger ego feeling is the starting point of empathy and the quest for Being and it represents "pre-Socratic thinking," wherein "the Being of beings is most apparent." It is best expressed in poetry (see Chapter 1). A defect in ego feeling is represented clinically by vague borderline complaints, concern about the meaningless of life, an inner deadness, and a quest for relief through holding, especially of physical contact, and in noncherishing relationships to the human and nonhuman environment (Searles 1960).

To avoid confusion, both ego consciousness and ego feeling should be carefully distinguished from the well-known ego mechanisms described by Freud and Anna Freud (1946). These latter are at an experiential (not metaphysical) level similar to the cognitive "categories of understanding" of Kant, and are defensive mechanisms utilized by the ego in everyday life. For Heidegger they could represent forfeiture and falling away from the authentic self and the being of man; for psychoanalysts they may lead to ordinary psychopathology, as the ego wrestles more or less successfully with its three harsh masters, and produces more or less stable compromise formations.

A typical pre-Kohut view of borderline patients (Sadow 1969) shows them as situated on something called the "ego axis," and sliding back and forth on this axis by the use of primitive or more structured defenses. Kernberg (1975) denied this "sliding" and fixed the employment of either "higher" or "lower" defenses each as constituting stable personality structures and determining psychopathology and diagnosis. Kernberg has been challenged clinically (Lichtenberg et al. 1984) over the question of whether there is such an entity as the borderline personality disorder, or whether it represents certain prevailing symptom clusters that appear in an intersubjective field, a view more compatible with those discussed in the present book.

Freud in his terminology mixed up these levels of higher and lower defenses; for example, he sometimes used *introjection* to refer to the well-known process of resolution of the Oedipus complex and superego formation, and at other times, under the influence of the work of Karl Abraham, used it as more typically preoedipal and primitive, and thought of introjection as an oral cannibalistic incorporative fantasy.

There are three terms that have been mixed up and that all represent subclasses of the classical mechanisms of internalization. They must be understood in order to distinguish them from Kohut's "transmuting internalization." *Identification* is the most mature of these mechanisms. It is less directly dependent on the drives and is more adaptively selective. It is the least ambivalent and represents a modeling process such as the original modeling we do on our parents. It is an automatic and usually unconscious mental process whereby an individual becomes like another person in one or several aspects. At times it can be consciously and deliberately employed. It is part of the learning process, but also part of adaptation to a feared or lost object, or is an attempt to improve one's skills in society. Identification is growth promoting and it leads to better adaptation, a crucial clinical point.

Introjection was originally used by Freud (1917) in "Mourning and Melancholia" as a process in which the lost object is taken in and retained as part of the psychic structure. Later he used it as a mechanism to explain the taking in of the parents' demands as if they were one's own in the formation of the superego at the time of the resolution of the Oedipus complex. Introjection does not simply copy selected aspects of the object as in identification; it is more encompassing. The original definition assumed a solid repression barrier, a cohesive sense of self, and a functioning ego, and this was Freud's use of the term.

Incorporation is a form or model of introjection, the taking into the mind of the attributes of another person, which in fantasy follows the model of oral ingestion and swallowing. Introjection, when it is accomplished by incorporation, implies change by fantasied cannibalism. A patient once told me, "I am devouring your book like a hungry wolf"; hence a primitive kind of interpersonal relations fantasy. It is primary process ideation, a form of "object relatedness." At one time it was thought this fantasy accompanies all introjection, but now this is not believed to be correct.

Schafer (1968) defines introjection as "the process whereby object representations are constituted as introjects or are changed into them" (p. 16). An introject, he goes on to explain, is an inner presence with which one feels in continuous or intermittent dynamic relationship.

The characteristics of introjects are:

1. They may be conceived as a personlike thing or creature.
2. They may be unconscious, preconscious, or conscious.
3. They may be experienced as exerting a pressure or influence on the subject's state or behavior independently of conscious efforts to control it.
4. They do not copy external objects, since they are shaped by "fantasies, projections, symbolizations, misunderstandings, idealizations, depreciations, and selective biases originating in the subject's past history and present developmental phase and dynamic position" (p. 73).
5. Once formed, introjects diminish the influence of the external object. This is a crucial clinical point. Introjects are formed owing to a severe ambivalence or some degree of disappointment in the attempt to modify distressing relations with an external object. Good introjects are also needed to counteract and protect one from the bad.
6. Once formed, the introject alters the relationship with the external object in a way not correctable by further experiences with the external object, since the external object's influence is diminished by the patient's attention turning inward toward the introject.
7. Introjection is an event, a change in psychic organization and in the psychic status of an object representation. Notice the active role of the mental processes in this, a capability assumed even of the infant. This is a highly controversial point, and is a problem also for Kohut's theory (Chessick 1985).
8. Introjection represents or expresses a regressive modification of the boundaries and reality testing function of the ego. Introjection perpetuates neediness and ambivalence and merely displaces it to the inside. It is not growth promoting per se. It is a passive mode of mastery and not adaptive in itself.

Splitting represents a failure in the synthesizing function of the ego. It is crucial to the turning away from reality in any condition (dreams, perversions, neuroses, psychoses) and it enables these processes to occur. The concept of splitting is used differently by almost every author (Pruyser 1975). For example, see Lacan's use of it, described in Chapter 5.

In *projection*, object representations and self representations, charged with energy or influence, that is to say, made into introjects, are experienced as coming from outside of the boundaries of the self, for example, from the analyst, and are ascribed to an independent object or creature or thing, for example, the influencing machine (see the great classic paper by Tausk 1948). This leads to a separation, in contrast to projective identification, in which the relationship to the projection from the individual is maintained. That is to say, in projective identification the patient must, for example, control or aggresively dominate the hated and feared object of his or her projection, the therapist. At the same time in the interaction, the patient exerts a steady unconscious pressure on the therapist to elicit behavior from the therapist congruent with the projection. It is important to understand these concepts also when we turn to the issue of transmuting internalization.

Kohut (1977), in *The Restoration of the Self*, refers to Lacan's (1953) work and agrees that their areas of investigation overlap, but Lacan and Kohut were opposed in many ways in both theory and practice. They do agree that cure is not the same as adaptation and that their theories are not compatible with traditional ego psychology, the predominant school in the United States' psychoanalytic establishment.

In fairness to Kohut's predecessors, remember what thinker (1) placed the developing self at the center of his theories, (2) insisted that the self can develop only when it receives intense recognition from another self, and (3) tried to show that self-development is ruled by forces out of our conscious awareness, like the unfolding of a seed into a plant, an unfolding that makes rational sense only by looking backward after the development has gone as far as it can. The answer to this is Hegel (1807). Again recall that Kohut was highly trained in German philosophy, having gone to school in Vienna before he came to the United States to study neurology and psychoanalysis. Kohut was an original and innovative psychoanalyst; Hegel was one of the great creative geniuses of all time.

9

KOHUT

IN FULL-TIME PSYCHOANALYTIC therapy practice for 35 years, treating borderline, narcissistic, and other various *DSM-III-R* types of personality disorders as well as other forms of psychopathology, patients that include mental health professionals of all sorts, many of whom have already had a traditional analysis and are now in re-analysis, I have found Kohut's concepts extremely valuable clinically, both in giving theoretical meaning to what I (and my analyst before me) did intuitively in practice for many years, and in suggesting new ways to understand clinical phenomena previously baffling or irritating, and often viewed pejoratively. I will now briefly discuss Kohut's basic premises, his ideas of what constitutes the subject or patient, and his use of these to conceptualize the curative process in psychoanalysis and psychotherapy. I (1985) have previously devoted an entire book to self psychology, which indicates how important I consider it to be.

There were four professional Kohuts in psychoanalysis. The first was the traditional analyst who was the president of the American Psychoanalytic Association from 1964 to 1965. The second was the Kohut of the early version of self psychology, produced in the late 1960s and the early 1970s and carefully presented in his first book, *The Analysis of the Self* (1971). The third Kohut was in a transition phase in the mid-1970s, manifest in his papers on empathy as the key to psychotherapy, contained in *The Search for the Self* (1978). In these papers

Kohut moved far away from the ego psychology school of psychoanalysis and from traditional psychoanalysis. The fourth or final Kohut was the later Kohut of *The Restoration of the Self* (1977), which marked his open split with traditional psychoanalysis. This was the first definitive theoretical statement of the later Kohut and was completed posthumously in his (1984) final book *How Does Analysis Cure?*. He lived from 1913 to 1981.

THE SELF AND ITS DEVELOPMENT

Here are some of Kohut's crucial concepts from his final theory, his last phase of work. The "self" is present at birth. It is an independent center of initiative, "not knowable in its essence" but manifested as the assertive, joyous baby. It is whole at birth and contains no "nuclei" or parts; it reaches out to the world for mirroring confirmation from the start of life (Kohut 1977). Others react to it as a self from the start of life. There is much experimental evidence for this, as Lichtenberg (1983) and Stern (1985) have reported, but that is not the same as demonstrating a "sense of self" that Kohut postulates, which can only be grasped empathically.

The infant experiences others (parents) as archaic selfobjects from the start, that is to say, as part of the infant's self. Their task is to (1) confirm, mirror, give a gleam in their eye, serve and obey in every way, and (2) be looked up to and be merged with as an image of calmness and omnipotence, not so different from Bion's (1963, 1967) "container" and "alpha function."

The blissful omnipotence of infancy while merged with the archaic selfobjects, according to Kohut (1977), is disturbed inevitably by the inadequacies of the selfobjects in the self/selfobject relationship. Between 8 months and 3 years of age this causes the formation of a grandiose self, the "grandiose exhibitionistic image of the self," and the idealized parent imago, the "image of an omnipotent calm parent with whom merger is desired." These are temporary narcissistic archaic configurations in the psyche and imagined as boundless in their power.

First the grandiosity is given up, and then the idealization of the external parents is given up slowly, so that owing to minor empathic failures and transmuting internalization there occurs the following: the grandiose self becomes integrated into the "ambitions pole" of the nuclear self at about the ages of 2 to 4 years, and the idealized parent imago becomes integrated into the "ideals pole" of the nuclear self at around the age of 4 to 6 years during the oedipal phase. In addition to this there is an "arc" or gradient of skills and talents that solidifies owing to the "twinship" experiences of the child between the ages of 4 and 10 years, a partaking in and modeling on the parental activities. This arc or gradient between the two poles of the self drives the individual to joyful creative activity, according to Kohut, an activity that provides a feeling that life has meaning, and involves the use of one's skills and talents at the service of an ambitious push towards idealized goals. When a cohesive bipolar self is so formed, the child is ready to resolve the oedipal phase without any significant Oedipus complex left over (Kohut 1977, 1984).

Kohut (1971) presents three stages of failure in early selfobject function, which cause what he calls a "narcissistic crisis" that must be resolved. In the first of these there is a phase-inappropriate disappointment in the idealized parent imago very early with the mother, in which case the patient later on shows an optimal need for soothing, and faulty tension regulation. This often leads to the search for drugs, addiction, alcoholism, interminable psychotherapy, and so forth.

In the late preoedipal period such phase-inappropriate disappointment eventually produces a patient who shows a resexualization of pregenital polymorphous, oral, anal, and genital drives, with perversions in fantasy or acts.

Phase-inappropriate disappointment in the selfobjects in early latency leads to patients who show a search for the external object of perfection, who are dependent on idealized outside figures, but who get only a transient good feeling when they are attached to them. The patients use these outside figures as a missing part of the psychic structure to bolster their self-esteem through the transient approval they can gain from such figures. All of these situations of transient approval are like pouring water into a sieve, and the patient's life becomes preoccupied with constantly renewing the search for the missing selfobject functions that should have been internalized.

All this implies, says Kohut (1978), "the double nature of man" (p. 754). He contrasts "guilty man," representing man against his drives, man in conflict, with "tragic man," reaching for realization of his nuclear self and blocked, humiliated, empty, depleted, "burned out," with low self-esteem.

With proper parental empathic response, one develops a normal self with appropriate ambitions and socially meaningful and enthusiastic ideals. This is true for the development of both men and women. Kohut is totally different from both Lacan and Freud on the subject of feminine psychology (Chessick 1983d). For him anatomy is not destiny, and healthy women do not suffer from any defect or lack or masochism as a function of their femininity. His view of women seems much more congruent with our clinical observations of women in our current culture.

The self needs mirroring confirmation and ideals all through one's life. For Kohut the proud "Lone Ranger" is sick, and represents an incorrect nineteenth century ideal. Similarly, Lacan, always standing alone, repeatedly cutting off support matrices and starting again, and often breaking with his friends, would be seen by Kohut as having a narcissistic personality disorder, not as a strong or healthy person. So for Kohut (1984) an empathic matrix of selfobjects, not experienced as primarily archaic selfobjects, but resonating with those of the past, is needed all through life. The selfobject needs of the infant are for a real person to provide direct responses. The selfobject needs of an adolescent are for human objects, symbols, and a peer subculture. Adult selfobject needs are for human objects, or for symbols such as the flag, or art, music, and literature.

Kohut (1977) states that the self in its essence cannot be defined. It is not the empirical self of Hume. It is a sense of cohesion and meaningfulness to one's life. If one is narcissistically wounded, as happens to all of us from time to time, one gets a sense of impending fragmentation of the self along with narcissistic rage. This produces, for example, the burned-out depression of middle age, low self-esteem, and a sense of empty depletion. The self of Kohut is not the transcendental or noumenal self of Kant, which Kohut calls the "axiomatic" self – although at times Kohut anthropomorphized his bipolar self, leading to much confusion and criticism. But it is also not a false image, as Lacan would insist. Kohut says that there is a center we are born with from the start, a sense of assertive, joyful, independent initiative that all infants have. Fragmentation is a disintegration of this original self, not a return, as Lacan would have it, to a premirror phase of initial chaos.

"Transmuting internalization," a controversial term, is defined by Kohut (1971) as taking place in the following manner. In a good-enough holding environment, minor failures in parental selfobject empathy lead to a bit-by-bit taking in of what the parent used to do. This occurs silently, gradually forming structures of drive regulation and drive channeling that make up, says Kohut, the fabric of the self.

More precisely, there are two aspects of transmuting internalization. The first aspect is that of acquiring functional capacities, for example, self-soothing. Kohut took this from Hartmann. Internalization for Hartmann is a process through which autonomous self-regulation replaces regulation by the environment. The second aspect of transmuting internalization is the structuring of the self experience, the formation of a cohesive sense of self. Kohut took this from Winnicott.

Transmuting internalization should be compared with introjection. In introjection, owing to an inappropriate disappointment in the selfobject's empathy, for example, in a poor analysis with a massive identification or taking in of the analyst, there occurs a massive incorporation and identification. An object is set up within, and a relation between the self and the object as introject continues. The structure of the self is not formed by this. It is rigid and maladaptive, but it removes the dependency on external objects, and it reduces vulnerability to disappointment from the failure of empathy by external objects.

Kohut (1984) says this helps to explain the constant "warring" groups of psychoanalytic schools and "the intensity with which theoretical beliefs are upheld" by each, and "their unpleasant behavior to each other" (pp. 164–165). This is due to an incomplete training analysis in the area of narcissism. An unanalyzed idealizing selfobject or narcissistic transference, for example, often improperly interpreted as a defense against oedipal rage, shifts to an idealizing of the "school" and the theories of the training analyst, or to a raging attack against the "school" or the theories of the training analyst with the formation of or joining a new idealized "school." This serves the function of perpetuating the unanalyzed idealizing selfobject transference (p. 166).

In narcissistic pathology, ubiquitous in today's world, the grandiose self and the idealized parent imago remain as unconscious unintegrated configurations with great energy attached, and consequently the self is empty and depleted, devoid of genuine ambitions and ideals. Also, its functioning is interfered with by the breakthrough and intrusion of these archaic structures with their archaic claims. This is a useful explanation of a common clinical picture.

Sometimes one pole will compensate for the other if one or the other selfobject was available, so there appears in clinical practice a variety of self pathology (Kohut and Wolf 1978). Such patients usually present with a vertical and horizontal split, two unfortunate geometric terms chosen by Kohut (1971) in his earlier version of self psychology that generated a lot of useless controversy. The "vertical split" is disavowal. It is based on a fusion with the mother's archaic grandiosity. The patient alternates between behavior and thoughts manifesting grandiosity, and a humble attitude. The "horizontal split" represents repression of the patient's grandiose self and idealized parent imago. This manifests itself clinically by a great shame propensity and a vulnerability to minor narcissistic failures.

THE TREATMENT PROCESS

In therapy the early material deals with undoing the vertical split, reducing disavowal and therefore increasing the pressure of repressed archaic configurations, the grandiose self and the idealized parent imago, under the horizontal split. These then become amalgamated to the representation of the analyst, so an idealizing or mirroring "selfobject transference" forms. In his last work, Kohut

(1984) also separated out a third type of "selfobject transference," the silent twinship transference.

Clinically one sees three types of mirroring transferences (the archaic merger, the alter-ego or twinship, and the mirror transference proper), and two types of idealizing transferences—archaic and overt. These transferences and the typical countertransferences they produce, according to Kohut, I (1985) have described in detail elsewhere, and they are quite well known. In Table 9-1 they are summarized for convenient reference.

There are certain crucial bits of clinical evidence that a selfobject transference has formed. The symptoms of an experienced failure of empathy after the idealizing transference has formed are a function of regression and a reactivated grandiose self. The disappointment shows itself by a cold, aloof, angry, raging withdrawal and a false sense of self-sufficiency, a grandiosity with affected speech and gestures, and an increase in arrogance. If further regression takes place, there may be feelings of fragmentation and hypochondriasis and even frantic erotized fantasies and activities, such as voyeurism with autoerotic and tension states.

Signs of disturbance of the mirror transference, again due to an experienced failure of empathy, are those of a sense of a crumbling self and hypochondriasis. So as to feel alive, there may be a hypercathexis of body parts or of mental functions, the appearance of so-called overwork—which is a symptom and not a cause of fragmentation—and a hypercathexis of activities that may even look like hypomanic excitement. If there is further regression, compulsive sexuality and perversions such as exhibitionism, and again autoerotic and tension states may develop. There also may be a compensatory reactivation of the idealized parent imago when a mirror transference is disturbed, leading to archaic idealizations and ecstatic or religious mystic feelings.

In the disturbance of any of these selfobject transferences, there is regression from higher levels of controlled assertiveness supporting normal ambitions and the wish for acclaim, to a regressive perception of the environment as hostile and dangerous. This may lead to narcissistic rage and chronic depression, which in turn hold the person back from steps to seek his or her own needed responsiveness from others. So we have a vicious cycle. The individual may end up cut off from all selfobjects and with paranoia and Hitlerian pseudoproductivity (Kohut 1978).

When the selfobject transferences have formed, the patient is ready to resume the development of the self, according to Kohut, driven forward by the so-called Zeigarnik phenomenon. This, according to Kohut, is the tendency to complete interrupted tasks if given a chance to do so. It is not necessarily a biological force, and it is not a drive (see Chessick 1985).

Table 9-1. Selfobject Transferences and Typical Countertransferences They Engender

Transference	Goal	Countertransference
Mirror transferences (Mobilized grandiose self)	To share with you the patient's exhibitionistic grandeur; either participate in your greatness or you reflect the patient's greatness.	Boredom, lack of involvement, inattention, leading to exhortations, impatience, sarcasm, and lecturing the patient out of our own exhibitionism and anger.
Archaic merger	You are part of patient and should know what is in his or her mind; expects total control of you.	
Alter-ego	You and patient look alike, or you look like him or his father (or her or her mother). Later separated out as a separate form of "twinship" transference by Kohut (1984).	
Mirror transference proper	The gleam in the mother's eye as she excitedly reflects the baby's magnificence: "How wonderful!"	
Idealizing transferences (Mobilized idealized parent imago)	To share magically in your power and omnipotence via a merger.	Embarrassed shame due to the mobilization of the therapist's grandiose self; straight-arm patient by denial of his or her idealization or by joking about it, etc.
Archaic	Mystical union with the mother, a silent merger	
Overt	A later formation, with the father, stresses the search for idealized parent imago; may mask a hidden silent archaic idealizing transference.	

For the later Kohut (1984) all pathology, including the oedipal neuroses, is grounded in disorders of the self. "Drives" are disintegration products of the fragmenting self, for examples, voyeurism on disappointment in the idealized parent imago, as when the analyst goes on vacation; or exhibitionism after disappointment in the grandiose self when the patient experiences some social or business failure or when the analyst makes an empathic mistake. Thus for Kohut the "drives" are not primary biology but are the disintegration products of normal joyfulness and assertiveness.

Crucial to the resolution of the oedipal phase, for Kohut, is parental acceptance and pride in the child's emerging development. Kohut (1982) compares Oedipus and Laius with Telemachus and Odysseus. Laius tried to kill his son and ends up being killed by his son, whereas Odysseus loves his son Telemachus and they end up shoulder to shoulder driving the suitors and intruders from their home.

In response to narcissistic wounds or the lack of empathy, or other experienced failure of idealized selfobjects, depending on the transference at the time, interpretations will deal with the patient's reactions of (1) regression to more archaic but cohesive forms, such as assertion becoming aggression (in which the patient often gets labeled borderline), idealization becoming voyeurism, or grandiosity becoming exhibitionism; (2) "enfeeblement of the self," a sense of empty depletion and a drop in self-esteem; or (3) a temporary fragmentation that manifests itself by irritability, fleeting paranoia, icy withdrawal, and hypochondriasis.

It should be noted that the selfobject transferences must be allowed to form first and not be interpreted as "defenses." This is in contrast to "traditional" interpretations of idealization as a defense against aggression, or grandiosity as a defense against frustrated oedipal wishes.

Here is a clinical example, provided only to illustrate these concepts, not to convince anybody of their validity. This is a dream from a case in which narcissism began dropping away in the second year of therapy and the patient formed a relatively good love affair, her first not totally pathological, with Don. She dreamed, "Don and his father [I think that really means Dr. Chessick] point out some imperfections in my housekeeping and some other matters, gently and tactfully. Next, I'm looking for my makeup kit [a narcissistic face mask to look beautiful and perfect], but I cannot find it." [Here after minor narcissistic wounding, she regresses to a search for grandiosity that does not work any more.] "Then my mother is there and gives me popcorn, which I don't like, and unpopped popcorn, to boot, to eat. My response is one of apathy and resignation—well, that's how she is. And then I felt great sadness." Other associations were, "This is typical of how my mother cared or met my needs. She couldn't stand infants and wanted to be a man."

The self psychological explanation of all this might be that when the narcissistic mask drops away, we see an empty, depleted self, as in Spitz's babies with anaclitic depression, not only rage. Under grandiosity there is Kohut's depleted, empty self, craving mirroring and merger. Therefore a clinical issue for the therapist to watch for and decide about is whether soothing through communicating empathic understanding to a depleted individual, rather than confronting the patient with interpretations, is the best technique. A crucial choice of theories is made here by the therapist, but *never* does Kohut advocate forced mirroring or encouraging idealization. This is not psychoanalytic treatment but simply narcissistic acting out by the therapist. Kohut does, however, speak of "reluctant compliance" at times with the patient's wish, and he leaves it open when and how to do this.

In therapy we interpret the patient's fears of humiliation and the loss of control and autonomy as these embarrassing transferences begin to appear. These fears are "defenses" against the selfobject transferences. We also interpret the patient's reaction to "empathic failures," defined as when the analyst is experienced by the patient as unempathic in the patient's selfobject transference expectation, such as when the analyst has to cancel a session because of illness. This requires, above all, empathy with the patient's narcissistically experienced world, *not* the correction of reality testing by confrontation, moral condemnation, or defense interpretations. These are the three crucial mistakes, and they lead to a borderline intersubjective field or an impasse or, at worst, breakup of the treatment. At best, the result is submission and massive introjection of the analyst.

PSYCHOTHERAPY AND PSYCHOANALYSIS COMPARED

Kohut introduces the concepts of "self-state dreams" and "traumatic states." These are often interpreted to the patient as reactions to empathic failures, in addition to the usual dream interpretations. There exist two types of dreams for Kohut. In self-state dreams the patient's associations lead nowhere, just laterally to vague fears. We leave the patient's "explanations" of these dreams alone and instead we investigate the narcissistic wounding that led to all this. Our focus is on the narcissistic wounding and not on "drives" or wishes expressed in the dreams and symptoms. Clinically, Kohut (1971) mentions that early dreams of climbing represent looking for an idealizing transference, while early dreams of falling represent looking for a merger mirror transference.

For Kohut (1977) cure is repair of the self, either through the rebuilding by a third chance in life via the selfobject transferences, or by strengthening of one pole of the self to compensate for the great weakness of the other. In this latter situation, "defensive structures" (for example, fantasies of sadistically enforced control and acclaim, pseudovitality, and pseudodrama that cover over defects in the self) are changed to more constructive pursuits of realistic goals and accomplishments. These latter are the "compensatory structures" and are more hopeful and autonomous. For example, I treated a very obese woman patient with an empty, depleted self, who sat around alone eating and fantasizing. After some years of therapy she lost much weight and changed her life to the active pursuit of political goals and immersion in an empathic matrix, working with others. This latter procedure Kohut calls "functional rehabilitation" of the bipolar self. He writes (1977), "Most frequently a weakness in the area of exhibitionism and ambitions is compensated for by the self-esteem provided by the pursuit of ideals" (p. 4).

There are two phases of treatment, according to Kohut, and both of these depend primarily on the analyst's empathy. The first phase is the understanding phase, which has three steps:

Step 1. Need activation and "optimal frustration." This occurs as a function of the psychoanalytic setting and permits the selfobject transferences to form as already described.

Step 2. Nonfulfillment of the need or "abstinence." There is no direct gratification of these demands by the analyst, or at least very little.

Step 3. A substitution for direct need fulfillment and a reestablishing of the bond of empathy between the self and selfobject. This occurs by interpretation from any school, even the Lacanian, as long as there is an empathic recognition of the need, and it takes place and is communicated by any kind of interpretation, wild or not, in any theory, says Kohut (1984). The communication of empathy and the interpretation of the disruption provide "limited structural accretion" and constitute psychotherapy. The results, Kohut insists, are ephemeral and incomplete, but a long period of this may be necessary to establish empathic bonding with very damaged patients. Just being empathically understood has a therapeutic effect, claims Kohut.

The second phase of treatment is called the explaining phase, in which the analyst explains and interprets the following:

1. The dynamics of the transference experience are explained: what was expected, what was experienced as failure, what was the patient's reaction, and so forth.

2. The genetic precursors of vulnerability of the patient are explained; the current situation is connected with failures of empathy from selfobjects of the past.

This moves psychotherapy into psychoanalysis, broadens and deepens the result, and establishes permanent change in psychic structure. Cure for Kohut rests not on an expansion of cognition but on the accretion of psychic structure through empathically based understanding and much explaining. The therapeutic ambience of empathy is the cornerstone of therapy and has a curative effect all by itself, according to Kohut.

For Kohut (1977) the validation that cure is taking place often is through "action thought." As the self coheres and the poles are strengthened, the patient seeks out at least one area of activity in which the patient's realistic skills can be employed to realize nuclear ambitions towards idealized goals. Furthermore, the patient establishes an empathic matrix of other people to mirror his or her accomplishments and confirm and share idealized goals. There is a sense of a meaningful life; joyful enthusiasm results, according to Kohut, and one can watch for this to develop clinically.

KOHUT'S CONCLUSIONS

To summarize, the self is constituted by two poles. The first pole is that of self-esteem, which usually comes from the mother's mirroring gleam, in contrast for example, to the face of the Medusa. The exhibitionistic and ambitious aspects of the self-esteem pole come from the integrated grandiose self. The other pole is that of guiding ideals, which usually come from the father and represent a fusion with the idealized parent imago, although they also stem earlier from the mother's omnipotent soothing. The archaic idealized parent imago leads to voyeuristic tendencies and the wish to fuse with power, and must be integrated into the guiding ideals pole. Between the self-esteem and guiding ideals pole there is an intermediate area of executive functions and skills needed to realize the patterns of both poles of the self. This is firmed up by the twinship experience between the ages of about 4 and 10 years. The goal of treatment is to fill out a defect in the self by way of transmuting internalizations after a transference revival of archaic selfobject needs, or to strengthen compensatory structures and so make them functionally reliable and autonomous, after a transference revival of selfobject needs. The psychology of the self essentially differs from traditional psychoanalysis in that Kohut positions the drive–conflict model within the vicissitudes of self-development, and he postulates a drivelike need for selfobject experiences from birth throughout life.

There are three functions for empathy, according to Kohut (1978). It is the crucial tool of psychoanalytic fact-finding. It expands the self to bonds between people, reducing aggression. It is an indispensable need from others throughout life.

The reason that sexual activity appears when self-fragmentation threatens is that sexual activity, through erotization, turns a painful affect initially endured as a child into a sense of active mastery, and orgasm is a discharge of narcissistic tensions.

Kohut (1977, 1984) distinguishes between the oedipal stage, in which there is a proudly achieved forward movement and development, and the Oedipus complex, a state of disruption of the normal due to faulty selfobject responses, so that aggressive and sexual aims appear in efforts to organize the fragmented self. Although Kohut never gives a very satisfactory definition of fragmentation, he (1982) describes how in fragmentation the self stands by helplessly as waves of "feverishly intensified" lust or aggression "achieve experiential primacy" (p. 401). *This can occur any time, even in late adult life.* The oedipal phase is a time-limited phase of life followed by latency around the age of 7, but Freud's oedipal phase is more emotional and less joyful and optimistic than Kohut's, and is infused with preoedipal experiences. For Freud every child's world becomes full of violence and sexuality at this time. Freud implies pessimistically that there exists a grim, dissatisfied, primitive child left in all of us, no matter what is accomplished.

The loss of vitality, seen so commonly in clinical work, represents the pathology of the self under stress. The typical symptoms pointing to self disorder are complaints of "existential malaise," "burnout," "midlife crisis," "menopausal depression," and so forth.

A mature selfobject matrix of relations is always different from object relations. Mature object relations represent a firm self expressing itself angrily, lovingly, and so forth, in the interest of achieving goals other than maintaining the strength and integrity of the self.

The narcissistic personality disorder differs from the normal in that the narcissistic patient is preoccupied with archaic selfobjects, so the patient's conduct is quite stereotyped, whereas the normal individual can share affective concerns with others on an equal footing, even within a selfobject matrix.

The self psychological stance shifts our focus to inside the patient and asks, "What is the patient experiencing?" If it is the grandiose self, the patient experiences absolute self-centeredness. If it is the idealized parent imago, the patient is less self-centered but feels union with another's power or ideals. We ask ourself, What feelings are stirred up in us as therapists? What is the patient asking us to be? How does the patient use us to maintain self-esteem? Some patients resist communicating this and protect the self by diminishing the therapist. This may cause therapeutic despair, but one must realize that sometimes the patient needs to consciously experience the therapist as of little value. The therapist's behavior must be reliable, predictable, and safe; in this way the therapist is used, sometimes even in the presence of overt devaluation, to channel excitation, aid in control and regulation, set goals, guide and direct activity, give vigor and enthusiasm, and enhance self-esteem.

Explanations reveal the analyst, his or her personality, and how well he or she has listened (Chessick 1989a). They also function to restore the empathic bond with the patient when there is an experienced failure in the selfobject transference. We must not have recourse to the traditional alibis such as "negative therapeutic reaction," "adhesiveness of the libido," "borderline patient," or "death instinct" when the analysis fails. In psychotherapy we encourage the patient to displace the selfobject transference to friends, family, and social organizations, forming a stable selfobject matrix that eventually takes the place of the therapist. But in psychoanalysis we concentrate more specifically on interpretations and explanations of the selfobject transferences.

Terman (1989) claims that Kohut, as he developed his theories and conception of what is crucially curative in treatment, shifted from the notion of transmuting internalization, a concept based on the mechanics and energetics in Freud's theories, to empathy, which Terman calls experiential and transactional. So in self psychology there are two approaches. The first is labeled by Terman the explanatory-interpretive, in which an attempt is made to articulate archaic affect states and to recognize and interpret failures of empathy within the selfobject transference, with the assumption that change will then more or less automatically take place, perhaps through transmuting internalization. The second approach has more of a relationship-experiential nature, emphasizing optimal responsiveness of the therapist rather than optimal frustration and, perhaps in the manner described by Loewald (1960) (although he was not a self psychologist), the experience of a new and better relationship enables and stimulates development automatically to resume.

CONTRIBUTIONS FROM INFANT RESEARCH

We need more understanding of archaic transferences and archaic mentation, of the phase from birth to 18 months which is "beyond interpretation," and of the earliest development of tension regulation. Lichtenberg (1983) delineates the first year as one in which the experiential exchange between the self and others has the crucial role; tension regulation and neurophysiological balance through this exchange are the primary phenomena. In the second year there is an apparent awareness on the part of the infant of a separate self from objects; this is a crucial development of self-consciousness, which in turn is a function of the neurophysiological development of imaging capacity. Only after all this comes the later development of conscious, articulate self-reflection. It follows that if there is serious empathic failure or trauma in the first 18 months of life, the patient later cannot sustain the psychoanalytic relationship itself, and this becomes the focus of the treatment. This is a stage "beyond interpretation" because it is prelinguistic, and one must reconstruct from nonverbal communications using empathic receptivity.

Lichtenberg concludes that the primary meaning of the psychoanalytic situation lies in the reverberation of it for the preoedipal child in the patient. Psychological holding and physicianly caring are crucial. The theories of both Klein and Kernberg, he says, are contradicted by infant research. Ranges of affect intensity, not splitting, are predominant. Early experienced regulatory defects may never be given image or language, as in the situation of alexithymia, or the incapacity to feel hunger as often found in very obese patients.

Stechler (1987, Stechler and Halton 1987) tried to distinguish, in studies of the infant, between "assertion," which is a constructive and intelligence-building behavior that is associated with euphoria, and "aggression," which is self-protective, reactive, and associated with fear and anger. Aggression represents a reactive wish to destroy a danger. Both of these appear in the second half of the first year of life and should not be confused in psychotherapy. When the parents react to assertion as aggression and thwart it, this is experienced by the infant as an empathic failure, constitutes a narcissistic wound, and engenders aggression.

Stern (1985) describes child development as taking place in the following manner. There is a sense of emergent self that begins at birth, so there is no autistic stage. An activity "of extracting meaningful information from a multitude of stimuli and experiencing the dependable rhythms . . . allows a sense of self to emerge" (Basch 1991, p. 6). From about 2 to 6 months of age occurs a sense of core self, of core relatedness, in which the body is separated from others. Schemas and patterns of behavior develop. From 7 to 15 months, the infant develops the sense of subjective self. This is established by "affect attunement" with the parent, an intersubjective exchange with the parent. After 15 months one has a verbal self, but before 18 months of age the Kleinian postulated intrapsychic mechanisms cannot occur, since there are no fantasies of wish fulfillment, and images are concerned only with events.

"Mirroring" during the sense of core self stage, between 2 and 6 months, is simply the appropriate response from the parent and proper regulation of the infant by the parent. "Mirroring" during the sense of subjective self stage, from about 7 to 15 months, as previously stated, is affect attunement. This can even be used by the parent pathologically, by selectively deciding what to respond to, leading or shaping the child to develop a false self as the price of affect attunement. "Mirroring" during the verbal self stage is represented by linguistic reinforcement, shaping through discussion, commands, attributions, or injunctions, and consensual validation.

Stern (1985) emphasizes the importance of what he calls an interaction that has become generalized. This represents the memory of an evoked companion that one is with intrapsychically, for the purpose of self-regulation. No drive theory is necessary in this developmental theory and the concept of splitting is seen as simplistic. Preoedipal pathology, says Stern, is based on deficits and not conflicts. These deficits are defective interpersonal operations that can be from misattunement that was undertaken to change a child or develop a false self, or from certain representations of interactions that have become generalized. All of this has substantially occurred before the verbal stage.

One can see from Stern's description of pathological self-development how the fragile structure of the self in these damaged individuals often must be protected against further damage, in the rough and tumble and intimacy of social intercourse, by either schizoid mechanisms to keep involvement shallow, or by paranoid mechanisms to surround the self with an aura of hostility and suspicion in order to keep noxious selfobjects at bay, a concept close to that of R. D. Laing (see Wolf 1988).

The field of infant research has much to offer to our further understanding of Kohut's psychology of the self and may prove very valuable in eventually correcting at least some of the minor points of disagreement among the alternative approaches to understanding humans. This is true even though Kohut did not rely on such research in his work, confining his psychoanalytic fact-finding to the use of empathy in the clinical situation. For an application of Stern's views to psychotherapy see Basch (1991).

There are three modes of clinical experience in psychoanalytic therapy, all of which require understanding and interpretation: (1) intrapsychic drives, defenses, and compromise formations, which represent the traditional approach to understanding the patient; (2) vicissitudes of the self and the sense of self, grasped using Kohut's method of empathic identification; and (3) phenomenological investigation of the mutual interaction with the patient, often expressed in terms of body experiences and tension regulation. The problem with theories such as those of object relations, which operate primarily from various postulated intrapsychic images, as Gedo (1979, 1988) points out, is that they ignore the early encoded action–affect patterns or archaic experiential patterns that generate behavior, which persist pervasively throughout life. These patterns can be best discovered through a phenomenological orientation to the study of the patient, to which I now turn.

10

HUSSERL AND
MERLEAU-PONTY:
PHENOMENOLOGY

STERN (1985) WRITES phenomenologically that "even though the nature of self may forever elude the behavioral sciences, the sense of self stands as an important subjective reality, a reliable, evident phenomenon that the sciences cannot dismiss. How we experience ourselves in relation to others provides a basic organizing perspective for all interpersonal events" (p. 6). Stern's infant is reality oriented, connected to and actively seeking of people, and capable of forming separate schemas of the self and others virtually from the beginning of life. Stern's is not primarily a phenomenological study because, as he admits, he makes certain leaps of inference, but there are no inferences necessary in grasping Stern's description of the ways in which all caretakers, intentionally or otherwise, shape for life the child's experience of himself or herself.

The term *phenomenology* has a difficult history, and over the years has come to have many meanings. It was first introduced into philosophy by Lambert, a German philosopher who was a contemporary of Kant, and who used the term simply to pertain to illusions. Kant called phenomenology the study of what appears to us in our experience. He (1781) contrasted experience, or "phenomena," with objects and events as they are "in themselves," a dichotomy Kant took for granted but which was broken down by the German idealists who followed him, culminating in Hegel's *Phenomenology of Spirit* in 1807. For Hegel phenomenology represented the discovery of Absolute Spirit through a study of the various stages in the historical development of the mind of the experience or phenomena of self-consciousness.

In the middle of the nineteenth century, however, phenomenology came to have the wider meaning of an attempt at a purely descriptive study of any given set of experiences. For example, the American philosopher Charles Peirce in 1902 used the term to mean a descriptive study of whatever appears before the mind, such as perceptions of so-called reality, dreams, imaginings, and even misperceptions.

PHENOMENOLOGY IN PSYCHIATRY

Edmund Husserl (1859–1938) introduced his phenomenological method as a way of doing philosophy in the early 1900s. His pupil, Martin Heidegger, took up this method, although he completely changed Husserl's orientation and applied it to investigating the human condition, in his so-called "existential analytic" (*Being and Time*, 1962a), reviewed in Chapter 1. This remarkable work spawned a school of psychiatric treatment on the European continent whose most prominent practitioners were Ludwig Binswanger and Menard Boss, among others. All of these in turn, however, presented a hodgepodge of approaches, each of which differed from Husserl's original method and intent (Kockelmans 1967). Their publications pose formidable difficulties for United States psychiatrists, who as a rule are not familiar with philosophy, in spite of Galen's (1952) famous treatise entitled "That The Best Physician Is Also A Philosopher," written about A.D. 160.

Phenomenology received a brief flurry of interest in the 1950s in the United States when a small school of so-called existential psychiatrists claiming an affinity to phenomenology appeared. Only after two further developments has the phenomenological approach again claimed attention here in psychiatry. The first of these two developments was Kohut's psychology of the self movement in psychoanalysis, discussed in the previous chapter, with its emphasis on the sense of self as it appears at birth and emerges with vicissitudes throughout various phases of development. This led to a resurgence of interest in infant research among psychiatrists, although Kohut confined his work to the clinical situation. Infant research lends itself nicely to a phenomenological approach, a description of the observed infant experience without prior logical or conceptual categories, since whatever is observed is prelinguistic. This is not to be confused with the famous pioneering work of Mahler and her co-workers (1975), who approached their infant observations with strongly held theoretical preconceptions (Tanguay 1977, Brody 1982). The second development came from a new generation of psychiatrists in Europe, mostly German, who took their starting point from the extensions and modifications of Heidegger's work by Gadamer (1982), discussed in Chapter 3.

Phenomenology requires the mental health professional to be tolerant of unfamiliar terms and ways of stating things, of difficult new concepts that are not easily and immediately grasped but require prolonged thought, and of ways of approach and presentation that, springing from the European and especially the German philosophical tradition, are different from the United States pragmatic tradition. Since we all tend to stay with the familiar and the comfortable, especially when we become older, a certain effort will be required to wrench oneself from routine thinking and to concentrate in a different manner. This effort is made more difficult by the current trend toward "medicalization" of psychiatry, which tends to lose vital information about the total patient that phenomenology attempts to retrieve.

WHAT IS PHENOMENOLOGY?

The Greek word φαινόμενον (phainomenon) comes from the verb φαίνεσθαι (phainesthai) which means "that which shows itself." Phenomenology attempts to return to the primordial data of experience, that which shows itself in the manner in which it shows itself. Phenomena are always prior to our theories and concepts; they are immediate data but they are not simply "appearances," for appearances are always appearances of something, whereas phenomena are that something which shows itself: they are primary, they are what is.

The most important feature of phenomenology is that it is in some ways a nonempirical science. It does not describe empirically observable "matters of fact" and it does not at all lend itself to what Heidegger called the "calculative thinking" which pervades our time. This is one of the reasons it is so unfamiliar to us. Thus phenomenological statements are not considered "true" if they correspond to the observation of "facts" thought of as "out there" in "reality"; they are considered true if they accurately describe phenomena experienced, and false if they do not. The phenomenologist does not frame theories; he or she examines and describes phenomena as they present themselves to a relatively unprejudiced view.

Husserl (1913) believed phenomenology offers us a presuppositionless form of inquiry, since it insists on no prior theoretical commitment and demands a dedication to try to operate without any unexamined assumptions. Husserl's main idea was that the examination of the phenomena yielded the truths of phenomenology directly; it brought us to the things themselves. Using his method, Husserl believed, things speak for themselves, that is to say, instead of understanding through controlled experiments based on scientific hypotheses, understanding is through an undergoing of experience. The Greeks called this πάθει μάθος, which I translate as "education is to have endured."

The confusing method of phenomenology, as stated in the Introduction, was originally developed by Husserl under the influence of Brentano, the previously mentioned philosopher-psychologist who developed the notion of "intentionality": all acts of consciousness are directed toward some intentional object. That consciousness is always a consciousness *of* something became a fundamental theme of Husserl's philosophy. Husserl first used the term "phenomenologic method" in 1900, and for him it was a way of achieving philosophic certainty. Husserl's (1913) mature method attempts what he calls *transcendental-phenomenological reduction*; as a starting point he does not permit the selection out of experience of certain specific things, sensations, feelings, and so on, since to do so would assume classificatory principles about the world. Thus phenomenological statements cannot be called empirical, because empirical scientific statements are about already assumed "things" out there. Phenomenological statements attempt what Husserl calls *presuppositionless inquiry*—no theories, just descriptions of phenomena as they present themselves to an unprejudiced view.

Husserl defined this starting point for phenomenological reduction as the "bracketing of experience," or *epoché*, the unbiased contemplation of phenomena without intellectual preconsiderations. Then, in a controversial methodological step, he proposed the use of "imaginative variations," in order to intuit the essence of the phenomena. So for Husserl phenomenological statements are not empirical in the traditional sense of the word; they are ultimately statements about the intuited essence of the phenomena, and in this way he claims they lead to philosophical certainty, and what he regarded as a radical form of empiricism. Most subsequent proponents of phenomenology have rejected this further step, a rejection which caused Husserl great disappointment.

From the point of view of the psychotherapist, the phenomenological stance is to examine one's reaction to what is simply there in a felt experience; the therapist does not disconnect, isolate, or interpret aspects of this experience. *Epoché*, or the bracketing of experience, demands refrainment from judgment about morals, values, causes, background, and even from separating the subject (patient) and objective observer (therapist). One pays special attention to one's experience or state of consciousness in the presence of a patient. The therapist must continue to observe and listen, staying with the patient's material and directly experiencing the patient rather than searching for hidden processes.

Phenomenologists warn that a distance can be created between the therapist and the patient by the standard interviewing technique, a gap that may be unproductively filled by abundant verbal material and analytic ideas, conceptions, and theories. They advise focusing on the emotional interchange, staying strictly with the phenomena presented by the patient, and concentrating on our experienced interaction with the patient.

Phenomenological reduction of the cognitive and emotional distance between the patient and the therapist, then, is the crucial procedure, leading to a true meeting or encounter (Jaspers 1972), hard to define but something we have all experienced. The application of phenomenology to psychotherapy raises the valid question of whether we as therapists can be sure that we are seeing and hearing our patients as they really are, rather than as projections of our theories about them. The aim of phenomenological study is to rediscover the whole living person and how being in the world is experienced by that person and those around that person.

Husserl hoped that from careful examination of the results of phenomenological inquiry we could, by using what he called our transcendental ego, intuit the essences of the phenomena. He thought he had developed a new and more exact method in philosophy, but his notion of a transcendental ego quickly came under fire for a variety of reasons. Sartre's (1957) *The Transcendence of the Ego* deals with this problem, but some experts (Kohák 1978) have argued that Sartre misunderstood Husserl.

Sartre's (1973b) later "existentialism" is based on Heidegger's use of the phenomenological method to ferret out not intuitive essences but the hidden background practices of human existence. For Heidegger the self is constituted by these cultural background practices, and as such provides a "clearing" in which Being appears. Sartre extended and changed Heidegger's findings to a point where the self becomes constituted solely within the phenomena and arises secondarily out of the description of the phenomena, rather than comprising some transcendental essence (Husserl) or manifestation of background practices (Heidegger); for Sartre, as we have seen in Chapter 6, the self is derivative and fugitive.

These philosophers stimulated the continental European psychiatric investigation of the self and its three important aspects of being in the world, modes of "being-with," as Heidegger called them: (1) *Umwelt*, our environment; (2) *Mitwelt*, our fellow humans; and (3) *Eigenwelt*, our relationship to ourselves. All of these modes can be described phenomenologically and all are interlocked with our constituted self, so that no hidden essences or entities are postulated. This eliminates the whole infrastructure of metapsychology, the disease classifications of *DSM-III-R*, and, above all, the classical notion of an independent neutral subject (e.g., the psychiatrist) observing the outside world (e.g., the patient) through collecting data and developing empirical and quantitative laws of cause and effect.

CLINICAL APPLICATIONS

Regardless of the various conceptions of phenomenology in philosophy—a dispute still going on today, and beyond the scope of this book—phenomenology has a useful application in psychiatry and psychoanalysis. We know that the phenomena of the encounter between one person and another, including that between the therapist and the patient, always is interactively or dialectically constituted, and that diagnoses and the postulation of psychic entities, commonly made on the basis of the phenomena generated in that encounter, are therefore relative to both the observer and the observed, or the therapist and the patient. This is consistent with quantum physics and the whole postmodern approach in philosophy and hermeneutics.

The famous Husserlian slogan, *"Zu den Sachen selbst!"* (to the things themselves) reflected Husserl's goal, to intuit the essences of the things themselves. Although not many philosophers still follow his methodology for that purpose today, *"Zu den Sachen selbst!"* could be taken as a slogan to admonish us to concentrate on treatment of the whole patient, examining and describing the whole of the phenomena the patient presents, including the phenomena of our interaction with the patient as we experience it. This *is* the patient!

In Husserl's terminology, the act of experiencing contains two phases. The first of these he labels *noesis* or the *noetic phase*, in which sense data are constituted as meaningful by the subject. In order to do this a second or *noematic phase* is necessary, in which the "objects" of experience are constituted by the intentionality of the experience. Such "objects," invested with the subject's meaning and emotions, are called *noemata* (a single such "object" is called *noema*). Human sciences must be built not on so-called natural objects, which are abstractions from *noemata* in which the intentional component is suspended, but on the *noemata* themselves. Otherwise we lose the vital human component and end up with less than the full, experienced reality. We also must know what kind of noematic world the person constitutes around himself or herself that makes his or her choice of behavior appropriate.

As a clinical example, Pao (1979) urged us to consider the diagnosis of schizophrenia not so much on the basis of Bleuler's famous criteria, but as a function of the kind of ambience the therapist experiences, that peculiar sensation of relating to someone who is both there and not there, which generates our considerable personal discomfort. We might extend this further by employing Kohut's (1971) method of empathy, to try to identify the self experience such a patient has by using trial identification, trying to see how we feel if we can empathize ourselves into the shoes of a patient who has to relate to us in this matter. Although Kohut's method of vicarious introspection (empathy) in this manner goes beyond phenomenology, one cannot avoid focus on the self-experience that is so central to Kohut's approach when one discusses phenomenology as it is applied to clinical work.

I do not know whether Pao was familiar with Heidegger, but he employs here Heidegger's (1962a) distinction between the "hermeneutic as" and the "apophantic as." Self psychologists and Sullivanians like Pao recognize the patient through participation, through experienced interaction subjected then to either Kohut's method of empathy or Sullivan's interpersonal process, and subsequently to hermeneutic exegesis. A shrug, a gesture, a facial expression, a reaction, the totality of such interpersonal phenomena directly conceptualize the patient for them. In contrast to this, Kleinians employ the "apophantic as." They make judgments about what goes on inside of the patient, from which they attempt to explain the interaction without direct reference to the therapist; the patient is judged as "projecting," using "projective identification," "splitting," enduring an unresolved "depressive position," and so on. For Heidegger this latter sort of theorizing is removed from the reality of the encounter and sets up a false subject–object (therapist–patient) dichotomy, often with the "therapist-scientist" as the sole arbiter of what is "reality."

Each psychiatrist (or philosopher) using phenomenology tends to employ it in his or her own way. Here is an example to clarify my use of it and how it may be distinguished from the standard clinical approach. I practice psychiatry very near the campus of Northwestern University in Evanston. A few years ago some of the shapeliest female students wore a fashionable T-shirt with the slogan "What You See Is What You Get" printed in large letters across that part of the front of the T-shirt that excited campus men as they experienced the phenomena of the young women's upper convex curvaceousness. To my knowledge none of the women wore this slogan over the seat of their pants, although to be consistent they might have done so—but that is a different philosophical discussion. As a philosophically inclined psychiatrist, I found myself pondering over and over again the "meaning" of this message.

"What You See Is What You Get" printed on top of the woman's upper convex curve, and my reaction of puzzled fascination—this comprised the phenomenological description. What did the young women "mean" by this? I must admit that today I still do not know. The standard empirical scientific point of view utilizing psychoanalysis might be that the young woman, from the drive of exhibitionist narcissistic libido with which her entire body-self was invested in lieu of a penis, was displaying her underlying breasts, in a compromise formation. They were hidden and yet attention was called to them by the tight-fitting T-shirt, and sometimes, when there was no bra, by the shape of the nipples outlined by the tight T-shirt. She then was forbidding the campus man to get at the underlying breasts, which she assumed, perhaps correctly, he would like to look at, caress, and so forth, leading to a sexual encounter. It was a polite way of expressing the combination of pride and annoyance at watching the man's eyes wander over her curves and of saying, "Beat it, you dirty old man." In this approach, as the objective neutral observer, I was postulating the presence of a naked body under the clothes as well as a psyche that was constituted of an ego, id, and superego. As in every single decision that we make, she had, through the use of ego apparatuses, arrived at a compromise formation satisfactory to those three "harsh masters"—id, superego, and reality—that both gratified and prohibited a forbidden narcissistic wish to exhibit herself, be admired, caressed, and perhaps sexually satisfied.

For a therapist this is a relatively anxiety-free explanation because it leaves the therapist out entirely and simply postulates certain entities and dynamic processes in the young woman. Of course the therapist could label it as countertransference if he or she spent much time pondering the matter, as I did above, but this could be theoretically removed by self-analysis of the infantile roots of the therapist's oedipal and preoedipal lust for the mother, and so forth, at which point it would disappear, and the therapist could be neutral and objective again.

From a phenomenological point of view, however, the matter is quite different, because in that approach the experience of reading "What You See Is What You Get" *is* the reality, it *is*, rather paradoxically, the truth. The medium is the message! There are no postulated essences or "breasts" under the observed phenomena to be thought about in terms of their psychic representations being invested with various energies by the mental apparatus of the young woman. There is only the interaction that is experienced by the observer or therapist, an interaction of titillation and frustration and puzzlement (in my case). The phenomenon is not a manifestation of something hidden "inside" either the woman or the observer but is the interaction itself, which has a certain—difficult to describe in words—experiential or phenomenological quality that all men and women have undergone at one time or another. But the kind of experience and the attributed meaning varies from person to person and does not represent some kind of fixed underlying "truth" or "reality" that can be described "scientifically" in terms of external objects like "breasts," or psychic mechanisms, or physiological laws of sexuality, or drives and so on. For the phenomenologist the "truth" of the situation is simply the *experience* of encountering "What You See

Is What You Get," and that is all there is. For the phenomenologist who follows Heidegger or Sartre, existence precedes essence, and our concept of essence is a secondary process by which we attempt to make sense out of the intrinsic ambiguity of experience.

The phenomenological task is not to provide some kind of mechanistic explanation of this experience, but to focus on the phenomena experienced in that particular situation by those particular people. Functioning as a phenomenologist, I cannot diagnose medically or mechanistically or scientifically what is going on "inside" of the woman at all, for if I try to do so I lose the essential holistic aspect of the interactive experience and also lose valuable phenomenological data by cancelling myself out of the picture. At the same time, the price I pay for this approach is lack of an orderly *DSM-III-R* scientific diagnosis of the woman; what I gain is *understanding by enduring what the experienced world is for us together at that moment*. Hopefully, if I am a therapist I can then begin, by the use of hermeneutic exegesis, to articulate this experience and, in a sense, raise it from a primary process level to a secondary process level so as to enable a discussion of it. The scientific and the phenomenological approaches are both valuable and can complement each other in the practice of psychotherapy.

For a phenomenologist the question, What did the young women "mean" by this? entails: How do the women wearing this message experience their interactive behavior? What does it mean to them in the context of their experience? What is it as a human way of being-in-the-world? We want to know the intentional structure of their experience, how they constitute the objects (men) toward whom they flash this signal, and what there is about their individualized constitution of the objects—perhaps as "dirty old men"—that causes them to imitate each other in this form of behavior and not in some other form. We would want to listen to them talk about it and to experience them in the encounter situation repeatedly before we could come up with some answers.

A phenomenologist would say, "I cannot theorize from *my* experience of the encounter anything about what goes on 'inside' the woman. All this would tell us is how *I* constitute the object and what the experience might mean for *me*, but it throws no light on the intrapsychic 'essence' of the woman; jumping to that becomes only a projection of our theories." The same point applies to ascertaining the "meaning" of suicide, or of paranoia. Here again phenomenologists ask, What self-conception or self-image would make suicide seem like a reasonable alternative for dealing with personal problems? Or, How can we make sense of paranoia as a way of being in the world—what experiences led the person to constitute the objects (*noemata*) of his or her experience in this manner?

A phenomenological approach to patients commonly labeled as "borderline" on the basis of the phenomenology of the interaction with them is, in my opinion, more fruitful than pinning a diagnosis on them, a pejorative diagnosis, which immediately shifts the interaction into an adversarial mode. Atwood and Stolorow (1984) have tried to apply their version of "psychoanalytic phenomenology" to this condition. As stated in Chapter 7, R. D. Laing called diagnosis a "political act," referring to what it means to have the diagnostic label of "schizophrenia" pinned on one—what it means to the world of the patient and also to the very therapy itself. It is more useful therapeutically for such patients if we try to articulate the phenomenology of the experience with the patient and convey an empathic understanding of it to the patient rather than try to "scientifically" explain it by postulating and interpreting the vicissitudes of intrapsychic split-off "all good" and "all bad" representations, and so forth.

Phenomenology with subsequent hermeneutic exegesis hopefully leads to better recognition for patients as to how others may experience them and how their difficulties in living come about through the generation of maladaptive interactional phenomena. It also removes the onus of being diagnosed as having secret malevolent representations carried about in one's psyche like some sort of poison that threatens to reach out and contaminate those around one. It allows the patient to preserve self-esteem during the investigation rather than to feel primitive and contemptible. It preserves the humanity of the patient and the vital sense of wholeness or autonomy of the self even during the investigation. In a recent book I (1989a) tried to indicate the clinical advantages and disadvantages of the traditional psychoanalytic, object-relations, self psychological, phenomenological, and interactional approaches. All are useful and necessary.

The greatest weakness of phenomenology is in its neglect of the unconscious realm of the psyche as envisioned by Freud. There is some room for argument that in phenomenology there is a similarity between Freud's "preconscious" and the manner in which phenomenologists speak of "unconscious," using it as a descriptive adjective. Husserl (1989), in a work recently published in English (which underwent revision after revision for about 20 years, with the last revision in 1928), discusses the "unconscious" to some extent. But in my opinion Husserl is curiously ambivalent on the topic and his discussion is ambiguous and open to several interpretations. Thorough and scholarly investigation of the problem of the unconscious in phenomenology has been carried out by Mishara (1989, 1990a, 1990b), but there remains a profound conceptual gap between Freud's concept of the unconscious and that of the phenomenological and existential traditions. At the present writing there seems to be a consensus among psychoanalysts in the United States that a serious disjunction exists between the phenomenological method and the method of exploring the unconscious that is used in psychoanalytical clinical work.

Husserl, Heidegger, Sartre, Merleau-Ponty, and so-called existential psychotherapists such as Binswanger and Boss each use a different conception of phenomenology, as do modern investigators (see Edie 1965, 1967, 1969).[1] They share very little in common, which, along with much obscure writing, accounts for some of the confusion in the field. For each investigator we must ask, What is your phenomenological method? and try to evaluate the method by the way the investigator actually applies it and by what information it provides us that is complementary to and enhances what can be obtained by the standard scientific approach. Unfortunately, sometimes a maximum of jargon conceals a minimum of information. As Merleau-Ponty explained, phenomenology, as it is used by each investigator, is only accessible through study of that investigator's work using the phenomenological method!

Phenomenology may be thought of as a style of thinking that suspends scientific explanation and attempts to get in touch with the primordial experiences underlying all our more mature constructions of the world. Infant research using phenomenology, and the unusual contribution of Merleau-Ponty from philosophy, which he developed without the benefit of modern infant research on the emerging sense of self, enhance our clinical study of borderline or preoedipal conditions. These conditions are generated in the period of development before acquiring speech, logical categories, and so on, have inserted the person's self into the symbolic order, as Lacan would put it. These conditions, in our age of technicity and narcissism, form the majority of disorders we see in outpatient psychiatry and psychoanalysis, and they often respond poorly to pharmacological agents, forcing us to lean more on the phenomenological approach.

WINNICOTT'S PHENOMENOLOGY

D. W. Winnicott (1965) moved away from Freud's depiction of the psyche of the infant as a separate autistic entity and replaced it with his notion of the "nursing couple" (p. 15). A pediatrician before becoming a psychoanalyst, he modeled his clinical orientation to the patient on what he called an ordinary and devoted mother's holding care of her infant, the "average expectable environment" (1966) essential to the health and growth of the personality of the child. He shifts from Freud's notion of the infant as a chaotic autistic aggregation of instincts to focus

---

[1]A thorough introduction to the different conceptions of phenomenology in Husserl, Heidegger, Sartre, Merleau-Ponty and others is presented by Kockelmans (1967). A review of phenomenology as it is used in psychiatry and psychology is offered by Spiegelberg (1972).

on a "continuously healthy fostering nursing environment" (Guntrip 1971), thus laying the groundwork for a phenomenological study of infancy. There is a "willingness as well as an ability on the part of the mother to drain interest from her own self onto the baby" (Winnicott 1965, p. 15), which he calls "primary maternal preoccupation" (p. 15); the self-experience of the individual develops in the context of the relationship between the mother and the infant. In another phenomenological statement Winnicott (1966) explains:

> Holding includes especially the physical holding of the infant, which is a form of loving. It is perhaps the only way in which a mother can show the infant her love. There are those who can hold an infant and those who cannot; the latter quickly produce in the infant a sense of insecurity, and distressed crying. All this leads right up to, includes, and coexists with the establishment of the infant's first object relationships and his first experiences of instinctual gratification. [p. 49]

If we describe the total experience of holding, and observations of both the holding of an infant that produces an obvious distressed crying, and the holding of an infant that produces an apparent sense of attunement, harmony, and contentment, we practice phenomenology. On the basis of his concept of holding, Winnicott distinguished between psychoanalysis for oedipal cases and "management" for preoedipal cases, where the initial good-enough mothering experience cannot be taken for granted. Guntrip (1968) depicts Winnicott as insisting that in the therapy of management cases we should attempt to imitate the natural phenomena that characterize the behavior of any mother with her own infant.

Winnicott in his publications confusingly, and for political reasons, kept one foot in the camp of the Kleinian theorists, who postulated various intrapsychic structures, but he was a clinical pioneer who reoriented psychoanalysis in the direction of study of the nursing couple, which lends itself more immediately to a phenomenological approach than to an approach based on Kleinian theory. Similarly, Winnicott emphasized the setting in which psychoanalytic work is carried out, and the importance of it, which suggests a phenomenological study of the frame of any psychotherapy or psychoanalysis, and of its effect on the interaction and mutual experience of the patient and the therapist (see Langs 1979).

There is an overlap between Winnicott's (1965) concepts of holding and the successful nursing couple, and his phenomenological observations of the "capacity of the infant to enjoy the experience of body functioning, and of BEING" (p. 19); as he puts it, "if the environment behaves well, the infant has a chance to maintain a sense of *continuity of being*" (p. 28). This links the earliest nursing-couple experiences with the whole quest for contact with Being that preoccupied Heidegger in philosophy, and forms a fertile cross-disciplinary unexplored area. Winnicott (1965) says that our sense of life being worth living, of being alive, of being real, of "BEING" (p. 19), comes out of the phenomena of the successful nursing couple, as does the very important capacity to be alone (Winnicott 1958). As is well known, all of these are defective in the preoedipal disorders (Chessick 1977, 1985, 1991).

In Winnicott's paper "The Mirror Role of the Mother and the Family" (Phillips 1988), the mother's face is seen as the precursor of the mirror; for Winnicott what is seen in the mirror depends on the prior experience of the mother's face. If the experience of the mother is in tune with the infant, no false mirror image takes place. The mother's recognition constitutes the sense of self in the infant; the infant sees a reflection of itself in the mother's expression. For Winnicott this prelinguistic interactive phenomena or prelinguistic sociability is crucial, and language is just something added later to the infant's primary capacity for communication, a sophisticated giving of signals. These conceptions are quite different from those of Lacan. However, Winnicott's emphasis on the nursing couple brings up the questions, What are the analyst's desires from the patient? and, How is the analyst using the patient?, which parallel for the analyst Lacan's emphasis on the discovery by the patient of the patient's own true desires. In contrast to Lacan, Winnicott sees the analytic setting as a transitional space for collaborative exchange, that is to say, an intermediate area of experiencing, which again lends itself to phenomenological investigation.

PHENOMENOLOGY IN INFANT RESEARCH

In his self psychology–oriented review of infant research, Lichtenberg's (1983) description is remarkably similar to Hegel's (1807) *Phenomenology of Spirit*, although I doubt if this was his intent. As discussed in the previous chapter, Lichtenberg points out that for the first 18 months the phenomena are prelinguistic and beyond interpretation. When we work with the many patients who have been damaged during that developmental period, we are forced to reconstruct from the phenomenology of our relationship with the patient, which is primarily nonverbal or which involves the use of reinstinctualized verbal communication (Lowenstein 1972, Chessick 1977), what must have happened during that first year or two of life. This clinical "reconstruction" is a hermeneutic exegesis of the phenomena in the same manner as Heidegger's

(1962a) "existential analytic" in philosophy (Chapter 1 and Chessick 1990); at its base is phenomenology.

A similar approach is taken by Stern (1985) in his investigation and exegesis of the phenomena of the nursing couple. As described in the previous chapter, he says there is a sense of emergent self manifest from birth in the infant, since phenomenologically the infant is never autistic. From 2 to 6 months there is an observed sense of core relatedness and an apparent separation of the infant's notion of its own body from its notion of others. From 7 to 15 months Stern emphasizes the sense of subjective self, as he calls it, which actually develops out of the intersubjective exchange or affect attunement between the mother and the infant, probably the most vital psychological nutrient, and which can be dramatically observed by phenomenological study. It is only after 15 months that a verbal self appears; before that time there are no enduring specific intrapsychic representations. Stern claims these require the development of language. If this is correct, it turns the work of Lacan and Mahler upside down, for Stern maintains that the infant must have a sense of separate self *before* it enters the symbolic order.

Misattunement that occurs before the verbal stage leads directly to what clinically we call preoedipal pathology. No postulates of splitting of images or representations in the infant's psyche are necessary to understand this preoedipal pathology, which basically represents adult maladaptation grounded on the persistence of distorted archaic action–affect patterns and behavior resulting from the infant's attempt to express or avoid the unpleasure of improper tension regulation and experienced misattunement during crucial preverbal stages. Stern (1985) writes, "It is the actual shape of interpersonal reality, specified by the interpersonal in variants that really exist, that helps determine the developmental course. Coping operations occur as reality-based adaptations. Defensive operations of the type that distort reality occur only after symbolic thinking is available" (p. 255).

If this phenomenological study of the nursing couple is correct, then, as Lichtenberg (1987) puts it, "psychoanalytic theoreticians need to reconsider their views on two points: first, infants are capable of many functions not previously believed possible, and, second, infants are not capable of other functions previously assumed" (p. 315). It is surprising that there has not been a more widespread understanding of the radical challenge to classical object relations theory that is inherent in the phenomenological investigations of the nursing couple that are accumulating in the literature.

Therapists familiar with these studies are influenced to shift their clinical approach to adult treatment. For example, Lichtenberg (1987) presents an anecdote of an observed interaction between a mother–infant pair which produces in him what he calls an affective feel of the exchange and evokes "a linkage to my clinical experience." Although Lichtenberg works from a self psychological point of view, his language and descriptions are close to phenomenology. He concludes, "More careful observations will increase the sensitivity with which we discern patterns, especially patterns of affectively rich presymbolic interactions that may underlie the symbolically-represented intersubjectivity of the adult" (p. 328).

THE PHENOMENOLOGY OF MERLEAU-PONTY

Merleau-Ponty (1908–1961) argued that there is a stratum of collectively accepted meanings that preevaluates the world and always stands between the subject and "things," and that there is a body representation of these preevaluative stances. He (1962) suggested that a study of art and the artistic process would be very important in helping to understand our perceptual rapport with the world, a rapport that a science-oriented culture represses but that constitutes a prelinguistic understanding of the world.

Merleau-Ponty concludes from his version of phenomenology that mental activities presuppose a body-subject and that perception is the mode of existence of the body-subject at a preconscious level; it constitutes a dialogue with the world that is already presupposed by the conscious. A preconscious level exists on which the human organism confers meaning to the world and which actually constitutes the milieu as the individual experiences it. It is a lived dialectic between the body-subject and the world, rather than some kind of division between subject and object. The human from the very beginning is a being in the world. Notice how similar this is to Winnicott's nursing-couple conception of the infant. The term Merleau-Ponty (1962, p. 140) uses for a prelinguistic understanding by the body-subject of its world is "praktognosis" *(praktognosie)*. He points out that the child has a prereflective perception of its mother in the dialogue of their behaviors, a concept quite similar to Stern's notion of affect attunement.

Merleau-Ponty wishes to explore a territory that underlies and is presupposed by various adult activities that give rise to the dualistic "subject" and "object" expressions of ordinary language. The phenomenological method as employed by him in this context cannot simply take the form of a faithful description of the immediate data of consciousness, because it involves delving into the region of obscurity of a preconscious body stance. Even Merleau-Ponty admits that any complete illumination of this obscure field is unobtainable, a conception similar to what we have earlier described as beyond interpretation in psychoanalytic practice.

It is not necessary to go into Merleau-Ponty's unfinished metaphysics here; it is sufficient to point out that his use of phenomenology differed from that of Husserl and centers around his argument that the primacy of perception is the mode of access to the *real*, that by a phenomenological analysis of perception we can reach a sort of conceptual encounter with the real world. This is an obscure philosophy, but his basic point is that all attempts, scientific and otherwise, to conceptualize the world remain dependent for their sense on our primordial perceptual milieu, which always contains a fundamental ambiguity.

Each person comes to have his or her own embodied understanding of what counts as real. So the illumination that makes possible our conscious and intellectual or conceptual skills and our adult communication really rests on the earliest preverbal bodily skills and bodily stance that we take toward people and things, a concept similar to Gedo's (1988) description of archaic affect–action states and behaviors mentioned above. Dreyfus (1988) explains, "In Merleau-Ponty's ontological view, pathology occurs when a particular way a person relates to some people or some objects becomes a way of relating to all people and all objects, so that it becomes the form or style of all relationships" (p. 241). When this happens, the person's world becomes restricted and rigid and the person suffers from a lack of possibilities that he or she cannot understand and over which he or she has no control. I have discussed Merleau-Ponty's phenomenological breadth psychology in contrast to Freud's depth psychology in Chapter 3.

What is challenging to psychoanalytically oriented clinicians is that Merleau-Ponty is offering a version of the unconscious that does not have to postulate fixed intrapsychic structures and imagos in order to explain personality disorders. It is phenomenologically sufficient to delineate preconscious and potentially changing body-subject images or attitudes in constant dialectic with the world as underlying our conscious thought and behavior; at a deeper level Merleau-Ponty (1962) characterizes this as a repressed habitual setting, a "prepersonal cleaving" (p. 84) to a general form of the world. There is a certain affinity of his notion of the body stance to Shapiro's (1965) more cognitive work on neurotic styles, but Shapiro emphasizes "a configuration of innate psychological equipment" (p. 178) rather than the phenomenology of the emerging sense of self. Dreyfus (1988) offers the example of a patient who relates to each person as if the issue were always one of determining who is inferior and who is superior. Merleau-Ponty (1964a) would say that such an individual's sense of inferiority is sedimented into his posture and other body-sets that structure his world, so that he unthinkingly responds in a similar way to each new situation. Here archaic affect states and behavior patterns are stated in a phenomenological way. Based on this approach Dreyfus recommends that in psychotherapy the patient must piece together an account of how his or her narrow version of reality developed through a series of accidental events and misunderstandings, and so the patient comes to realize that what he or she takes to be "destiny" is not objective reality but an arbitrary interpretation.

Merleau-Ponty (1968) moves farther away from the usual use of phenomenology by also postulating what he calls a paradigmatic object, which has the effect of reorganizing the background in which all contents appear. Often such a paradigmatic object or "emblem" (p. 270) may focus a person's world by closing it down, which sets the patient on the road to psychopathology.

This is based on Heidegger's notion that a culture's shared practices, embedded in tools, language, and institutions, produces a *clearing* in which entities can then show up for us. It represents an acquired context, which opens and limits what things show up *as*. Merleau-Ponty has compared this clearing with the illumination in a room, which allows us to perceive objects but is not itself an object. This illumination, according to Merleau-Ponty, correlates with our body skills and the stance that our body takes towards people and things, and thus he calls it "an embodied understanding." When the way a person relates to some people and some objects becomes a way of relating to all people and all objects, then this stance becomes the clearing itself. This phenomenon occurs due to what Merleau-Ponty calls "generalization," for example, a jealous style that produces a restricted rigid clearing.

In therapy, parallel to what Winnicott recommended as management for preoedipal disorders, the patient must be shown that he or she did not always view things that way, and through the experience with the therapist, the patient must be shown that such a view does not fit and that the patient is reacting inappropriately. This leads to reconstruction, which attempts to show how the patient came to think this arbitrary way, a process that may be called a genealogy of the patient's world. One then focuses on marginal other stances that the patient still possesses and may serve as a positive paradigm for the patient. This has a certain parallel to Heidegger's philosophy and contains no depth-psychological causal theory and no assumptions about intrapsychic functioning components of the personality. It may be called a phenomenological investigation and an experiential repair of archaic distortions.

MERLEAU-PONTY AND SARTRE CONTRASTED

For Merleau-Ponty the child is already situated in an intersubjective cultural world and from infancy develops habitual modes of relating to its human world through bodily powers. It is in and through such prereflective interaction that the child gradually develops a concept of subjectivity. Others and the cultural world become part of the body image and are understood prior to any conscious reflection. For Merleau-Ponty it is the phenomenal body-self that comprehends, appropriates and precipitates the world into its dynamics; in the normal individual there is a continual preconscious dialectic between the body-self or body image, and experienced reality. Langer (1989) contrasts this to Sartre's (1973b) phenomenological description of our relations with others. Sartre's view is based on the experience of conflict leading to our consciousness of others, whereas for Merleau-Ponty the experience of conflict is derivative while that of community, the nursing couple, has ontological priority and reveals an essential dimension of our real existence.

For Merleau-Ponty the body itself or our self- (body-subject) representation already outlines the fundamental features of the world, and there is an internal relationship between the body and the world out of which all meaning emerges through the process of a dialectic beginning with the nursing couple. We are a network of relationships, and from infancy we dialectically receive a particular style that becomes embedded in our body image and body stance, a prereflective bond with others. This contrasts sharply with Sartre's concept of the fundamental alienation of each individual. Merleau-Ponty argues that prior to any rejection of other people, our bodily being or body-subject establishes a prepersonal unity with them; without that unity selfhood cannot develop at all. Therefore when we study the preoedipal disorders we need to look at what has gone wrong in that prepersonal unity that constitutes the ground out of which a sense of self emerges.

This contrast between Merleau-Ponty and Sartre has a parallel in psychoanalysis, in the attitudes of Winnicott and Kohut on the one hand and the Kleinians on the other. The former group of psychoanalysts view life beginning as a mutually enhancing nursing couple, a prereflective unity of mother and infant, whereas the latter group views life beginning as a war in which the infant has to deal with its innate self-destruction by projecting outward and developing the paranoid-schizoid position with its accompanying sense of alienation and fear. Merleau-Ponty, like Kohut, would say that the processes described by Klein are secondary to an archaic failure in the prereflective unity of the nursing couple, and represent an attempt by the infant to deal with the rage and disappointment of such a failure, with its fundamental calamitous effect on the self and body image.

Sense and Non-Sense (1964b), a book of articles that introduce Merleau-Ponty's thought, focuses on how to understand the emergence of sense from nonsense, another way of looking at the phenomenological investigation of the emerging sense of self. Merleau-Ponty claims this form of investigation was started by Hegel, who attempted to explore the irrational and integrate it into an expanded reason. In another publication, "The Child's Relations with Others,"

Merleau-Ponty (1964a) attempts to compare his work with that of Lacan, especially with regard to the mirror stage. His basic contention in these publications is that we make sense out of our experience from within it, and all of our rational concepts grow out of perception and therefore reflect the irreducible contingency of perception. There is no such thing as absolute knowledge and no guarantee that, as Hegel and Marx thought, order will ultimately be achieved in history. No aspect of culture or personality can be understood in isolation. There is a continuing and unending dialectical relationship between the human and the world in which the human exists, which begins at birth and continues until death.

PREOEDIPAL PATHOLOGY

The phenomenological approach is exceptionally suitable to an understanding of the preoedipal disorders generated during the prelinguistic period of life, as already recognized by such psychoanalytic pioneers as Federn and Winnicott. Working from the background of German philosophy, Merleau-Ponty arrived at a philosophical position which, although vague and obscure, has a remarkable parallel to recent psychoanalytic work. This lies in his emphasis on the primacy of perception and the inseparability of the body and the conscious mind, enhancing our understanding of archaic affectual states and of behavior due to a misattunement of the early nursing couple, as well as of the development of maladaptive preoedipal behavior patterns that bring the patient into treatment as an adult. There is a remarkable overlap of descriptions of the ground of our experience using the phenomenological method in both psychiatry and philosophy, a fertile field for further study.

The phenomenology of Merleau-Ponty becomes clear in his distinction between the body as object and the body as subject. We study the body purely as an object in general medical practice. However, the objective body is not the truth of the phenomenal body, the truth of the body as we live it. It is only an impoverished image and has only a conceptual existence, in contrast to the phenomenal body, which is the body as lived and experienced, the body-subject. As Merleau-Ponty (1962) puts it, "This past which remains our true present does not leave us but remains constantly hidden behind our gaze instead of being displayed before it" (p. 83). The reason for this is found in Merleau-Ponty's conception of the body as comprising two distinct layers—the "habitual body" and the "present body." The habitual body signifies the body as it has been lived in the past, in virtue of which it has acquired certain habitual ways of relating to the world and thus already projects a habitual setting around itself and outlines, prior to all reflection, those objects that it "expects" to encounter. In this form of intentionality it already lays down the general form of a future that it antici- pates. So the present is always haunted by the past and shaped by the past, as well as by expectations of the future, as first emphasized by Heidegger (1962a).

The example Merleau-Ponty uses of this is the familiar phenomenon of the "phantom limb." In that phenomenon, as in many instances of preoedipal psychopathology also, there is a body image that involves a primordial prereflective orientation and motility, one's awareness of where one's limbs are as one's body projects itself toward the world of its tasks. This body image has a crucial effect on future experiences, for it carries with it an intentionality or expectation of what will be encountered; thus it determines one's entire way of being in the world. In this sense Merleau-Ponty speaks of the body as "an expressive space" that subtends our entire existence as human beings. There is no pure contemplative conscious or "psyche" in a thinglike body. As Merleau- Ponty (Kockelmans 1967) concludes:

The philosopher . . . is a perpetual beginner. This means that he holds nothing as established which the popular majority or the scientists believe they know. It also means that philosophy cannot consider itself as definitively established in any of the truths which it can utter, that it is a renewed experience of its own beginning, and that it consists entirely of a description of this beginning. It means, finally, that this radical reflection is consciousness of its own depen- dence upon a nonreflective life which is its initial, constant and final situation. [p. 346]

11

EPILOGUE

$\mathbf{G}$REENBERG AND MITCHELL (1983) explain that "only by analysis of an analyst's vision of human experience can his theoretical position be accurately assessed" (p. 348). This is consistent with the views of Heidegger and of Jaspers that each major thinker (and each of us) embodies a basic vision of human experience and reality in his or her work. Ricoeur, using hermeneutics, as we saw in Chapter 4, attempted to ferret out Freud's "unthematized teleology." Here I will briefly focus on Freud's notion of the death instinct and its use and misuse by subsequent thinkers, and then discuss the future of the human insofar as he or she is constituted by the culture or by "instincts."

THE DEATH INSTINCT

In *Beyond the Pleasure Principle*, Freud (1920) attempted to demonstrate the great primacy of the "drive" toward death or return to inorganic matter, and he characterized the life "instincts" only as somehow fighting a delaying or holding action while all organic matter—the individual and the species—speeds on towards its own destruction. In his later writing, and without argument or explanation, Freud gave a more equivalent status to the life and death instincts, but this was a gratuitous change and was not supported by any arguments or clinical evidence (Chessick 1980a). In his original formulation he made it clear that the dominant force in biological organisms has to be the death instinct (Meissner 1985). Elsewhere I (1992) have explored the ambiguity in Freud's developing concept of the death instinct and attempted to retrieve what he was struggling to articulate.

Melanie Klein (Grosskurth 1986) recognized the full consequences of Freud's theory. If Freud is correct, a person's greatest and most serious problem is in having to deal with the "death instinct," which begins operation from the moment of conception of life. She concluded, in an unfortunately applied version of Freud's speculative concept, that from birth the powerful innate self-directed aggressive drives of a person posed the fundamental obstacle to life. She took seriously Freud's theory that with the individual, as with the species, there is a brief flicker of life and then ultimately extinction and destruction as the death instinct prevails and all organic matter returns to the inorganic form. Gedo (1986) points out that her view reflects a "deep pessimism about the human condition" (p. 85) and fails because it involves a concretization of Freud's metaphysical forces, representing a return to the outmoded "doctrine of vitalism" (p. 98) in biology.

Certain humanistic disciplines, including a lot of traditional philosophy and theology, can be understood as an effort to disavow, deny, or transcend in one way or another this "being-towards-death" direction of human life both in the individual and in the species. The overwhelming difficulty in struggling with such a powerful trend generates the consistent historical pattern of never-ending dissatisfaction with one philosophy after another as it gains ascendancy and is then discarded and replaced by the next. The same phenomenon sometimes occurs in the history of religion. The reason for this is that as time passes, no philosophy and no religion can withstand careful critical analysis that eventually demonstrates it to be based on uncertain assumptions or "illusions" or "revelations," and in that sense, as Nietzsche pointed out, each represents an unconscious attempt to deny the truth of our existential dilemma. So Nietzsche (Chessick 1983a) wrote, founding the postmodern era, that behind every philosophy there is a hidden philosophy. Religions solve this problem by requiring faith in their revelations as their foundation, but since the Middle Ages philosophers on the whole have tried to avoid postulating their systems on faith or divine revelation, appealing instead to so-called self-evident premises—which Freud suspected as based on infantile wishes and disavowed hopes.

The same career is marked by psychoanalysis, as a variety of alterations have been attempted by depth psychologists desiring to escape from Freud's rather pessimistic view of humans. Central to Freud's later metapsychology is the postulated power of aggression either as a basic drive or, as he finally thought of it, as representing the force of the death instinct. A study of Freud reveals—in contrast to what his critics have claimed—that he was telling the truth when he insisted that his famous pessimism about humans was the consequence and not the cause of the formation of his psychoanalytic theories (see Kohut 1978).

In *Civilization and Its Discontents* (1930), better translated as "The Uneasiness Inherent in Culture," Freud wrote, "the evolution of civilization may therefore be simply described as the struggle for the life of the human species" (p. 122). He concluded already in 1930:

> The fateful question for the human species seems to me to be whether and to what extent their cultural development will succeed in mastering the disturbance of their communal life by the human instinct of aggression and self-destruction. It may be that in this respect precisely the present time deserves a special interest. Men have gained control over the forces of nature to such an extent that with their help they would have no difficulty in exterminating one another to the last man. They know this, and hence comes a large part of their current unrest, their unhappiness and their mood of anxiety. [p. 145]

Eissler (1971, 1975) defends Freud's notion of the death instinct. No better theory has been devised that fits so well with the rest of Freud's discoveries and theories; to reject it leaves an impossible paradox in psychoanalytic metapsychology, as Freud (1920) himself pointed out. The death instinct theory, says Kohut (1984), "cannot be removed from the magnificent edifice of Freud's theoretical system without seriously changing its cohesion and internal consistency" (pp. 35–36). This is true regardless of the fact that Freud, over his long and productive life, shifted his notion of "instinct" from a more simply biological reflex-arc or tension-discharge model to an almost Bergsonian metaphysical force model. This shift has produced a mass of secondary literature from several disciplines on the subject, but little light and much speculation.

Rapaport (1967) explains that "the historical links between the problems of narcissism, masochism, the instinctual vicissitude of 'turning round upon the self', the self and identity, the death instinct, the aggressive drive, instinctual drive-fusion and defusion, the superego's turning upon the self, and the energies of the superego form a Gordian knot" (p. 707). Gedo (1979) more recently has maintained that in discarding the death instinct, "psychoanalysts have failed to offer an alternative that could fill its previous role within the metapsychological realm. No concept now performs the basis for the phenomena attributable to the repetition compulsion" (p. 249).

HUMAN AGGRESSION

In most of modern civilization, children in their education and social milieu are deprived of the two known traditional cultural counterforces to human lust and aggression: some sort of parentally and pedagogically inculcated and culturally reinforced humanistic attitude toward all people, and those sincere religious faiths stressing reverence for life. Freud (1921) wrote, "Even those who do not regret the disappearance of religious illusions from the civilized world of today will admit that so long as they were in force they offered those who were bound by them the most powerful protection against the danger of neurosis" (p. 142).

Current education for many reasons tends to deemphasize the study of the western classics and classical languages, and even if it did not, only a small percentage of students show any aptitude in that direction. Many American students enter college barely able to read and write, and are utterly bewildered by the ideas in the "great books," as Bloom (1987) has trenchantly pointed out. It is extremely difficult for parents to inculcate their children with religious faith in the manner of days gone by because few adults in our culture today believe that the details and day-to-day regulations of their religion have any validity; they regressively reach for religion only in times of acute crises. Most of the time most people live as if religion had no meaning for them at all. Although a small number of deeply religious countries still try to persist, even they are disrupted by sects and schisms and by interminable, irrational, acrimonious battles between orthodoxy and reform.

Wallace (1986), reviewing Freud's *Civilization and Its Discontents*, described five sources of the aggressiveness of the enculturated person's superego. These are (1) an identification with an actually aggressive parent; (2) the person's own aggression, projected onto the parent and then reinternalized; (3) aggression bottled up because of the injunction of external authority against it; (4) aggression released as a result of the defusion process occurring during identification; and (5) aggression due to frustration by authority figures, imposing instinctual deprivation. Wallace concludes, "Freud's thesis that man's aggression is an 'original and self-subsisting disposition', his diagnosis of the problematic nature of culture's means of controlling it, and his suggestion that groups maintain their cohesion in part by externalizing their aggression toward out-groups and neighboring societies do not bode well for the future" (p. 115).

It is possible to argue, as does Jaffe (1982), that Freud's view of the death instinct is wrong, and that aggression has a constructive component. The trouble with such arguments is that they are unsupported by clinical experience, significantly deviate from the main half-century thrust of Freud's entire metapsychology, and are contradicted again and again by historical experience. Nowhere is this more beautifully illustrated than in Thurber's (1956) little story *The Peacelike Mongoose*. When, in cobra country, a mongoose is born who does not want to fight cobras or anything else, he is reminded that it is the "duty of every mongoose to kill cobras or be killed by cobras." "Why?" asks the peacelike mongoose, and he is immediately labeled crazy, sick, a coward, and a mongoosexual. When he replies that he is trying to use reason and intelligence, he is accused of being a traitor and is exiled.

LACAN'S CONCEPT OF THE ORIGIN OF AGGRESSION

The Lacanians have given a fundamental signification to the death instinct, a signification directly connected with the subjective incoherence they consider specific to the child before its entry into language. For them "primordial signifiers" conceal the surfacing of the void they call the death instinct, establish desire, and give the subject his or her organic and psychical coherence. For Lacan (1977), in *Ecrits*, 16, what is primordial to the birth of symbols is death. The Lacanian analyst Leclaire (Lemaire 1981, p. 167) labels the death instinct an "ecstatic void" around which the subject gravitates. For Lacanians "the antinomy of the one" refers to the subject when he or she has been able to maintain a (false) "I" in consciousness with the help of some "letter," a term defined loosely by Lacanians as the structure of language. I will try to explain this in the following discussion.

As described in Chapter 5, for Lacan the entrance into the symbolic order, the social and cultural constituting of humans, has the effect of alienating the human from what Lacan considers to universally be the human's true fragmented subjectivity. It is here, as mentioned in Chapter 5, that the origin of human aggression is to be sought. Lemaire (1981) explains, "Obliged to fashion himself with reference to and in rivalry with the other, obliged to wait for recognition from or judgment by the other, man is naturally inclined to a whole range of aggressive behaviour, from envy, morbid jealousy and real aggression to mortal negation of self or other" (p. 181).

For Lacanians aggression and the death instinct are removed from Freud's biological substrate and arise from the human developmental process of becoming, which begins already in "the mirror stage" as a narcissistic identification with one's mirror image. This identification alienates the person from his or her true fragmented subjectivity by adopting a false whole-self representation of the "I" seen in the mirror double. For Lacan, therefore, the alienation of the ego or "I" in the mirror stage always has as its corollary the sacrifice of the "truth" of ourselves. The inevitably progressive discordance between the false ego and the true chaotic being of the subject has destruction as its corollary. In this sense humans devote themselves to their own death, consummating this death in the very movement whereby they seek to assert themselves in the social and cultural world, a path forced by the symbolic and cultural order on the developing child. Even before birth, claims Lacan, the human individual is caught up in and completely assimilated into a causal chain of which he or she can never be any more than an effect.

Therefore the history of the subject, who, Lacan claims, is inevitably decentered from himself or herself, is an endless Hegelian dialectic of the vain search for the self. The person must "struggle against his fellow in his search for a position of strength and prestige, he must appear one thing or another under the right-minded gaze of the other, and he must therefore mask his truest and innermost tendencies in order to be answerable to a universal morality" (Lemaire 1981, p. 183).

TRILLING'S OPPOSITION TO THE POSTMODERN APPROACH

Trilling (1955), in an approach opposite to that of Lacan, made a heroic attempt to use Freud's consistent adherence to biology and natural science investigation as a "bedrock" or "fixed point" from which any person or culture could be criticized. He hoped this would serve as an antidote to those even in his day (before Derrida, Lacan, and Foucault were known in America) who viewed the self as decentered, false, and entirely formed by culture. He (1965) foresaw, before Kohut, that the crucial issue of our time in both psychoanalysis and literature would be the problem of the self: "And there is no reality about which the modern person is more uncertain and more anxious than the reality of himself" (1965, p. 41). In contrast to the radical use of Freud's concept of the life and death instincts by authors such as Marcuse (1955) and Brown (1959), Trilling emphasized the biological and conservative nature of Freud's notion of the death instinct, pointing out, as Krupnick (1986) explains, "All that the organism wants is to be beyond wanting" (p. 123).

Trilling's solution also took Freud himself as a moral ideal, stressing his fierceness, boldness, honesty, and independence, as well as his sense of tragedy and stoical resistance, viewing both the preservation of civilization against the breakdown of modern culture and the death instinct as a value-based challenge: "Like Nietzsche, Freud thought that life was justified by our heroic response to its challenge" (1965, p. 21). As our culture became more and more heterogeneous and resistant to reductionistic interpretation, Trilling retreated to essays of high generality and an abstract concept of the self, and wore himself out in struggling with these problems (see Kupnick 1986).

KOHUT'S CONCEPT OF AGGRESSION

We reviewed in Chapter 9 how Kohut brought the problem of the self to the center of his psychology and offered a meticulous study of it, which led some to a new orientation in his discipline. His differentiation between "Guilty Man," caught up in the conflict between drives and defenses, and "Tragic Man," preoccupied, like Trilling, with problems of the search for a self, pointed the way to his criticism of the traditional but now obsolete value systems of our culture, values that stress independence and private autonomy rather than empathy with others and joy in living. Kohut also noted the shift in our culture that Trilling (1971) had already described and deplored, from sincerity based on shared moral values, to preoccupation with an "I want" so-called authenticity. Kohut (1982) explained this shift as a consequence of the modern incipiently fragmenting self suffering since infancy from a lack of mirroring and idealizing selfobjects.

Kohut, along with many others, criticized the confusing mixture of biology and psychology in Freud's notion of the death instinct. In Kohut's thinking, as we saw in Chapter 9, aggression is a byproduct of the failure of empathy from others, and chronic narcissistic rage—which leads to the most dangerous form of indiscriminate and terrorist destruction—arises from an increasing dearth of empathic bonding among all members of the human species. Heidegger (1962a) similarly proclaimed that when humans "devote themselves to the same affair in common, their doing so is determined by the manner in which their *Dasein*, each in its own way, has been taken hold of. They thus become *authentically* bound together" (p. 159); but Heidegger's approach is entirely different than the humanism of Trilling or the self psychology of Kohut.

Rage and destructive aggression are not, says Kohut (1977), from a "primary given—an 'original sin' requiring expiation, a bestial drive that has to be 'tamed' " (p. 124), as held by the Kleinian school, but such a "drive" appears as a disintegration product when joyful assertiveness fails to bring an empathic parental response. Basch (1985) maintains that Lichtenberg's (1983) careful current review of infant studies (discussed in previous chapters) supports Kohut's view.

Kohut is more hopeful about the reduction of aggression, since he does not view it as the product of a basic fixed drive. At the same time he emphasizes the great difficulty in changing human value systems. This is because such ideals as insular nationalism, jingoistic patriotism, and the whole American wild west or "Rambo" adolescent mentality that pervades each national body politic in the world become invested with all the imagined perfection of the parents from whom we obtained them. Whenever such values are challenged, the reaction is rage as if one's cherished parents were insulted—narcissistic rage—as illustrated in Thurber's story. As Nietzsche pointed out, values that at one time were adaptive tend to become rigid and maladaptive, but remain guarded like a precious flag: "My country, right or wrong." Thus Nietzsche called for a revaluation of all values. Instinct or no instinct, the problem of controlling aggression is an extremely difficult one, regardless of how humans are constituted.

Hamburg (1991) compares Kohut and Lacan, emphasizing Lacan's contempt "for the empathic, sustaining, two-person function of the analyst" (p. 351). Hamburg argues that self psychology "subtly devalues" (p. 353) vast regions of human experience, especially "disconnexion, disharmony, disruption, desire, aggression, hatred and schism" (p. 353). He regards Kohut's contention that aggression is not a fundamental human attribute as "something that must astound most survivors of the twentieth century" (p. 354) and he concludes that "the cocoon concept of the whole self embedded in its fabric of selfobjects left out a harsh world, both exterior and interior, and promised a fullness of being that has little resemblance to the prevailing chronicles, even the most optimistic ones, of life in our times" (p. 354).

THE ERASURE OF HUMANS

It is certainly feasible that the twenty-first century will mark the end of the human species, since the effectiveness of weapons of destruction has reached a point where only a very small trigger is necessary to quickly wipe out the world's population. Because there are no effective instinctual checks on human aggression as there are in the wolf, for example, and there are no effective rational, humanistic, or religious checks, there is no compelling reason to believe that human aggression will be checked. On the contrary, there is an evident worldwide trend toward increasingly isolated and fanatical religious and cultural ethnocentrism and away from empathic feelings for the human community as a whole and for the planet that is our common home.

Time is running out. Schell (1982) presents an apocalyptic vision of impending nuclear war and offers a typical humane idealistic solution, suggesting that humans will have to become rational animals and transcend their own history; they will have to develop respect for human life, respect for the earth, and respect for God, Nature, or Being. These are wonderful values, but how can they be attained? Or, as Ricoeur (1983) eloquently puts it, "we must protect the ecosystem to which history belongs" (p. 31). This is what Keys (1982, p. 119) calls "eco-consciousness," a reverence for life, simplified living—traveling through life lightly and joyfully, unburdened by material possessions. But such a great transformation of values, following Heidegger in viewing the earth as our fragile, precious dwelling place, will require a spectacular reorientation that is nowhere in evidence today.

With Nietzsche and Freud melioristic idealism in philosophy, humanities, and psychology comes to an end. Just as Nietzsche predicted that human barbarism would soon break out of the false veneer of hypocritical bourgeois Victorian morality, and that the twentieth century would tear the world of the nineteenth century to pieces, we can now predict on the same grounds, and with almost another hundred years of experience, that this trend will continue into the next century and threaten the end of the human species. In the nineteenth century, as Nietzsche put it, our anthropomorphic God died, and in the twenty-first century there are good reasons to believe that barbarous humanity will also die. It is clear that the only way this definitely would not take place would be through the profound change Einstein hoped for in the minds and hearts of humans, and this change can only take place through an unforeseen miracle.

Therefore it is at least not unreasonable for Heidegger (Sheehan 1981) to have insisted that the next move in the history of humankind is up to a god. The only ray of hope that logical or historical analysis of this problem affords us arises when we remember that the explosion of science in the twentieth century is beyond anything anyone in the nineteenth century could imagine – and it is still continuing, for example, in the areas of genetic engineering, microchip technology, and artificial intelligence. Therefore it is possible that in the twenty-first century some unforeseen explosion of our knowledge will occur that will enable us in some unimaginable way to alter our basic psychology, a task perhaps requiring some sort of genetic or spiritual changes in the entire world's population. Total worldwide alteration of the human species would offer definitive hope of saving the species from extinction, but there is little evidence now to believe this will be possible in time.

As Caputo (1985) explains, Nietzsche, Heidegger, and Derrida are "ultimately united by an experience of the abyss: of what is variously called by Nietzsche, the tragic, by Heidegger, *das Nichts*, and by Derrida, the *ébranler*, the trembling" (p. 74). In the face of this "irreversible going under," Nietzsche advocates a capacity for suffering and for "laughter which is the measure of the genuine strength of the spirit"; Heidegger speaks of "the need for openness to the mystery of withdrawal," and Derrida insists upon "a vigilance" in order to "remain alert to the self-induced illusions of presence" (p. 74). Caputo argues that for Nietzsche and Derrida the "metaphorics of dance and celebration, of Dionysian play, prevails" whereas for Heidegger, "a metaphorics of quiet calm, meditative stillness, silence and mystery" (p. 76) are offered. Sheehan (1979) adds that Heidegger's "deconstruction of the Western tradition requires a violent reconstruction of the meaning of man's essence no longer as the 'subject' which the West has taken man to be . . . but as temporal and historical self-transcendence and becoming, as 'self-exceeding' in the communally held world of purpose and action, language and work" (p. 184).

SOLUTIONS

One need not conclude from this, as Heidegger did, that there is nothing to do but sit and wait: "*Wir sollen nichts tun sondern warten*" (Richardson 1974, p. 641n). As species-beings, if we follow Feuerbach (see Introduction), we owe it to each other and to our children to keep working to bring about this change in the minds and hearts of humans in every way we can. Physicians, especially psychiatrists, as well as all mental health professionals, have a special obligation to participate in this work actively and personally, since clearly preservation of humanity and the earth on which we dwell is to be the central public health problem of the coming century. Who can tell how and through what agency a miracle might be produced? Who could predict in the darkest days of the Roman empire that Christianity would spread like wildfire and completely transform the western world? Who dared to guess in the historical nadir of the tenth century that humanity had any future? Matthew Arnold (Super 1981, vol. V) wrote: "Culture looks beyond machinery, culture hates hatred; culture has one great passion, the passion for sweetness and light. It has one even yet greater! the passion for making them *prevail*" (p. 112).

The critical survival problem of our dark time, as Kohut (1978) emphasized, requires all the academic disciplines to cooperate in helping us to attain a greater control over our historical destiny. Our university departments must develop a common empathic matrix aimed towards the solution of this problem; the isolating effects of the "tool and method pride" that predominates in each academic discipline must be overcome.

The authors discussed in this book approach survival by extolling the notion of *praxis*, in which philosophical and psychological theories, and the actions based on their consequences, form a mutually corrective interrelated feedback system. See, for example, Sartre's concept of dialectical reason, discussed in Chapter 6. The psychological model of such a system is Freud's psychoanalysis, in which metapsychological theory was formed and re-formed as a consequence of clinical experience; new theories in psychoanalysis lead to different attitudes and interactions with patients that result in different clinical data and, in turn, the correction of theories.

Merleau-Ponty (Descombes 1980) explains, "What Marx calls *praxis* is the meaning which appears spontaneously at the intersection of the actions by which man organises his relationship with nature and with others" (p. 17). In this way writing becomes a "signifying practice" and philosophy a "theoretical practice." So for Althusser (1971), "Philosophy is a *practice* of political *intervention* carried out in a theoretical form" (p. 107). Whether we like it or not, the same is true for intensive psychotherapy. As in psychoanalysis, philosophical theories become ways of organizing our experience and the experiential consequences of these theories suggest new ways of organization; hence we develop new and corrected philosophical theories. This brings philosophy and psychology back to the center of human living where they belong, and focuses the best brains of the world on the problems of modern humanity, which are so crucial and pressing. There is no intrinsic reason to be pessimistic about where this modified dialectic can lead; in psychoanalysis, as we have seen in this book, it has indeed led to more and more effective techniques of treatment and problem solving, and to an ever-widening scope of application to patients.

Loewald (1980) points out the similarity between Nietzsche's and Freud's view of civilization, that it is a product of internalization or turning inward of human aggressiveness. But this internalized struggle, this inner conflict, is not necessarily a bad development. Utilizing Hartmann's concept of change of function, for Loewald it "becomes a hallmark, valued in itself, of human nature" (p. 318). In general, as Rieff (Bloom 1985) explains, Freud, in viewing pleasure as the basic motivation of humans, seldom elevates—he digs at the foundations, and his basic doctrine is resignation to reality. For example, Freud (1932) considers war "scarcely avoidable" and ironically (?) suggests that perhaps we should adapt ourselves to it, although he admits that we rebel against it because "we cannot help doing so—" but he does not explain or follow the implications of that comment. Similarly, in *Civilization and Its Discontents* (1930) he argues against the utopian Marxists that no social action or form of society could guarantee a happy life, owing to the irrational cruelty of the superego inevitable in members of civilization.

Thus a curious and unexpected parallel occurs in the later thinking of Freud and Heidegger; both imply a certain resignation, a sense of hopelessness about the role of people's active efforts to basically improve the status of civilized life. This may constitute a pernicious and dangerous attitude. Zimmerman (1981) writes, "Against Marx, Heidegger denies the efficacy of human *praxis* in bringing about the fully human world" (p. 252). Should we then have "adapted" to slavery, the oppression of women, and gladiatorial contests, and not have bothered to fashion the world's first democratic form of government on a large scale?

Dreyfus (1980) tries to rescue some hope from Heidegger's theories, insisting that he "holds open the possibility that there still exists in our microactices an undercurrent of a pretechnological understanding of the meaning of Being, presumably once focused in the Greek Temple" (p. 22). Heidegger (1975b) points out that we should strengthen these practices and extols the artist as especially devoted to preserving them. This argument has a curious resemblance to Arnold's (Trilling 1949) point in "Culture and Anarchy": "What if our urgent want now is, not to act at any price, but rather to lay in a stock of light for our difficulties?" (p. 502). But Dreyfus (1980) admits that Heidegger claims there is nothing we can do to produce the emergence from our age of technicity into a new focus based on these micropractices; the hope is in that they do exist and form the potential of a new paradigm. Their existence cannot be proved by philosophical arguments, explains Dreyfus, but "only their existence and continued efficacy would account for our otherwise mysterious preference for anything rather than the disciplinary technological society" (p. 22). This illuminates Freud's comment quoted above that we rebel against war because "we cannot help doing so."

THE IMPORTANCE OF PRAXIS

Perhaps the problem is between those hoping to produce a utopia in one miraculous stroke (surely Heidegger is correct that only a god can do that) and those who advocate the value of smaller but significant changes, what Heidegger might label ontic changes. For example, it is reasonable to hope that by *praxis* the next step up the ladder will be the forced attention of the rich and privileged few in this world to the masses of poor, homeless, and starving, those whom the psychoanalyst Fanon (1963) called "the wretched of the earth," discussed in Chapter 6. How many psychiatric residents or student mental health professionals are asked to study his work? Yet whether peacefully or by violence, whether with the churches' approval of "liberation theology" or without it, whether the psychoanalytic goal of adaptation agrees with it or not, this revolutionary change is surely welling up in the "third world," and among the underprivileged and ignored people of the so-called advanced societies. No professional, as Foucault said, can be "apolitical" any more, since those who do not actively fight oppression, injustice, and all the evils of current society are, by their passivity, allowing these evils to persist, which expresses a value system. And our patients soon become aware of our values, whether we like it or not.

Heidegger's claim that this is all still within the realm of the age of technicity is true, but there is much that humans can do, even while trapped in that realm and waiting for a miracle, that will significantly improve the human condition. As Schur (1966) points out, appeal to the "death instinct" provides an easy out when a psychoanalysis fails; similarly, it can be used as an excuse for resignation and failure to act to improve the human condition.

A further argument could be made that the very essence of Eros is the fight against the death instinct, and that refusal to fight, refusal of energetic *praxis* for the betterment of the human lot, represents a neurosis of a little discussed type because it is culturally sanctioned in the narcissistic society in which we are immersed, where success comes to those who "fit in" and who "don't make waves." Is this mental health? Can a therapist be empathic with his or her patients and yet not respond empathically with action to the plight of the "wretched of the earth?" What about those psychoanalysts who, as Kohut (1984) puts it, refuse to let their sleep be disturbed by the possibility of an impending nuclear winter and who confine their concerns to their patients and perhaps their loved ones—are these to be our models, our training analysts, or is this a subtle form of unanalyzed narcissism?

The shadow of the Holocaust falls inexorably across all psychology and philosophy in this century. Even the father of deconstruction, Derrida, holds back from speaking directly about it. Megill (1985) explains, "For Derrida it is the Holocaust, both in its immediate and in an extended, metaphorical sense, that is the most striking manifestation of the horror that he sees lurking within modern history. . . . In this he accords with those modern critics who have seen it as an event so terrible that it exhausts the powers of language" (p. 317). Even Lacan, that master of language, would blanch on reading Gilbert's (1986) description of the Holocaust; Foucault (1973b) would identify the "testimonies" carried in Gilbert's book as the prototypical "serious discourse" of the era of the end of civilization. How many psychiatric residents or student mental health professionals have studied this? How many realize that a similar horror is being carried out today against the peaceful Baha'i community in Iran? What about the Chinese unarmed students? Or whole segments of the Cambodian population? Or the Kurds in Iraq? Should we sleep well?

Historians and psychoanalysts have been exasperatingly slow in attempting to make connections between regressive tendencies in the human psyche and the horrors of the century in which they have lived. Jacoby (1983) describes how that minority of European psychoanalysts who had a strong social conscience were forced to conform and communicate underground with each other internationally by a sort of *samizdat* because they needed to survive in their host countries as refugees. These "political Freudians" had to avoid the label of rebels and radicals if they wished to practice at all. At almost 50 years of age one of the best known of the psychoanalysts, Otto Fenichel, who had not studied general medicine for many years, was required to undertake an arduous one-year full-time internship in order to become licensed to practice in California. He died within 6 months of starting the internship. Jacoby writes, "He was working rotating night shifts as an intern. He complained frequently of fatigue; and he hoped to transfer to a hospital where night duty was not required. He was also overweight, and very much unlike himself, he expressed doubts about his command of medical knowledge. A visitor recalled him somewhat tragically: an older German-Jewish intellectual in a tight ill-fitting white uniform" (p. 132). He died of a stroke just after his 48th birthday, a death raising important questions about this requirement for "medicalization" that threatens to overwhelm the entire field of contemporary psychiatry.

Franz Alexander worried a great deal about social matters. About 3 months before he died, he pointed out that one of the most remarkable qualities of psychoanalytic treatment was in its capacity to give a contemporary meaning to the motto of the Renaissance humanists: "Respect for the dignity of the individual." Alexander (1964) wrote:

> Psychotherapy aims not only at enabling a person to adjust himself to existing conditions, but also to realize his unique potentials. Never was this aim more difficult and at the same time more essential. Psychoanalysis and psychotherapy in general are among the few still existing remedies against the relentlessly progressing levelization of industrial societies which tend to reduce the individual person to becoming an indistinguishable member of the faceless masses. [p. 243]

There must always be room in psychiatry for psychoanalysis, which represents, as Rangell (1988) maintains, "the last stronghold of the interior of the individual, the ultimate respecter of the privacy of the self" (p. 337).

CAN HUMAN AGGRESSION BE "TAMED"?

The challenge that faces us today was, as one might expect, already outlined by Freud. In "The Economic Problem of Masochism" (1924) he discusses the concept of the taming (Bändigung) of one instinct by another—the action by which the libido can make the death instinct innocuous. In "Analysis Terminable and Interminable" (1937) he explains this concept: "The instinct is brought completely into the harmony of the ego, becomes accessible to all the influences of the other trends in the ego and no longer seeks to go its independent way to satisfaction. If we are asked by what methods and means this result is achieved, it is not easy to find an answer" (p. 225). This is supported by the work of Parin and Morgenthaler (1972), who argue on the basis of a study of the Dogin and Agni tribes in West Africa that the ego, molded under the influence of specific cultural influences, ultimately determines the way in which destructive aggression is managed. Thus the Western ego, based on repression and internalization of aggressive strivings and the expression of them in what Heidegger (1954) calls the age of technicity, is not the necessary or even the "normal" destiny of aggression.

Werman (1985) points out that "most human misery appears to be, usually and for most people, the bitter fruit of object loss, disease, death, war, and poverty—what Freud called the unhappiness of everyday life" (p. 251). The problem is that, although there are healthy sublimatory channels available to all of us in work, art, religion, and so forth to alleviate these miseries, "The dangerous innocence generally proposed by civilization's stewards denies the reality around us and in us; repeatedly society makes tragic decisions based on a mythology that emanates from wishful thinking and ideology" (p. 253). This represents what Steiner (1985) from the Tavistock Clinic in London has called "turning a blind eye." He writes, "Unemployment at home and poverty and starvation in the third world are examples, but it seems to be above all the buildup of nuclear weapons which poses such a threat that neither we nor our leaders can properly comprehend it. Yet all the information pointing to the seriousness of the situation is available and we seem to have to avoid drawing the unhappy conclusions which a realistic appraisal would demand. We can only carry on our lives as normal by turning a blind eye" (p. 169). Is this massive disavowal not the indispensable basis of the current regressive cultural narcissistic preoccupation that characterizes affluent people of the Western world? Is it not the prime obligation of mental health professionals and above all psychiatrists, as physicians and citizens, to call attention to the explosive dangers of such massive disavowal, even if it disturbs everybody's sleep? Even if it "makes waves" and requires personal sacrifice?

Werman (1985), like Trilling, claims that Freud's own life history contradicts any recommendation for regression and resignation in the face of dour reality: "The life Freud himself lived is a superb model of devotion to the individual, to a search for truth, and to the duty of being human. . . . This model was to be Freud's response to Einstein's deep pessimism regarding the prevention of war, and it inherently embodies a commitment to the preservation of civilization, that most elegant and most enslaving of human products" (p. 253).

All mental health professionals have the social and professional obligation to urge humankind to look squarely and honestly at the truth about our plight and to stop trying to escape, through narcissistic disavowal and politically popular but obsolete nineteenth century illusions, from the grim reality of the

world-historical moment in which we exist. Utilizing philosophical and psychological theories as the basis of a self-correcting *praxis*, we must wander over the
world and labor, inquiring from all we meet with the spirit of Wotan:

> In bondage to the world
> do the Norns spin:
> nothing can they alter nor change.
>
> But of your knowledge
> gladly would I learn
> how to arrest a turning wheel.
>   *Siegfried* (Act III)

As Freud in *Civilization and Its Discontents* (1930, p. 145) concludes, "Who can
foresee with what success and with what result?"

REFERENCES

Alexander, F. (1964). Social significance of psychoanalysis and psychotherapy. *Archives of General Psychiatry* 11:235–244.

Alexander, F., and Selesnick, S. (1966). *The History of Psychiatry: An Evaluation of Psychiatric Thought and Practice from Prehistoric Times to the Present*. New York: Harper and Row.

Althusser, L. (1971). *Lenin and Philosophy and Other Essays*. Trans. B. Brewster. New York: Monthly Review Press.

Aronson, R. (1980). *Jean-Paul Sartre: Philosophy in the World*. London: Verso.

Atwood, G., and Stolorow, R. (1984). *Structures of Subjectivity: Explorations in Psychoanalytic Phenomenology*. Hillsdale, NJ: Analytic Press.

Bacon, F. (1620). *Novum Organum*. In *The English Philosophers from Bacon to Mill*, ed. E. Burtt, pp. 24–128. New York: Modern Library, 1939.

Barnes, H. (1981). *Sartre and Flaubert*. Chicago: University of Chicago Press.

Basch, M. (1985). Some clinical and theoretical implications of infant research. *Psychoanalytic Inquiry* 5:509–516.

—————— (1991). Are selfobjects the only objects? Implications for psychoanalytic technique. In *The Evolution of Self Psychology: Progress in Self Psychology*, vol. 7, ed. A. Goldberg, pp. 3–15. Hillsdale, NJ: Analytic Press.

Bell, D. (1991). After the age of sinfulness: Lukács and the mystical roots of revolution. *Times Literary Supplement*, July 26, 1991, pp. 5–8.

Benvenuto, B., and Kennedy, R. (1986). *The Works of Jacques Lacan*. London: Free Association Books.

Bernauer, J., and Rasmussen, D., eds. (1990). *The Final Foucault*. Cambridge, MA: MIT Press.

Bernstein, R. (1988a). Interpretation and its discontents: the choreography of critique. In *Hermeneutics and Psychological Theory*, ed. S. Messer, L. Sass, and R. Woolfolk, pp. 87–108. New Brunswick, NJ: Rutgers University Press.

———— (1988b). Metaphysics, critique, and utopia. *Review of Metaphysics* 42:255–273.

Bernum, J. (1984). The unfortunate case of Dr. Z: how to succeed in medical practice in 1984. *New England Journal of Medicine* 310:729–730.

Bettelheim, B. (1982). *Freud and Man's Soul*. New York: Knopf.

Biemel, W. (1976). *Martin Heidegger: An Illustrated Study*. Trans. J. Metha. New York: Harcourt Brace Jovanovich.

Binswanger, L. (1963). *Being-in-the-World*. Trans. J. Needleman. New York: Basic Books.

Bion, W. (1963). *Elements of Psycho-analysis*. New York: Basic Books.

———— (1967). *Second Thoughts: Selected Papers on Psycho-analysis*. London: Heinemann.

Bloom, A. (1987). *The Closing of the American Mind*. New York: Simon and Schuster.

Bloom, H., ed. (1985). *Modern Critical Views: Sigmund Freud*. New York: Chelsea House.

Boss, M. (1963). *Psychoanalysis and Daseinanalysis*. Trans. L. Lefebre. New York: Basic Books.

———— (1979). *Existential Foundations of Medicine and Psychology*. Trans. S. Conway and A. Cleaves. New York: Jason Aronson.

Bowie, M. (1979). Jacques Lacan. In *Structuralism and Sense: From Levi-Strauss to Derrida*, ed. J. Sturrock, pp. 116–153. New York: Oxford University Press.

———— (1991). *Lacan*. Cambridge, MA: Harvard University Press.

Boyers, R., and Orill, R., eds. (1971). *R. D. Laing and Anti-Psychiatry*. New York: Harper and Row.

Breuer, J., and Freud, S. (1893–1895). Studies on hysteria. *Standard Edition* 2:1–308.

Brody, S. (1982). Psychoanalytic theories of infant development and its disturbances: a critical evaluation. *Psychoanalytic Quarterly* 51:526–597.

Brown, L., and Hausman, A. (1981). Intentionality and the unconscious: a comparison of Sartre and Freud. In *The Philosophy of Jean-Paul Sartre*, ed. P. Schlipp, pp. 539–581. LaSalle, IL: Open Court.

Brown, N. (1959). *Life Against Death*. Middletown, CT: Wesleyan University Press.

Bruns, G. (1989). *Heidegger's Estrangements: Language, Truth, and Poetry in the Later Writings*. New Haven: Yale University Press.

Buber, M. (1958). *I and Thou*. New York: Scribners.

Cannon, B. (1991). *Sartre and Psychoanalysis: An Existential Challenge to Clinical Metatheory*. Lawrence, KS: University Press of Kansas.

Caputo, J. (1985). Three transgressions: Nietzsche, Heidegger, Derrida. *Research in Phenomenology* 15:16–78.

———— (1987). *Radical Hermeneutics: Repetition, Deconstruction, and the Hermeneutic Project*. Bloomington, IN: Indiana University Press.

———— (1988). Demythologizing Heidegger: Alētheia and the history of Being. *Review of Metaphysics* 41:519–546.

Catalano, J. (1980). *A Commentary on Jean-Paul Sartre's Being and Nothingness*. Chicago: University of Chicago Press.

Caws, P. (1977). *Sartre*. Boston: Routledge and Kegan Paul.

Chessick, R. (1977). *Intensive Psychotherapy of the Borderline Patient*. New York: Jason Aronson.

———— (1980a). *Freud Teaches Psychotherapy*. Indianapolis, IN: Hackett.

———— (1980b). Some philosophical assumptions of intensive psychotherapy. *American Journal of Psychotherapy* 34:496–509.

———— (1981). The relevance of Nietzsche to the study of Freud and Kohut. *Contemporary Psychoanalysis* 17:359–373.

———— (1983a). *A Brief Introduction to the Genius of Nietzsche*. Washington, DC: University Press of America.

———— (1983b). *Why Psychotherapists Fail*. New York: Jason Aronson.

———— (1983c). *The Technique and Practice of Intensive Psychotherapy*. New York: Jason Aronson.

———— (1983d). Marilyn Monroe: psychoanalytic pathography of a preoedipal disorder. *Dynamic Psychotherapy* 1:161–176.

———— (1984). Sartre and Freud. *American Journal of Psychotherapy* 38:229–238.

———— (1985). *Psychology of the Self and the Treatment of Narcissism*. Northvale, NJ: Jason Aronson.

———— (1986). Heidegger for psychotherapists. *American Journal of Psychotherapy* 40:83–95.

———— (1987a). Lacan's practice of psychoanalytic psychotherapy. *American Journal of Psychotherapy* 41:571–579.

———— (1987b). *Great Ideas in Psychotherapy*. Northvale, NJ: Jason Aronson.

———— (1988a). A comparison of the notions of self in the philosophy of Heidegger and the psychoanalytic self psychology of Kohut. *Psychoanalysis and Contemporary Thought* 11:117–144.

———— (1988b). Prolegomena to the study of Paul Ricoeur's book *Freud and Philosophy*. *Psychoanalytic Review* 75:299–318.

———— (1989a). *The Technique and Practice of Listening in Intensive Psychotherapy*. Northvale, NJ: Jason Aronson.

———— (1989b). The death instinct and the future of humans. *American Journal of Psychotherapy* 43:546–561.

———— (1990). Hermeneutics for psychotherapists. *American Journal of Psychotherapy* 44:256–273.

———— (1991). The unbearable obscurity of Being. *American Journal of Psychotherapy* 45:576–593.

———— (1992). The death instinct revisited. *Journal of the American Academy of Psychoanalysis* 20:3–28.

Chomsky, N. (1972). *Language and Mind*. New York: Harcourt Brace Jovanovich.

Clément, C. (1983). *The Lives and Legends of Jacques Lacan*. Trans. A. Goldhammer. New York: Columbia University Press.

Cohen-Solal, A. (1987). *Sartre: A Life*. Trans. A. Cancogni. New York: Pantheon.

Congdon, L. (1983). *The Young Lukács*. Chapel Hill, NC: University of North Carolina Press.

Conway, D. (1987). *A Farewell to Marx: An Outline and Appraisal of His Theories*. New York: Viking.

Copleston, F. (1977). *History of Philosophy*. Vol. 9, part 2, pp. 9–277. Garden City, NY: Image.

Danto, A. (1975). *Jean-Paul Sartre*. New York: Viking.

De Beauvoir, S. (1984). *Adieux: A Farewell to Sartre*. Trans. P. O'Brian. New York: Pantheon.

De Man, P. (1983). *Blindness and Insight*. Minneapolis: University of Minnesota Press.

Descombes, V. (1980). *Modern French Philosophy*. New York: Cambridge University Press.

Detmer, D. (1988). *Freedom as a Value: A Critique of the Ethical Theory of Jean-Paul Sartre*. LaSalle, IL: Open Court.

Dilthey, W. (1978). *The Critique of Historical Reason*. Trans. M. Ermarth. Chicago: University of Chicago Press.

Dreyfus, H. (1980). Holism and hermeneutics. *Review of Metaphysics* 34:3–24.

_____ (1988). Foucault versus Freud. In *Die Philosophen und Freud*, ed. H. Vetter and L. Nagl, pp. 227–249. Munich: Oldenbourg Press.

Dreyfus, H., and Rabinow, P. (1983). *Michel Foucault: Beyond Structuralism and Hermeneutics*. Chicago: University of Chicago Press.

Dreyfus, H., and Wakefield, J. (1988). From depth psychology to breadth psychology: A phenomenological approach to psychopathology. In *Hermeneutics and Psychological Theory*, ed. S. Messer, L. Sass, and R. Woolfolk, pp. 272–288. New Brunswick, NJ: Rutgers University Press.

Edie, J., ed. (1965). *An Invitation to Phenomenology*. Chicago: Quadrangle.

_____ , ed. (1967). *Phenomenology in America*. Chicago: Quadrangle.

_____ , ed. (1969). *New Essays in Phenomenology*. Chicago: Quadrangle.

Eissler, K. (1971). Death drive, ambivalence, and narcissism. *Psychoanalytic Study of the Child*, 26:25–78. New Haven: Yale University Press.

_____ (1975). The fall of man. *Psychoanalytic Study of the Child*, 30:589–646. New Haven: Yale University Press.

Eribon, D. (1991). *Michel Foucault*. Trans. B. Wing. Cambridge, MA: Harvard University Press.

Evans, R. (1976). *R. D. Laing: The Man and His Ideas*. New York: Dutton.

Fanon, F. (1963). *The Wretched of the Earth*. New York: Grove.

Farias, V. (1989). *Heidegger and Nazism*. Trans. P. Burrell and G. Ricci. Philadelphia: Temple University Press.

Federn, P. (1952). *Ego Psychology and the Psychoses*. New York: Basic Books.

Feenberg, A. (1981). *Lukacs, Marx and the Sources of Critical Theory*. Totowa, NJ: Rowman and Littlefield.

Fell, J. (1979). *Heidegger and Sartre: An Essay on Being and Place*. New York: Columbia University Press.

Feyerabend, P. (1989). Realism and the historicity of knowledge. *Journal of Philosophy* 86:393–406.

Foucault, M. (1971). Nietzsche, genealogy, history. In *Michel Foucault: Language, Counter-*

Memory, Practice: Selected Essays and Interviews, ed. D. Bouchard, pp. 139–164. New York: Cornell University Press, 1977.

_____ (1972). *The Archaeology of Knowledge.* Trans. A. Smith. New York: Pantheon.

_____ (1973a). *Madness and Civilization.* Trans. A. Smith. New York: Vintage.

_____ (1973b). *The Order of Things.* New York: Vintage.

_____ (1975). *The Birth of the Clinic: An Archaeology of Medical Perception.* Trans. A. Smith. New York: Vintage.

_____ (1979). *Discipline and Punish: The Birth of the Prison.* Trans. A. Sheridan. New York: Vintage.

_____ (1980a). *Power/Knowledge: Selected Interviews and Other Writings,* ed. C. Gordon. New York: Pantheon.

_____ (1980b). *The History of Sexuality.* Vol. 1. Trans. R. Hurley. New York: Vintage.

_____ (1984). What is an author? In *The Foucault Reader,* ed. P. Drabinow, pp. 101–120. New York: Pantheon.

_____ (1985). *The Use of Pleasure: The History of Sexuality.* Vol. 2. Trans. R. Hurley. New York: Pantheon.

Frankl, V. (1962). *Man's Search for Meaning.* New York: Simon and Schuster.

Freud, A. (1946). *The Ego and the Mechanisms of Defense.* New York: International Universities Press.

Freud, S. (1895). Project for a scientific psychology. *Standard Edition* 1:283–378.

_____ (1900). The interpretation of dreams. *Standard Edition* 4/5: 1–62.

_____ (1909). Notes upon a case of obsessional neurosis. *Standard Edition* 10: 153–319.

_____ (1912). Recommendations to physicians practicing psychoanalysis. *Standard Edition* 12:109–120.

_____ (1914). On narcissism: introduction. *Standard Edition* 14:67–104.

_____ (1917). Mourning and melancholia. *Standard Edition* 14:237–258.

_____ (1920). Beyond the pleasure principle. *Standard Edition* 18:3–66.

_____ (1921). Group psychology and the analysis of the ego. *Standard Edition* 18:67–144.

_____ (1924). The economic problem of masochism. *Standard Edition* 19:157–172.

_____ (1928). Dostoevsky and parricide. *Standard Edition* 21: 173–196.

_____ (1930). Civilization and its discontents. *Standard Edition* 21:59–148.

_____ (1932). Why war? *Standard Edition* 22:197–199.

_____ (1937). Analysis terminable and interminable. *Standard Edition* 23:209–254.

_____ (1940). An outline of psycho-analysis. *Standard Edition* 23:144–207.

Friedenberg, E. (1973). *R. D. Laing.* New York: Viking.

Friedman, L. (1976). Cognitive and therapeutic tasks of a theory of mind. *International Review of Psycho-Analysis* 3:259–275.

Fromm, E. (1969). *Escape from Freedom.* New York: Avon.

_____ (1980). *Marx's Concept of Man.* New York: Ungar.

Fukuyama, F. (1992). *The End of History and the Last Man.* New York: Free Press.

Gadamer, H. (1976). *Hegel's Dialectic: Five Hermeneutical Studies.* Trans. C. Smith. New Haven: Yale University Press.

_____ (1977). *Philosophical Hermeneutics*. Trans. D. Linge. Berkeley: University of California Press.

_____ (1980). *Dialogue and Dialectic: Eight Hermeneutical Studies On Plato*. Trans. C. Smith. New Haven: Yale University Press.

_____ (1982). *Truth and Method*. New York: Crossroad.

_____ (1984). *Reason in the Age of Science*. Trans. F. Lawrence. Cambridge, MA: MIT Press.

_____ (1985). *Philosophical Apprenticeships*. Trans. R. Sullivan. Cambridge, MA: MIT Press.

_____ (1986). *The Idea of the Good in Platonic-Aristotelian Philosophy*. Trans. P. Smith. New Haven: Yale University Press.

_____ (1991). *Truth and Method*. 2nd ed. Revised by J. Weinsheimer and D. Marshall. New York: Crossroad.

Galen (1952). Selections. In *Great Books of the Western World*, vol. 10, ed. R. Hutchins, pp. 167–215. Chicago: Encyclopedia Britannica.

Gallop, J. (1985). *Reading Lacan*. Ithaca, NY: Cornell University Press.

Gedo, J. (1979). *Beyond Interpretation: Toward a Revised Theory for Psycho-analysis*. New York: International Universities Press.

_____ (1986). *Conceptual Issues in Psychoanalysis: Essays in History and Method*. Hillsdale, NJ: Analytic Press.

_____ (1988). *The Mind in Disorder: Psychoanalytic Models of Pathology*. Hillsdale, NJ: Analytic Press.

Gerassi, J. (1989). *Jean-Paul Sartre: Hated Conscience of His Century*, Vol. I: *Protestant or Protester?* Chicago: University of Chicago Press.

Gilbert, M. (1986). *The Holocaust: A History of the Jews During the Second World War*. New York: Henry Holt.

Gill, M. (1978). Metapsychology is irrelevant to psychoanalysis. In *The Human Mind Revisited*, ed. S. Smith, pp. 349–368. New York: International Universities Press.

Giovacchini, P. (1967). The frozen introject. *International Journal of Psycho-Analysis* 48:61–67.

Gluck, M. (1985). *George Lukács and His Generation 1900–1918*. Cambridge, MA: Harvard University Press.

Goldmann, L. (1979). *Lukács and Heidegger: Towards a New Philosophy*. Trans. W. Boelhower. London: Routledge and Kegan Paul.

Gramsci, A. (1985). *Selections from the Prison Notebooks of Antonio Gramsci*. Trans. Q. Hoare and G. Smith. New York: International Publishers.

Greenberg, J., and Mitchell, S. (1983). *Object Relations in Psychoanalytic Theory*. Cambridge, MA: Harvard University Press.

Grosskurth, P. (1986). *Melanie Klein: Her World and Her Work*. New York: Knopf.

Grünbaum, A. (1983). Freud's theory: the perspective of a philosopher of science. *Proceedings of the American Philosophical Association* 57: 5–31.

_____ (1984). *The Foundations of Psychoanalysis: A Philosophical Critique*. Berkeley: University of California Press.

Guntrip, H. (1968). *Schizoid Phenomena, Object Relations and the Self*. New York: International Universities Press.

_____ (1971). _Psyhoanalytic Theory, Therapy and the Self._ New York: Basic Books.

Gutting, G. (1989). _Michel Foucault's Archaeology of Scientific Reason._ New York: Cambridge University Press.

Habermas, J. (1971). _Knowledge and Human Interests._ Boston: Beacon.

Halliburton, D. (1981). _Poetic Thinking: An Approach to Heidegger._ Chicago: University of Chicago Press.

Hamburg, P. (1991). Interpretation and empathy: reading Lacan with Kohut. _International Journal of Psycho-Analysis_ 72:347–361.

Havel, V. (1988). _Letters to Olga._ New York: Knopf.

_____ (1990). History of a public enemy. _New York Review of Books,_ May 31, 1990, pp. 36–46.

Hayman, R. (1987). _Sartre: A Life._ New York: Simon and Schuster.

Hegel, G. (1807). _Phenomenology of Spirit._ Trans. A. Miller. Oxford, England: Clarendon Press.

_____ (1976). _Hegel's Philosophy of Right._ Trans. T. Knox. New York: Oxford University Press.

Heidegger, M. (1954). _The Question Concerning Technology and Other Essays._ Trans. W. Lovitt. New York: Harper and Row.

_____ (1958). _The Question of Being._ Trans. W. Kluback and J. Wilde. New Haven: College and University Press.

_____ (1961). _An Introduction to Metaphysics._ Trans. R. Manheim. New York: Anchor.

_____ (1962a). _Being and Time._ Trans. J. Macquarrie and E. Robinson. New York: Harper and Row.

_____ (1962b). _Kant and the Problem of Metaphysics._ Trans. J. Churchill. Bloomington, IN: Indiana University Press.

_____ (1968a). _Existence and Being._ Intro. by W. Brock. Chicago: Henry Regnery.

_____ (1968b). _What Is Called Thinking?_ Trans. J. Gray and F. Wieck. New York: Harper and Row.

_____ (1969). _Discourse on Thinking._ Trans. J. Anderson and E. Freund. New York: Harper and Row.

_____ (1975a). _Early Greek Thinking._ Trans. D. Krell and F. Capuzzi. New York: Harper and Row.

_____ (1975b). _Poetry, Language, Thought._ Trans. A. Hofstadter. New York: Harper and Row.

_____ (1977a). _Basic Writings,_ ed. D. Krell. New York: Harper and Row.

_____ (1977b). _On Time and Being._ Trans. J. Stambaugh. New York: Harper and Row.

_____ (1982). _The Basic Problems of Phenomenology._ Trans. A. Hofstadter. Bloomington: Indiana University Press.

_____ (1985a). _History of the Concept of Time._ Trans. T. Kisiel. Bloomington: Indiana University Press.

_____ (1985b). The self-assertion of the German university and the rectorate 1933/34: facts and thoughts. Trans. K. Harries. _Review of Metaphysics_ 38:467–502.

Holt, R. (1973). On reading Freud. In _Abstracts of the Standard Edition of the Complete_

Psychological Works of Sigmund Freud, ed. C. Rothgeb, pp. 3–79. New York: Jason Aronson.

———— (1981). The death and transfiguration of metapsychology. *Journal of the American Psychoanalytic Association* 25:835–872.

Hunter, P. (1977). Sartre's existential humanism and Freud's existential naturalism. *Psychoanalytic Review* 64:289–298.

Husserl, E. (1913). *Ideas: General Introduction to Pure Phenomenology.* Trans. W. Gibson. New York: Macmillan, 1952.

———— (1970). *The Crisis of European Sciences and Transcendental Phenomenology.* Evanston, IL: Northwestern University Press.

———— (1989). *Ideas Pertaining to a Pure Phenomenology and to a Phenomenological Philosophy. Second Book: Studies in the Phenomenology of Constitution.* Trans. R. Ojcewicz and A. Schuwer. Dordrecht, Netherlands: Kluwer Academic Publishers.

Hyppolite, J. (1969). *Studies on Marx and Hegel.* New York: Basic Books.

Jacoby, R. (1983). *The Repression of Psychoanalysis: Otto Fenichel and the Political Freudians.* New York: Basic Books.

Jaffe, D. (1982). Aggression; instinct, drive, behavior. *Psychoanalytic Inquiry* 2:77–94.

Jakobson, R., and Pomorska, K. (1983). *Dialogues.* Cambridge, MA: MIT Press.

Jaspers, K. (1932a). *Philosophy.* Vol. 1. Trans. E. Ashton. Chicago: University of Chicago Press, 1969.

———— (1932b). *Philosophy.* Vol. 2. Trans. E. Ashton. Chicago: University of Chicago Press, 1970.

———— (1932c). *Philosophy.* Vol. 3. Trans. E. Ashton. Chicago: University of Chicago Press, 1971.

———— (1962). *The Great Philosophers.* Vol. 1. Trans. R. Manheim. New York: Harcourt, Brace and World.

———— (1966). *The Great Philosophers.* Vol. 2. Trans. R. Manheim. New York: Harcourt, Brace and World.

———— (1972). *General Psychopathology.* Chicago: University of Chicago Press.

Jay, M. (1984). *Marxism and Totality: The Adventures of a Concept from Lukács to Habermas.* Berkeley: University of California Press.

Jones, E. (1953). *The Life and Work of Sigmund Freud.* Vol. 1. New York: Basic Books.

Kadarkay, A. (1991). *Georg Lukács: Life, Thought, and Politics.* Cambridge, MA: Basil Blackwell.

Kaelin, E. (1988). *Heidegger's Being and Time: A Reading for Readers.* Tallahassee, FL: Florida State University Press.

Kant, I. (1781). *Critique of Pure Reason.* Trans. N. Smith. New York: St. Martin's Press, 1965.

Kernberg, O. (1975). *Borderline Conditions and Pathological Narcissism.* New York: Jason Aronson.

Keys, D. (1982). *Earth at Omega: The Passage To Planetization.* Boston: Branden Publishers.

Kierkegaard, S. (1946). *The Concept of Dread.* Trans. W. Lowrie. Princeton, NJ: Princeton University Press.

———— (1954). *Fear and Trembling* and *Sickness unto Death.* New York: Anchor.

Kockelmans, J., ed. (1967). *Phenomenology*. Garden City, NY: Anchor.
_____ (1984). *On the Truth of Being: Reflections on Heidegger's Later Philosophy*. Bloomington: Indiana University Press.
_____ (1985). *Heidegger on Art and Art Works*. The Hague: Martinus Nijhoff.
Kohák, E. (1978). *Idea and Experience*. Chicago: University of Chicago Press.
Kohut, H. (1971). *The Analysis of the Self*. New York: International Universities Press.
_____ (1977). *The Restoration of the Self*. New York: International Universities Press.
_____ (1978). *The Search for the Self*. Ed. P. Ornstein. New York: International Universities Press.
_____ (1982). Introspection, empathy, and the semi-circle of mental health. *International Journal of Psycho-Analysis* 63:395–407.
_____ (1984). *How Does Analysis Cure?* Chicago: University of Chicago Press.
Kohut, H., and Wolf, E. (1978). The disorders of the self and their treatment: an outline. *International Journal of Psycho-Analysis* 59:413–425.
Kojève, A. (1969). *Introduction to the Reading of Hegel*. Trans. J. Nichols. Ithaca, NY: Cornell University Press.
Krupnick, M. (1986). *Lionel Trilling and the Fate of Cultural Criticism*. Evanston, IL: Northwestern University Press.
Kuhn, T. (1962). *The Structure of Scientific Revolutions*. Chicago: University of Chicago Press.
Kuper, A., and Stone, A. (1982). The dream of Irma's injection: a structural analysis. *American Journal of Psychiatry* 139:1225–1234.
Kurzweil, E. (1980). *The Age of Structuralism: Lévi-Strauss to Foucault*. New York: Columbia University Press.
Lacan, J. (1953). Some reflections on the ego. *International Journal of Psycho-Analysis* 34:11–17.
_____ (1968). *Speech and Language in Psychoanalysis*. Trans. A. Wilden. Baltimore, MD: Johns Hopkins University Press.
_____ (1977). *Ecrits: A Selection*. Trans. A. Sheridan. New York: Norton.
_____ (1978). *The Four Fundamental Concepts of Psycho-analysis*. Trans. A. Sheridan. New York: Norton.
_____ (1988a). *The Seminar of Jacques Lacan, Book 1: Freud's Papers on Technique 1953–1954*. Trans. J. Forrester. New York: Norton.
_____ (1988b). *The Seminar of Jacques Lacan, Book 2: The Ego in Freud's Theory and in the Technique of Psychoanalysis 1954–1955*. Trans. S. Tomaselli. New York: Norton.
_____ (1990). *Television: A Challenge to the Psychoanalytic Establishment*. Trans. D. Hollier, R. Krauss, A. Michelson, and J. Mehlman. New York: Norton.
Laing, R. (1965). Mystification, confusion and conflict. In *Intensive Family Therapy*, ed. I. Boszormenyi-Nagy and J. Framo, pp. 343–363. New York: Harper and Row.
_____ (1967). *The Politics of Experience*. New York: Pantheon.
_____ (1969a). *The Divided Self*. New York: Pantheon.
_____ (1969b). *Self and Others*. New York: Pantheon.
_____ (1971). *Knots*. New York: Pantheon.
_____ (1972). *The Politics of the Family and Other Essays*. New York: Vintage.
_____ (1976). *The Facts of Life*. New York: Pantheon.

_____ (1985). *Wisdom, Madness and Folly: The Making of a Psychiatrist.* New York: McGraw-Hill.

Laing, R., and Cooper, D. (1971). *Reason and Violence: A Decade of Sartre's Philosophy 1950–1960.* New York: Pantheon.

Laing, R., and Esterson, A. (1971). *Sanity, Madness and the Family.* New York: Pantheon.

Langer, M. (1989). *Merleau-Ponty's Phenomenology of Perception: A Guide and Commentary.* Tallahassee, FL: Florida State University Press.

Langs, R. (1979). *The Therapeutic Environment.* New York: Jason Aronson.

Leakey, R., and Lewin, R. (1978). *People of the Lake.* Garden City, NY: Anchor.

Leavy, S. (1980). *The Psychoanalytic Dialogue.* New Haven: Yale University Press.

Lehman, D. (1991). *Signs of the Times: Deconstruction and the Fall of Paul de Man.* New York: Poseidon.

Lemaire, A. (1981). *Jacques Lacan.* Trans. D. Macey. London: Routledge and Kegan Paul.

Lévi-Strauss, C. (1969). *The Savage Mind.* Chicago: University of Chicago Press.

Lichtenberg, J. (1983). *Psychoanalysis and Infant Research.* Hillsdale, NJ: Analytic Press.

_____ (1987). Infant studies and clinical work with adults. *Psychoanalytic Inquiry* 7:311–330.

Lichtenberg, J., Bornstein, M., and Silver, D. (1984). *Empathy.* Vols. 1 and 2. Hillsdale, NJ: Analytic Press.

Lichtheim, G. (1970). *Georg Lukács.* New York: Viking.

Llewelyn, J. (1985). *Beyond Metaphysics? The Hermeneutical Circle in Contemporary Continental Philosophy.* Atlantic Highlands, NJ: Humanities Press.

Locke, J. (1690). *An Essay Concerning Human Understanding.* New York: Meridian, 1969.

Loewald, H. (1960). On the therapeutic action of psychoanalysis. *International Journal of Psycho-Analysis* 41:16–33.

_____ (1980). *Papers on Psychoanalysis.* New Haven: Yale University Press.

Loewenstein, R. (1972). Ego autonomy and psychoanalytic technique. *Psychoanalytic Quarterly* 41:1–23.

Lukács, G. (1969). On the responsibility of intellectuals. *Telos* 2:123–131.

_____ (1976). *The Young Hegel: Studies in the Relations between Dialectics and Economics.* Trans. R. Livingstone. Cambridge, MA: MIT Press.

_____ (1980). *The Destruction of Reason.* Trans. P. Palmer. London: Merlin Press.

_____ (1982). *History and Class Consciousness: Studies in Marxist Dialectics.* Trans. R. Livingstone. Cambridge, MA: MIT Press.

_____ (1991). *The Process of Democratization.* Trans. S. Bernhardt and N. Levine. New York: State University of New York Press.

Macey, D. (1988). *Lacan in Context.* London: Verso.

Mahler, M., Pine, F., and Bergman, A. (1975). *The Psychological Birth of the Human Infant.* New York: Basic Books.

Marcuse, H. (1955). *Eros and Civilization.* Boston: Beacon.

_____ (1964). *One-Dimensional Man.* Boston: Beacon.

Marx, K. (1844). *Early Writings.* Trans. T. Bottomore. New York: McGraw-Hill, 1963.

_____ (1867). *Capital.* Vol. I. New York: Vintage, 1977.

May, R. (1958). *Existence.* New York: Basic Books.

McInerney, P. (1979). Self-determination and the self. *Journal of Philosophy* 76:663–676.

McLellan, D. (1979). *Marxism After Marx: An Introduction*. Boston: Houghton Mifflin.

Megill, A. (1985). *Prophets of Extremity: Nietzsche, Heidegger, Foucault, Derrida*. Berkeley: University of California Press.

Mehta, J. (1971). *The Philosophy of Martin Heidegger*. New York: Harper and Row.

──────── (1976). *Martin Heidegger: The Way and the Vision*. Honolulu: The University Press of Hawaii.

Meichenbaum, D. (1988). What happens when the "brute data" of psychological inquiry are meanings: nurturing a dialogue between hermeneutics and empiricism. In *Hermeneutics and Psychological Theory*, ed. S. Messer, L. Sass, and R. Woolfolk, pp. 116–130. New Brunswick, NJ: Rutgers University Press.

Meissner, W. (1971). Freud's methodology. *Journal of the American Psychoanalytic Association* 19:265–309.

──────── (1985). Classical psychoanalysis. In *Comprehensive Textbook of Psychiatry*, ed. H. Kaplan, A. Freedman, and B. Sadock, 4th ed., pp. 337–418. Baltimore: Williams and Wilkins.

Merleau-Ponty, M. (1962). *Phenomenology of Perception*. Trans. C. Smith. Atlantic Highlands, NJ: Humanities Press.

──────── (1964a). *The Primacy of Perception*. Ed. J. Edie. Evanston, IL: Northwestern University Press.

──────── (1964b). *Sense and Non-Sense*. Trans. H. Dreyfus and P. Dreyfus. Evanston, IL: Northwestern University Press.

──────── (1968). *The Visible and the Invisible*. Trans. A. Lingis. Evanston, IL: Northwestern University Press.

Messer, S., Sass, A., and Woolfolk, R., eds. (1988). *Hermeneutics and Psychological Theory: Interpretive Perspectives on Personality, Psychotherapy, and Psychopathology*. New Brunswick, NJ: Rutgers University Press.

Miller, M. (1991). *Plato's Parmenides: The Conversion of the Soul*. University Park, PA: Penn State Press.

Mishara, A. (1989). "Phenomenology and the unconscious—the problem of the unconscious in the phenomenological and existential traditions: E. Husserl, V. Von Weizsaecker, and L. Binswanger." Doctoral dissertation. Pennsylvania State University, Dept. of Philosophy. Netherlands: Kluwer Academic Publishers—in press.

──────── (1990a). Husserl and Freud: time, memory, and the unconscious. *Husserl Studies* 7:29–58.

──────── (1990b). The problem of the unconscious in the later thought of L. Binswanger: a phenomenological approach to delusion in perception and communication. *Analecta Husserliana* 31:247–278.

Mitcham, C. (1985). What is the philosophy of technology? *International Philosophical Quarterly* 25:73–88.

Mitchell, J., and Rose, J., eds. (1982). *Feminine Sexuality: Jacques Lacan and the Ecole Freudienne*. New York: Norton.

Modell, A. (1978). The nature of psychoanalytic knowledge. *Journal of the American Psychoanalytic Association* 26:641–658.

Muller, J., and Richardson, W. (1982). *Lacan and Language: A Reader's Guide to Ecrits*. New York: International Universities Press.

_____ (1988). *The Purloined Poe: Lacan, Derrida, and Psychoanalytic Reading*. Baltimore, MD: Johns Hopkins University Press.

Murray, M., ed. (1978). *Heidegger and Modern Philosophy*. New Haven: Yale University Press.

Pao, P. (1979). *Schizophrenic Disorders*. New York: International Universities Press.

Parin, P. (1972). Contribution of ethnopsychoanalytic investigation to the theory of aggression. *International Journal of Psycho-Analysis*. 53:251-257.

Parkinson, G. (1977). *Georg Lukács*. London: Routledge and Kegan Paul.

Patočka, J. (1989). *Philosophy and Selected Writings*. Trans. E. Kohák. Chicago: University of Chicago Press.

Peterfreund, E. (1971). *Information, Systems, and Psychoanalysis*. New York: International Universities Press.

Phillips, A. (1988). *Winnicott*. Cambridge, MA: Harvard University Press.

Piaget, J. (1970). *Genetic Epistemology*. New York: Columbia University Press.

Pöggeler, O. (1987). *Martin Heidegger's Path of Thinking*. Trans. D. Magurshak and S. Barber. Atlantic Highlands, NJ: Humanities Press.

Poole, R., and Strangerup, H., eds. (1989). *The Laughter is on My Side: An Imaginative Introduction to Kierkegaard*. Princeton, NJ: Princeton University Press.

Poster, M. (1982). *Sartre's Marxism*. New York: Cambridge University Press.

Pound, E. (1949). *Selected Poems*. New York: New Directions.

Pruyser, P. (1975). What splits in "splitting"? *Bulletin of the Menninger Clinic* 39:1-46.

Rabinow, P., ed. (1984). *The Foucault Reader*. New York: Pantheon.

Ragland-Sullivan, E. (1986). *Jacques Lacan and the Philosophy of Psychoanalysis*. Urbana, IL: University of Illinois Press.

Rangell, L. (1988). The future of psychoanalysis: the scientific crossroads. *Psychoanalytic Quarterly* 57:313-340.

Rapaport, D. (1967). *The Collected Papers of David Rapaport*. New York: Basic Books.

Rescher, N. (1973). *Conceptual Idealism*. Oxford, England: Basil Blackwell.

Richardson, W. (1965). The place of the unconscious in Heidegger. *Review of Existential Psychology and Psychiatry* 5:265-290.

_____ (1974). *Heidegger: Through Phenomenology to Thought*. 3rd ed. The Hague: Martinus Nijhoff.

Ricoeur, P. (1969). *The Symbolism of Evil*. Trans. E. Buchanan. Boston: Beacon.

_____ (1970). *Freud and Philosophy*. Trans. D. Savage. New Haven: Yale University Press.

_____ (1974). Consciousness and the unconscious. Trans. W. Domingo. In *The Conflict of Interpretations: Essays in Hermeneutics*, ed. D. Ihde, pp. 99-120. Evanston, IL: Northwestern University Press.

_____ (1977). The question of proof in Freud's psychoanalytic writings. *Journal of the American Psychoanalytic Association* 25:835-872.

_____ (1981). *Hermeneutics and the Human Sciences*. Trans. J. Thompson. New York: Cambridge University Press.

_____ (1983). On thinking about the unthinkable. *University of Chicago Magazine*, Fall, pp. 29-31.

Rilke, R. (1984). *The Selected Poetry of Rainer Maria Rilke*. Trans. S. Mitchell. New York: Vintage.

Roberts, J. (1988). *German Philosophy: An Introduction*. Atlantic Highlands, NJ: Humanities Press.

Roqué, A. (1988). Non-linear phenomena, explanation and action. *International Philosophical Quarterly* 28:247–255.

Rorty, R. (1979). *Philosophy and the Mirror of Nature*. Princeton, NJ: Princeton University Press.

_____ (1991). The Seer of Prague. *The New Republic*, July 1, 1991, pp. 35–40.

Roudinesco, E. (1990). *Jacques Lacan and Company: A History of Psychoanalysis in France 1925–1985*. Trans. J. Mehlman. Chicago: University of Chicago Press.

Sadow, L. (1968). Ego axis in psychopathology. *Archives of General Psychiatry* 21:15–24.

Sartre, J. (1947). *Existentialism*. Trans. B. Frechtman. New York: Philosophical Library.

_____ (1948a). *The Emotions: Outline of a Theory*. Trans. B. Frechtman. New York: Philosophical Library.

_____ (1948b). *The Wall and Other Stories*. Trans. L. Alexander. New York: New Directions.

_____ (1949). *No Exit and Three Other Plays*. New York: Vintage.

_____ (1953). *Existential Psychoanalysis*. Trans. H. Barnes. Chicago: Henry Regnery.

_____ (1955). *Literary and Philosophical Essays*. Trans. A. Michelson. New York: Collier Books.

_____ (1957). *The Transcendence of the Ego*. Trans. F. Williams and R. Kirkpatrick. New York: Farrar, Straus & Giroux, 1957.

_____ (1963a). *Saint Genet: Actor and Martyr*. Trans. B. Frechtman. New York: Pantheon.

_____ (1963b). Preface. In *The Wretched of the Earth*, F. Fanon, pp. 7–31. New York: Grove.

_____ (1964a). *Nausea*. Trans. L. Alexander. New York: New Directions.

_____ (1964b). *The Words*. Trans. B. Frechtman. New York: George Braziller.

_____ (1965). *Anti-Semite and Jew*. Trans. J. Becker. New York: Schocken.

_____ (1968). *Search for a Method*. Trans. H. Barnes. New York: Vintage.

_____ (1973a). *The Age of Reason*. Trans. E. Sutton. New York: Vintage.

_____ (1973b). *Being and Nothingness: A Phenomenological Essay on Ontology*. Trans. H. Barnes. New York: Washington Square Press.

_____ (1973c). *The Reprieve*. Trans. E. Sutton. New York: Vintage.

_____ (1973d). *Troubled Sleep*. Trans. G. Hopkins. New York: Vintage.

_____ (1978). *Sartre by Himself*. Trans. R. Seaver. New York: Urizen.

_____ (1981). *The Family Idiot: Gustave Flaubert 1821–1857*. Vol. 1. Trans. C. Cosman. Chicago: University of Chicago Press.

_____ (1984). *The War Diaries of Jean-Paul Sartre, November 1939–March 1940*. Trans. Q. Hoare. New York: Pantheon.

_____ (1985). *The Freud Scenario*. Trans. Q. Hoare. Chicago: University of Chicago Press.

_____ (1987). *The Family Idiot: Gustave Flaubert 1821–1857*. Vol. 2. Trans. C. Cosman. Chicago: University of Chicago Press.

_____ (1988). *What is Literature? and Other Essays*. Cambridge, MA: Harvard University Press.

_____ (1989). *The Family Idiot: Gustave Flaubert 1821–1857*. Vol. 3. Trans. C. Cosman. Chicago: University of Chicago Press.

Saussure, F. (1989). *Course in General Linguistics*. La Salle, IL: Open Court.

Schafer, R. (1968). *Aspects of Internalization*. New York: International Universities Press.

_____ (1983). *The Analytic Attitude*. New York: Basic Books.

Schell, J. (1982). *The Fate of the Earth*. New York: Avon.

Schneiderman, S. (1980). *Returning to Freud: Clinical Psychoanalysis in the School of Lacan*. New Haven: Yale University Press.

_____ (1983). *Jacques Lacan: The Death of an Intellectual Hero*. Cambridge, MA: Harvard University Press.

_____ (1986). *Ratman*. New York: New York University Press.

Searles, H. (1960). *The Nonhuman Environment in Normal Development and in Schizophrenia*. New York: International Universities Press.

Shapiro, D. (1965). *Neurotic Styles*. New York: Basic Books.

Sheehan, T. (1979). Philosophy and propaganda: response to Professor Bronner. *Salamagundi* 43:174–199.

_____ , ed. (1981). *Heidegger: The Man and the Thinker*. Chicago: Precedent Publishing.

Sheridan, A. (1980). *Michel Foucault: The Will to Truth*. London: Tavistock.

Smart, B. (1985). *Michel Foucault*. London: Tavistock.

Smith, J., and Kerrigan, W. (1983). *Interpreting Lacan*. New Haven, CT: Yale University Press.

Soll, I. (1981). Sartre's rejection of the Freudian unconscious. In *The Philosophy of Jean-Paul Sartre*, ed. P. Schlipp, pp. 582–604. LaSalle, IL: Open Court.

Spence, D. (1982). *Narrative Truth and Historical Truth*. New York: Norton.

Spengler, O. (1962). *The Decline of the West*. Trans. C. Atkinson, abridged by A. Helps. New York: Knopf.

Spiegelberg, H. (1972). *Phenomenology in Psychology and Psychiatry: A Historical Introduction*. Evanston, IL: Northwestern University Press.

Stechler, G. (1987). Clinical applications of a psychoanalytic systems model of assertion and aggression. *Psychoanalytic Inquiry* 7:348–363.

Stechler, G., and Halton, A. (1987). The emergence of assertion and aggression during infancy: a psychoanalytic systems approach. *Journal of the American Psychoanalytic Association* 35:821–838.

Steele, R. (1979). Psychoanalysis and hermeneutics. *International Review of Psycho-Analysis* 6:389–411.

Steiner, G. (1979). *Martin Heidegger*. New York: Viking.

_____ (1982). Making a homeland for the mind. *Times Literary Supplement*, January 22, 1982, p. 67.

Steiner, J. (1985). Turning a blind eye: the cover up for Oedipus. *International Review of Psycho-Analysis* 12:161–172.

Stern, D. (1985). *The Interpersonal World of the Infant: A View from Psychoanalysis and Developmental Psychology.* New York: Basic Books.

Strenger, C. (1991). *Between Hermeneutics and Science: An Essay on the Epistemology of Psychoanalysis.* Madison, CT: International Universities Press.

Sulloway, F. (1979). *Freud, Biologist of the Mind: Beyond the Psychoanalytic Legend.* New York: Basic Books.

Super, R. (1981). *The Complete Prose Works of Matthew Arnold.* Ann Arbor: University of Michigan Press.

Tanguay, P. (1977). Review of "The Psychological Birth of the Human Infant." *Journal of the American Academy of Child Psychiatry* 16:542–544.

Tausk, V. (1948). On the origin of the "influencing machine" and schizophrenia. In *The Psychoanalytic Reader,* ed. R. Fliess, pp. 52–85. New York: International Universities Press.

Terman, D. (1989). Therapeutic change: perspectives of self psychology. *Psychoanalytic Inquiry* 9:88–100.

Thurber, J. (1956). *Further Fables For Our Time.* New York: Simon and Schuster.

Toulmin, S. (1986). Self psychology as a "postmodern" science. *Psychoanalytic Inquiry* 6:459–477.

Trilling, L., ed. (1949). *The Portable Matthew Arnold.* New York: Viking.

_____ (1955). *Freud and the Crisis of our Culture.* Boston: Beacon.

_____ (1965). *Beyond Culture.* New York: Harcourt Brace Jovanovich.

_____ (1971). *Sincerity and Authenticity.* Cambridge, MA: Harvard University Press.

Turkel, S. (1978). *Psychoanalytic Politics.* New York: Basic Books.

Vergote, A. (1983). From Freud's "Other Scene" to Lacan's "Other." In *Interpreting Lacan,* ed. J. Smith and W. Kerrigan, pp. 193–222. New Haven: Yale University Press.

Wakefield, J. (1988). Hermeneutics and empiricism: commentary on Donald Meichenbaum. In *Hermeneutics and Psychological Theory,* ed. S. Messer, L. Sass, and R. Woolfolk, pp. 131–148. New Brunswick, NJ: Rutgers University Press.

Wallace, E. (1986). Freud as ethicist. In *Freud: Appraisals and Reappraisals. Contributions to Freud Studies,* vol. 1, ed. P. Stepansky, pp. 83–142. Hillsdale, NJ: Analytic Press.

Warnke, G. (1987). *Gadamer: Hermeneutics, Tradition and Reason.* Stanford, CA: Stanford University Press.

Waterhouse, R. (1981). *A Heidegger Critique.* Atlantic Highlands, NJ: Humanities Press.

Weinsheimer, J. (1985). *Gadamer's Hermeneutics: A Reading of "Truth and Method."* New Haven: Yale University Press.

Werman, D. (1985). Freud's *Civilization and Its Discontents*—a reappraisal. *Psychoanalytic Review* 72:239–254.

White, D. (1978). *Heidegger and the Language of Poetry.* Lincoln, NE: University of Nebraska Press.

Whitehead, A. (1967). *Science and the Modern World.* New York: Free Press.

Winnicott, D. (1958). On the capacity to be alone. In *The Maturational Process and the Facilitating Environment,* pp. 29–36. New York: International Universities Press, 1968.

_____ (1965). *The Family and Individual Development.* London: Tavistock.

_____ (1966). *The Maturational Process and the Facilitating Environment*. New York: International Universities Press.

Wolfe, T. (1987). *The Bonfire of the Vanities*. New York: Farrar, Straus, Giroux.

Wynne, L., Ryckoff, I., Day, J., and Hirsch, S. (1958). Pseudomutuality in the family relations of schizophrenics. *Psychiatry* 21:205–220.

Young-Bruehl, E. (1982). *Hannah Arendt: For Love of the World*. New Haven: Yale University Press.

Zimmerman, M. (1981). *Eclipse of the Self: The Development of Heidegger's Concept of Authenticity*. Athens, OH: Ohio University Press.

_____ (1990). *Heidegger's Confrontation with Modernity: Technology, Politics, and Art*. Bloomington, IN: Indiana University Press.

INDEX